YEADON'S REGISTER

of

L N E R

LOCOMOTIVES

Volume Forty-Eight

Classes J64, J65, J66, J67, J68, J69, J70 & J92

The Great Eastern 0-6-0Ts

YEADON'S REGISTER OF L.N.E.R. LOCOMOTIVES - VOLUME 48

EDITORS NOTE AND ACKNOWLEDGEMENTS

Many of you will be wondering why this particular volume has appeared in print before the planned publication of volumes 47A and 47B. Others will be wondering why it has taken so long to bring out this volume after the publication of Volume 46B. Most of you will, we hope, be glad that a volume of Yeadon's Register has at last appeared anyway. So, we make our apologies and carry on with the job of producing what is arguably the longest running and most comprehensive history of any of the locomotives which ran on any British railway sytem. We could give you many reasons why 47A&B has been late in appearing but suffice to say that everything is now back in place and ready for production. In the fullnes of time we will get back on course and bring the two parts of Volume 47 into the public realm - the first quarter of 2010 is indeed the projected period when both will 'see the light of day.'

So, what does this tome hold within its covers? The Great Eastern Railway 0-6-0 tank engine classes of J65 to J69, the J70 tram engines, the J92 crane tanks and the three inherted J64s. As many of you are already aware, the history of the GE 0-6-0T, particularly J67 and J69 classes, is somewhat complex and hopefully we have presented here a version which is fully understandable even in its complexity and diversity.

Once again Eric Fry has played an important role in production, and this volume has brought out his knowledge of GER 0-6-0 tank engines. His teaching skills were tested to the full but he eventually managed to get the far-from-straightforward history over to us so.

Sadly, Mike Lake, one of our typesetting team, passed away recently and his contribution and enthusiasm for the Register will be greatly missed. Being a NER afficianado, Mike took on the setting of the whole of Volume 47 and the results of that labour-of-love will soon be available.

Judy Burg and the staff at Hull University Archive continue to produce the goods when asked and we thank them for their continued profesionalism in dealing with our requests.

Jean and Simon endure some harsh winters in Canada but occassionally, when the post gets through, a parcel arrives from Nottingham indicating yet another volume of *Yeadon's Register* has got to publication. They have had a rather long wait for this one but we are sure they will not be dissappointed.

Finally, thanks to you the reader who keep this important and mammoth series on track to completion.

The catalogue reference for the locomotives featured in this volume are as follows:
DYE 1/48; DYE 1/49; DYE 1/52; DYE 2/6.

We would also like to acknowledge the contribution from the following photographers, most of whom, sadly, are no longer with us: I.C.Allen, J.W.Armstrong, R.J.Buckley, W.A.Camwell, H.C.Casserley, G.Coltas, A.J.Cook, R.C.Copeman, A.B.Crompton, A.W.Croughton, D.A.Dant, C.E.Dixon, A.G.Ellis, N.Fields, A.G.Forsyth, E.V.Fry, P.H.Groom, L.Hanson, T.G.Hepburn, B.H.Hilton, P.J.Hughes, W.M.J.Jackson, J.M.Jarvis, H.N.James, C.Lawson-Kerr, R.A.Panting, H.Percy, L.W.Perkins, L.R.Peters, P.Ransome-Wallis, S.J.Rhodes, J.Robertson, J.F.Robinson, C.L.Romane, C.J.B.Sanderson, E.E.Smith, J.L.Smith, N.E.Stead, Rail Archive Stephenson, W.H.Tate, D.L.Wilkinson, P.Wilson, W.H.Whitworth, W.B.Yeadon.

Volume 49 of Yeadon's Register will feature the 0-6-2 tanks of Great Central origin - N4, N5, N6.

In the early part of 2010 the Yeadon Collection is being relocated to the new Hull History Centre and will available for inspection there. Anyone who wishes to inspect any part of the collection should contact -

Judy Burg, The Archivist, Brynmor Jones Library
University of Hull, Hull, HU6 7RX
Tel: 01482 465265.
e-mail j.burg@hull.ac.uk
archives@hull.ac.uk
A catalogue of the Yeadon Collection is available.

First published in the United Kingdom by
BOOK LAW PUBLICATIONS 2009 in association with Challenger
382 Carlton Hill, Nottingham, NG4 1JA
Printed and bound by The Amadeus Press, Cleckheaton, West Yorkshire.

INTRODUCTION

Class J64

The Mid-Suffolk Light Railway had been in administration since 1907 and was not absorbed into the LNER until 1st July 1924. Its entire locomotive stock consisted of three Hudswell Clarke 0-6-0 tanks of that maker's standard designs. Nos.1 and 3 (of 1904 and 1909 respectively) were similar. No.2 (1905) was slightly smaller and was constructed as a 2-4-0T but altered to six coupled on delivery to the MSLR. It was 6ins. shorter, as was the wheelbase at 5ft 9in. + 5ft 9in., instead of 6ft 0in. + 6ft 0in., as on Nos.1 and 3. Although of the same age, the boiler barrel was likewise 6in. shorter. The cylinder diameter was one inch less.

The engines of the CV&HR had been given LNER numbers 8312, 8313 and 8314, and their boilers were numbered 1312, 1313 and 1314 in the Stratford lists. The engine number 8315 remained blank (the boiler No.1315 also was not used until 1930 when a replacement boiler for an F7 took it).

MSLR No.1 became LNER 8316 and No.2 became 8317. No.3 was condemned in August 1924, soon after the take-over, without being renumbered. Some previously published accounts have suggested that the number 8315 was allotted by the LNER but it is far more likely to have been 8318, for two reasons. Firstly, if Nos.1, 2 and 3 were to have been renumbered 8316, 8317 and 8315 they would have been out of numerical order. The second, and compelling, reason is that the boiler from No.3 was actually retained at Stratford and renumbered 1318. It was not used and was cut up in October 1930 after engines 8316 and 8317 had been withdrawn. Everything therefore points to 8318 as No.3's intended number on the LNER.

Besides steam brakes, these engines also carried Westinghouse equipment used for train braking.

Shortly after the LNER took control of the MSLR, the two surviving engines found employment elsewhere from their native patch, with No.8316 shunting at Ipswich whilst Parkeston gave similar work to No.8317. Their original duties on the nineteen mile line between Haughley and Laxfield were taken over by J65 tanks.

Classes J65 to J69 - The Holden 0-6-0Ts.

Until 1867 all shunting work on the Great Eastern Railway was performed by main line tender engines or a few passenger tank locomotives, and even by 1886 the company possessed only nineteen 0-6-0 tanks. From that year a dramatic change took place when James Holden put into service the first ten Class T18 (LNER J66) six-coupled tanks designed specifically for shunting work. Further batches quickly followed and during 1887 one engine (No.294) was equipped with Westinghouse brake for passenger work. Success was immediate and paved the way for large scale construction, the new engines taking over much of the suburban passenger workings out of London. More were also constructed for shunting and short distance goods duties.

Eventually these Holden designed engines totalled 260 (a fifth of the GER locomotive fleet), the last ten being turned out to GER order by the LNER in 1923. There were of course improvements and minor alterations down the years, but the basic design remained unchanged.

Despite their modest size and weight (40 ton as first built), they established themselves as the mainstay of the intensive 'Jazz' services to Enfield and Chingford until 1925-26 when the LNER built large numbers of N7 class 0-6-2Ts. However, the role of the 0-6-0Ts was far from over, many being put to work on shunting and pilot duties elsewhere on the LNER system, twenty even going to Scotland. The final withdrawals from service took place in 1962. Fortunately, one of these versatile engines has been preserved as GER No.87.

Construction and Rebuilding 1886 to 1923:

1886 - Class T18 (LNER J66) introduced. Fifty built to 1888, forty of which for goods.

1887 - No.294 fitted for passenger work.

1888 - The last ten T18s built as passenger engines.

1889 - First ten of Class E22 (LNER J65) built. Smaller version of T18 class - 1ft shorter at the rear, smaller cylinders and side tanks, but same boiler. Passenger engines. Further ten constructed in 1893.

1890 - Class R24 (LNER J67) introduced. Like T18, but 1ft shorter at rear. Wheelbase lengthened by 6in. at rear. 140 built down to 1901, of which 100 were for passenger work and forty for goods.

1902 - Rebuilding of R24 to R24 Rbt. (LNER J69) began. Boiler with larger firebox and higher working pressure (180 instead of 160 p.s.i), and wider side tanks fitted. By 1921 (when such rebuilding ceased) 95 of the passenger engines had been converted. None of the goods R24s were ever given large tanks, although some got the 180 lb. boiler in LNER days.

1904 - Twenty passenger engines of Class S56 (also LNER J69) built. Similar to R24 Rbt. but had wide cabs and bunker to match the side tanks.

1912 (1) - The first ten R24s were altered from passenger to goods, eight of which had previously been converted to R24 Rbt. and kept their wide tanks.

1912 (2) - Class C72 (LNER J68) - ten passenger engines built, followed in 1913/14 by ten for goods. Same as S56 class but had better cab with side windows and large square spectacle windows, also built up in place of stovepipe chimneys.

1923 - Ten more J68 class, for shunting, built by LNER to a GER order.

Boilers

Diagram 39 - This type originated in 1886 on the first T18 class (J66) engines and was also used on the E22 (J65) and R24 (J67) classes subsequently introduced.

The basic size was 4ft 2in. diameter, with a barrel length of 9ft 1in. and outer firebox length of 4ft 6in. The working pressure of the first examples was 140 p.s.i. and the grate area was 12·4 sq. ft. As was usual with Holden's smaller engines, the dome was positioned well forward, on the front ring of the barrel which consisted of butt jointed rings. The inner firebox was made of copper, but steel fireboxes were tried from 1889 onwards on E22 Nos.159, 245 to 254 (1889); R24 Nos.407 to 416 (1890), and 265 to 274 (1896).

The boiler was redesigned in 1898 when the barrel was made from two telescopic rings (the maximum outside diameter remaining at 4ft 2in.) and working pressure raised to 160 p.s.i. The first examples were used for reboilering classes T18 and E22 (J66 and J65). New R24 class engines from 1899 came out with this type of boiler and all subsequent replacements on the three classes were of this pattern.

Steel fireboxes were again fitted from time to time and some boilers so equipped lasted into LNER days. They could be identified by the position of the twin Ramsbottom safety valves which were on the back ring of the boiler barrel instead of on the firebox (This was in the same position as the later Diagram 37 boiler, but these had 4-column Ramsbottom valves in a much larger casing).

Under LNER ownership Ross pop safety valves were substituted for the Ramsbottom type. At first these were mounted on the same raised base, complete with cover plate, as the Ramsbottom valves. Boilers built from 1934 onwards had the pop valves mounted directly on the boiler, still in the same position. A few boilers still with Ramsbottom valves survived into BR days. As far as is known, none of the boilers with steel firebox received pop valves.

The year 1914 saw the start of boiler exchanging on the GER, also commencement of a new boiler numbering series for replacements. All of the J65, J66 and J67 engines hitherto carried boilers bearing the same number as the engine, and when replacement had become due the new boiler took the same number as its predecessor. For Diagram 39 the new series began at 2800 and by Grouping had reached 2844. The LNER continued the series which reached 2919 in 1938 when further construction ceased. By then withdrawal of all three engine classes was well under way, twenty-nine having been condemned during 1937. This resulted in many recently built boilers becoming available for further use, not only on existing engines but also to convert a number of J69s to J67.

When the BR boiler renumbering scheme came into effect in September 1950, the Stratford maintained boilers took numbers 23900 to 23933. Those shopped at Gorton became 23950 to 23956 and the pair in Scotland which Cowlairs looked after became 23960 and 23961.

Diagram 37 (*used on classes J68 and J69*) - Replacement of the original boilers on the oldest class R24 engines had begun in February 1899 using the latest 160 lb. version referred to above. Eight of the passenger engines were dealt with as follows: 1899 - Nos.347, 356, 361; 1900 - Nos.352, 358; 1901 - 338; 1902 - 330, 336. Then in July 1902 No.332 was given a new boiler in which the outer firebox was lengthened from 4ft 6in. to 5ft 2Z\ zn in. The grate area was enlarged from 12·4 sq. ft. to 14·5 and the working pressure raised from 160 to 180 p.s.i. Otherwise the dimensions were similar to the earlier Diagram 39 type. No change was required to the superstructure of the locomotive, the boiler merely protruded further back into the cab.

Nos.329, 341 and 342 were likewise rebuilt to Class R24 Rebuilt later in the same year and it was the start of the intended systematic rebuilding of all R24 passenger engines. After a peak of 24 such conversions in 1904, rebuilding proceeded steadily until 1921 when 95 out of the original 100 had been done. Nos.161, 164 and 169 were not rebuilt, nor Nos.330 and 336 (given new 160 lb. boilers in 1902 - *see above*) these two having been converted to goods category in 1912. In addition twenty new engines (classified S56) were constructed with 180 lb. boilers

in 1904 and twenty C72 (LNER J68) in 1912-14, completed by a final ten J68s to GER order in 1923.

Except for the first few (possibly as many as ten) rebuilds, four-column Ramsbottom safety valves were fitted enclosed in a large rectangular casing positioned on the back ring of the boiler barrel. Even when the LNER adopted a pair of Ross pop valves in their place these were still positioned on the boiler barrel, so that visual identification of the boiler type was still possible because Diagram 39 boilers had their pop valves on the firebox. A few boilers with Ramsbottom valves survived into the BR period. These were maintained by Cowlairs works (e.g. No.68623 to November 1952 and No.68551 to May 1954).

As with Diagram 39, prior to 1914 the 180lb. boilers took the same number as the engine on which they were installed. This of course led to replacement Diagram 37 boilers carrying the same number as their predecessor Diagram 39 type, which of course were cut up so there was no duplication in fact.

When exchanging of boilers became the practice from July 1914 onwards, Diagram 37 boilers built thereafter were numbered 2950 upwards and 3017 had been reached by Grouping. The construction of Class J68 Nos.31 to 40 in 1923 continued the GER practice of, where possible, still giving new engines boiler numbers coinciding with the engine numbers. However, there must have been some delay in making the boilers for these engines because boiler numbers 31 to 35 went onto engines 36 to 40, and engines 31 to 35 came out with boilers numbered 3024 to 3028. When they did appear, boilers 36 to 40 were used to reboiler engines numbered 274, 387, 45, 341 and 30 respectively.

As with the Diagram 39 boilers, construction of Diagram 37 ceased in 1938 after 3105 was fitted to engine 7362 in March of that year. At that time there were many Diagram 39 boilers available due to withdrawal of J65, J66 and J67 engines, so some were utilised on classes J68 and J69 resulting in reclassification to J67.

By 1944 it had become obvious that more boilers were needed to prolong the life of the Holden 0-6-0Ts during wartime and it was decided that further construction should be of the 180 lb. Diagram 39 to be used to keep the remaining J65, J66 and J67 engines in service. So the previous decision was reversed and boilers built from 1944 onwards were not only used on classes J68 and J69 but also to convert some J67s to Class J69, which included a number of reversions.

The new boilers took numbers 3153 upwards, this being due to the series 3100 to 3152 having originally been allotted to Class D13, although only a few remained in stock (3100 to 3105 were reused in 1938 because these numbers were then blank). Of the first ten constructed in 1944, four were sent from Stratford to Cowlairs but three of these were not actually put to use by Cowlairs until 1947. Prior to the start of the BR boiler numbering scheme in September 1950, the Stratford series had reached 3207. New boilers numbered 23800 to 23819 followed in 1951/2 and the final nine, Nos.23820 to 23828, during 1955-7, the last newly built boiler going to engine No.68498 in February 1957.

Under the BR scheme, existing Diagram 37 boilers were renumbered 23700 to 23796 for those maintained at Stratford and 23840 to 23843 for Gorton's stock of them. Cowlairs used the series 23860 to 23883, though not all these numbers were taken up.

Earlier, from 1929, Cowlairs had renumbered some of the Diagram 37 boilers into their own system and these are dealt with separately.

Mid-Suffolk Light Railway No.1 was built in November 1904 by Hudswell, Clarke & Co. Leeds and was acquired by the LNER on the 1st July 1924 when it became Class J64. It had 14in. cylinders and 12ft 0in. wheelbase.

The initial ten engines of what was to become LNER Class J65, Nos.150 to 159 were built at Stratford from February to June 1889.

Cowlairs maintained Diagram 37 boilers - Soon after the last of the twenty J69s were received in Scotland in November 1928, Cowlairs began to renumber their boilers into their own series, taking numbers 1683 to 1702 (*Note* - that the tables show the prefix C for these boilers to indicate they were in the Cowlairs series but in reality the prefix did not show in official records, nor on the boiler plates themselves.) The Cowlairs numbers were allotted in the same order as the engine numbers and the list must therefore have been drawn up some time after November 1928 when the final engine arrived in Scotland - January 1929 seems likely.

When replacements were required for worn out boilers, these were obtained from Stratford, who constructed all boilers for the Holden 0-6-0 tanks. Previously used boiler No.3011 was the first to go north early in 1933, but was not given a fresh number. However, when three brand new boilers were received from Stratford in 1934 they were given Cowlairs numbers 1829, 1830 and 1831, their intended numbers 3074 to 3076 being left blank in the Stratford list (1829 and 1830 were fitted to 7391 and 7356 in September 1934, but 1831 remained spare until put on 7341 in August 1937). A further new boiler, 3096, went north in 1937 but was not given a fresh number by Cowlairs, and the same happened to previously used Nos.2982, 3018, 3019, 3029 and 3070 which followed during 1938-40. New boilers 3153, 3158, 3160 and 3161 were sent to Cowlairs in 1944 (the last three not being utilised until 1947) and these too kept their Stratford numbers.

Eventually some of the J69s in Scotland were returned south, including those then carrying Cowlairs numbered boilers 1686 and 1692 in 1944, and 1689, 1690 and 1700 in 1951/2. None of these were further renumbered back into the Stratford series.

The BR numbers 23860 to 23879 were allotted to all the Diagram 37 boilers still on the Cowlairs lists in September 1950. These included some that had gone south as mentioned above. The order of allotment was firstly the remnants of the twenty that had been renumbered 1683 to 1702 in 1929, then followed the later acquisitions in construction date order. Nos.23880 to 23883 were given to four new boilers built at Stratford in 1951 for use in Scotland, and put to use between October 1951 and March 1953. In the event only the relatively few boilers that actually passed through works after September 1950 got their BR numbers, the rest going for scrap still carrying their old numbers.

Cowlairs boiler renumbering:

.1.	.2.	.3.	.4.	.5.	.6.	.7.
1683	2963	8/30	1916	10/28	7057	Cut up 1932.
1684	3003	1/29	1921	5/28	7089	Cut up 1938.
1685	3002	4/31	1920	2/28	7337	Cut up 1938.
1686	3051	1/30	1928	11/28	7338	Off 68579 in 12/51, then reno. BR*.
1687	39	3/29	1924	11/28	7341	Cut up 1947.
1688	2950	12/30	1914	10/27	7342	Cut up 1938.
1689	3044	11/31	1928	5/28	7343	Off 68552 in 1/56, then reno. BR*.
1690	42	?	1912	9/28	7347	Cut up 1954 as 23862.
1691	2992	1/30	1920	2/28	7348	Cut up 1947.
1692	28	?	1914	3/28	7356	Cut up 1947.
1693	2956	6/32	1915	5/28	7357	Cut up 1937.
1694	3022	?	1923	3/28	7358	Cut up 1956 as 23865.
1695	3000	?	1920	7/28	7368	Cut up 1946.
1696	2969	5/31	1918	8/28	7374	Cut up 1946.
1697	270	-/31	1910	2/28	7375	Cut up 1934.
1698	3004	4/29	1921	11/27	7376	Cut up 1944.
1699	2952	3/29	1914	9/28	7379	Cut up 1932.
1700	395	?	1910	12/27	7386	Off 68499 in 8/51, then reno. BR*.
1701	388	1/30	1904	11/27	7391	Off 68503 in 9/52, then reno. BR*.
1702	165	10/29	1912	10/27	7392	Cut up 1937.
1829	*3074*	new	1934	- *to* 7391 9/34		Off 68568 in 2/56, then reno. BR*.
1830	*3075*	new	1934	- *to* 7356 9/34		Cut up 1957 as 23871.
1831	*3076*	new	1934	- *to* 7341 8/37		Off 68504 in 4/52, then reno. BR*.

Key:-
1 - Cowlairs number; 2.- Ex Stratford number; 3.- Date renumbered; 4.- Built; 5.- To Scotland;
6.- Received on engine; 7.- Disposal.
3074-3076 these numbers not carried. * Some of these may have been scrapped, and not renumbered.

Class J65

Ten engines, numbered 150 to 159, were built at Stratford in 1889, with Westinghouse brake. Similar to Class J66 of 1886-88 but of lighter construction for use on the Fenchurch Street to Blackwall passenger services and the smaller branch lines in East Anglia. The boiler and wheelbase were the same, but the cylinders were smaller, as were the side tanks. A shortening of the frames at the rear end by 1ft. resulted in a shorter cab. No.159 had a steel firebox with the twin Ramsbottom safety valves mounted much further forward, on the rear ring, of the barrel.

In 1893 ten more engines (Nos.245 to 254) were built. They had wider, but lower, side tanks (with cabs and bunkers widened to match), increasing the water capacity from 600 to 650 gallons. Like No.159 they all had steel fireboxes.

All twenty were reboilered between 1899 and 1912 with copper fireboxes which had the safety valves in the normal position on the firebox. From 1915 heavier smokebox doors began to be fitted. However, from 1918 new boilers with steel fireboxes reappeared on a few engines such as Nos.156 and 250 (boiler Nos.2814 and 2815).

During 1924-25, six engines were fitted with vacuum ejectors. In 1931 two more of the class received the same equipment but withdrawals had started in the preceding year. 1930 also saw cast iron chimneys being fitted as replacements of the stovepipe type.

Although withdrawals continued unabated, improvements were still carried out on the class and during 1933 a start was made to replace the original wooden pattern cab roofs with steel roofs. By the end of 1937 only five of the class remained in stock and so it was to stay as such for the following ten years but in 1956 the class became extinct.

Class J66 (GER T18)

1886-88 - Forty (out of an eventual fifty) new 0-6-0Ts (Nos.275 to 316) put into service by James Holden. These were the foundation of all futures 0-6-0Ts for the GER and were designed for shunting and short distance goods duties and, at first, had only hand brakes.

1887 - No.294, only three months after being built, was equipped with Westinghouse brake for passenger work. No.296 entered traffic four months late due to retention at Stratford works providing power for the Wheel Shop.

1888 - The success of No.294 on suburban passenger work resulted in the final ten engines (Nos.317 to 326) of the class being built as passenger engines. To increase their coal capacity they were given 6ins. longer bunkers at the expense of the cab i.e. the frames were not lengthened.

1890 - The slightly modified R24 class were introduced in that year, also for passenger work, whereupon T18 class Nos.317-326 were demoted to goods engines and the brake gear from them was used on R24 Nos.337 to 346, then under construction.

1893 - No.281 transferred to Service Stock at Stratford works, where it worked for a further 69 years. Unlike all the others, it never got coal rails.

1895-99 - All (except No.294) fitted with steam brake (they had only hand brakes previously).

1898-1908 - All reboilered with 160 p.s.i. in place of 140 p.s.i. boilers. The same pattern was used on classes J65 and J67 (None of the J66s ever carried 180lb. boilers).

1915 - Heavier smokebox doors began to be fitted.

1918 - A few received new boilers with steel fireboxes. As with such earlier boilers, the safety valves (Ramsbottom type) were ahead of the firebox.

1930 - Cast iron chimneys began to be fitted. No.294 converted to a goods engine, so the whole class were then alike in having steam brake only.

1933 - Steel cab roofs began to be fitted.

1936 - Withdrawals started - some were sold.

1948 - Eighteen entered BR stock, plus Mersey Electric Railway No.3 (ex 7297) which had been sold in 1939. It was withdrawn from LM Region Service Stock in 1950 and cut up at Stratford.

1955 - Last engine in Running Stock withdrawn.

1962 - Last engine in Service Stock withdrawn.

Class J67 (GER R24) and J69 (GER R24 Rebuilt and S56)

1890 - In 1890 a development of the GER Class T18 (LNER J66) saw twenty engines, numbered 327 to 346, turned out by Stratford and classified R24. The rear section of the wheelbase was lengthened by 6in. but the rear overhang was one foot less making them shorter than the T18 class. Accordingly the side tanks were positioned further forward and the length of the cab was shortened. The water capacity remained at 1000 gallons. Note that the front footsteps on Class T18 were just ahead of the tanks whereas on class R24 they were in line with the smokebox. Westinghouse brakes were fitted, as was wheel reverse. The wheels were made of cast steel with ten spokes and had balance weights.

1890-91 - Twenty more engines, numbered 397 to 416, were turned out later that year and into 1891 but these were for goods working and differed in having hand brakes only, lever reverse and unbalanced cast iron wheels with fifteen spokes. Nos.407 to 416 had steel fireboxes and on these the twin column safety valves were mounted well forward, on the rear end of the boiler barrel.

1892 - During 1892 a further twenty engines for passenger work, Nos.347-366, were built at Stratford.

1893 - The existing passenger engines, Nos.327 to 366, were fitted with condensing apparatus, which required a rectangular chamber on top of each tank about 6ins. deep and stretching from the cab to a point about three-quarters forwards on the tanks. These chambers were visible above the side sheets of the tanks and this was never changed, even when the tanks were widened on rebuilding to Class J69.

1894-96 - In this period another forty passenger engines, Nos.367 to 396 and 265 to 274, were built. These too had condensing gear but the side sheets in the vicinity of the chambers were extended upwards in order to obscure them. Nos.265 to 274 had steel fireboxes, like Nos.407 to 416 of the goods variety.

1899-1900 - Twenty more goods engines, Nos.255 to 264 and 199 to 208, were delivered during 1899 and 1900. Their boilers worked at 160 p.s.i. instead of the previous standard 140 p.s.i. They had steam brakes from new, the earlier twenty goods engines having by then been so fitted.

1899 onwards - All replacement boilers of the same type were pressed to 160 p.s.i.

1900-01 - The years 1900 and 1901 saw yet more passenger engines put into traffic with twenty, Nos.189 to 198 and 160 to 169, coming out of Stratford. These were like the 1894-96 engines. Class R24 now totalled 100 passenger and 40 goods engines.

1902-21 - From 1902 to 1921 the rebuilding of the passenger engines took place but none of the goods engines were affected. The rebuilding involved fitting new boilers pressed to 180 p.s.i.

Thirty engines built at Stratford from June 1886 in September 1887 were numbered 275 to 304. They all had fifteen spoke cast iron wheels and lever operated reversing gear as they were only for shunting. The LNER classified them J66.

Twenty goods engines built at Stratford between November 1890 and January 1891 formed the basis of what was to become LNER Class J67. Their initial numbers were 397 to 416 but in January 1920 Nos.407 to 416 were changed to Nos.11 to 20. They all had 15-spoke cast iron unbalanced wheels and tanks holding 1000 gallons.

and with fireboxes some 8in. longer, increasing the grate area from 12·4 to 14·5 sq. ft.; these boilers merely projected further back into the existing cab. An outward point of difference was the use of 4-column Ramsbottom safety valves in a large rectangular casing, positioned well forward on the back ring of the boiler barrel, instead of the 2-column type on the firebox in the case of the original boilers (except for those with steel fireboxes and the first few rebuilds - see above). The reboilered engines were designated R24 rebuilds.

The first R24 to carry the redesigned boiler was No.332 (in July 1902), soon followed by Nos.329, 341 and 342. The side tanks remained unaltered, with 1000 gallons capacity. In February 1903 No.334 was rebuilt and on this engine the side tanks were widened by 4in. so that they projected beyond the width of the cab and bunker. The capacity was increased to 1140 gallons. Down to January 1904, ten more (Nos.335, 340, 343, 345, 346, 348, 351, 354, 360 and 379) were likewise altered. All those rebuilt subsequently, starting with No.386 in February 1904, had their tanks widened further, by 5in., giving a capacity of 1180 gallons. The first four rebuilds (Nos.329, 332, 341 and 342) subsequently received 5in. tank extensions, but the eleven with the 4in. type retained this slightly smaller type. The original side tanks were evidently retained because the difference between those built down to 1893, and No.367 onwards remained, i.e. the raised tank side sheets on the later engines.

As many as twenty-four R24 class were rebuilt in 1904. Thereafter a small number were converted year by year until in January 1922 some 95 of the 100 engines had been done. Of the five that remained unaltered, Nos.161, 164, and 169 got new boilers of the original type when first reboiled in 1920/21, whilst Nos.330 and 336 (which had been altered from passenger to goods engines in 1912 - see below) also kept 160lb. boilers. This was the situation when the LNER was formed in 1923.

1904 - In 1904 twenty new passenger engines (Nos.51 to 60 and 81 to 90) were built. In these, not only was the 180lb. boiler fitted, but the cabs and bunker were made the same width as the tanks, which held 1200 gallons of water, thus avoiding the noticeable step of the rebuilds. They were separately classified S56 by the GER. It will be noticed that the building of these engines in 1904 coincided with the peak year of rebuilding Class R24.

1909 - During January 1909 No.189 was renumbered 305, its old number being required for a new F4 2-4-2T.

1912 - The final development of the Holden 0-6-0T design appeared in this year when A.J.Hill built Class C72 Nos.41 to 50 (see J68). At the same time the ten oldest R24 engines, Nos.327 to 336, were downgraded from passenger to goods category. Their Westinghouse brake gear was removed and steam brake substituted, lever reverse replaced the wheel type, condensing gear was removed (though the chambers on the top of the tank remained), and new 15-spoke unbalanced cast-iron wheels replaced the 10-spoke balanced cast steel ones (which were reused on the new engines, 41 to 50).

The working pressure of their boilers was 160 p.s.i. However Nos.327, 328, 329, and 331 to 335 had already been converted to Class R24 Rebuilt, with 180lb. boilers and larger tanks. When converted to goods engines, the large tanks were kept (Nos.334 and 335 had the 1140 gallon type, the rest 1180). In the case of No.327 a brand new 160lb. boiler was provided whilst all the others merely had their working pressure reduced to that figure. Nos.330 and 336 were still in their original state, with 160lb. boilers and 1000 gallon tanks, so needed no alteration.

In February 1917 No.328 had its 180lb boiler uprated again to that figure and No.335 got a new 180lb boiler, working at that pressure. These two differed from the other eight.

The remaining five which had derated 180lb. boilers (with of course 4-column Ramsbottom safety valves mounted in front of the firebox - some later had 'pop' valves, also in this position) kept them for some time: No.7329 to October 1931, 7331 to May 1940, 7332 to June 1929, 333 to December 1920, and 7334 to April 1930.

The complexity of the history of these ten engines was to cause confusion to later generations of the keepers of official records, particularly regarding the size of the tanks and there were a number of incorrect entries, which was hardly surprising.

1915 - Saw the start of heavier pattern smokebox doors being fitted.

1920 - In January 1920 Nos.407 to 416 were renumbered 11 to 20 so that Class E4 could be accommodated in a single block of 100 numbers.

1923 - Under the LNER the classifications J67 and J69 were allotted to these engines, the former for those with boilers pressed to 160 p.s.i. and the latter for those working at 180 p.s.i. This equated roughly into Class J67 for the R24 goods engines and J69 for the R24 Rebuilt and S56 passenger engines. The exceptions were J67 Nos.7161, 7164 and 7169, the only passenger engines to have escaped rebuilding with large tanks and high pressure boilers, and Nos.7328 and 7335 which had been converted to goods engines in 1912 but had been restored to 180lb. pressure in 1917 and thus became Class J69.

The position may be summarised as follows:-

J67 Westinghouse brake - 7161/4/9 (3); J67 Steam brake - 7011-20, 7199-7208/55-64, 7327/9-34/6, 7397-7406 (48)

J69 Westinghouse brake - 7051-60/81-90, 7160/2/3/5-8, 7190-8, 7265-74, 7305, 7337-96 (107) Steam brake - 7328/35 (2).

The LNER boilers diagrams were 39 for the 160 p.s.i. boilers and 37 for the high pressure 180 p.s.i. type with the longer firebox. It will be noticed that engines from the 7327-36 series running with Diag.37 boilers set to blow off at 160 p.s.i. were included in Class J67, i.e. the type of boiler did not affect the engine classification, only the working pressure did. No changes were made to the above classifications until 1938 - see later.

1923-24 - Over the course of a year from November 1923, twenty-four of the passenger J69s in the Stratford district were equipped with ejectors to allow them to handle vacuum as well as Westinghouse stock.

This was the start of numerous changes to their brake arrangements which continued until 1942, after which year no further alterations were made. Only two passenger J69s escaped these changes and remained as Westinghouse only engines - No.7364 withdrawn as a result of an accident in January 1931 and No.7056 sold to the Government in October 1940.

The steam braked J67s were unaffected and remained as such.

1926-33 - Large scale construction of Class N7 0-6-2Ts to take over the work of the J69s on the GE suburban services resulted in redundancy for the latter. The LNER realised that they had a large class of still useful engines which could be used to replace aged tank engines on shunting and trip work elsewhere on the system and thus avoid new construction. So, in August 1926, conversion to steam brake and lever reverse, and in some cases with vacuum ejector added, began and fifty-nine were dealt with down to 1933. These alterations involved also removal of the condensing gear, though the prominent chambers on the top of the side tanks were left in place.

These converted J69s were despatched to various sheds on the GN, GC and CLC sections as well as ten to the NB section of the Scottish Area. Ten more conversions to shunting also went to Scotland, but these retained their Westinghouse brake with the addition of vacuum ejectors (it will be remembered that the NBR, like the GER, was a Westinghouse line). Full details of these changes are listed separately.

1926-30 - Additional coal rails were added to all the J67 and J69 engines. These filled in the gaps between the existing rails around the tops of the bunkers.

1927 onwards - Condensing gear was stripped from those still retaining it except for those J69s that worked the East London line beneath the Thames to the Southern Railway.

1930 onwards - Cast iron chimneys, with lipped rim, replaced the stovepipe type.

1933 onwards - The wooden cab roofs were replaced by a higher profile steel pattern with sliding ventilator. (Note the twenty engines sent to Scotland, and hence on Cowlairs maintenance, escaped this and the chimney alteration).

1935-39 - The 'odd' J67s (Nos.7161/4/9) and J69s (Nos.7328/35) received vacuum ejectors, the J67s becoming W+VE (7164 in 1936, 7161/9 in 1939) and J69s 7328/35 became S+VE in 1935.

1937 - Withdrawals began of Class J67, eleven being condemned.

1938-44 - In March 1938 No.7396 of Class J69 was fitted with a 160 p.s.i. Diagram 39 boiler, the large side tanks being retained and was given the classification J67/2. The original J67s then became J67/1. Down to 1944 a total of twenty engines were converted to Class J67/2 - nineteen from J69 and one J68. The new classification J67/2 consequently also embraced engines 7327/9/31-4 (converted to goods engines in 1912), although at times official records failed to recognise the fact.

The reason why these conversions from J69 to J67 took place is not altogether clear. It may be noted that construction of Diagram 39 boilers ceased in 1938 following the commencement of withdrawal of Class J67 during the previous year, and it was probably realised that nearly new Diagram 39 boilers (twenty-four had been made in 1934-35 and five in 1938) were to become available for reuse. Construction of the 180lb. Diagram 37 type also ceased temporarily in 1938 and was not resumed until 1944. Reconversion of some of the J67/2 back to J69 and J68 took place from 1940 to 1954, even before rebuilding to J67/2 ceased - *see* below.

1940 - Thirteen J69s and one J68 were sold to the Government in October having been on loan to the WD since October 1939.

1944-54 - The fact that no new boilers of either the Diagram 37 or 39 type had been built since 1938, coupled with the cessation of the withdrawal of J67 engines because of the 1939-45 War, began to cause problems. Replacement boilers were urgently required to keep engines in traffic and it was decided henceforth to build only the 180lb. Diagram 37 type when a resumption was at last made in 1944. From then on, an average of ten new boilers a year were made, the last one being fitted in February 1957 to No.68498.

The further construction of Diagram 37 boilers resulted in fourteen of the J67/2 engines reverting to Class J69, together with the single J68 (No.7047) returning to that class also from J67/2. These reversions took place mainly during the years 1944-54, though No.7332 had been dealt with in 1940 this being one of the 1912 conversions from passenger to goods and thus a J67 at Grouping. Nos.7327/31 also figured amongst those rebuilt to Class J69 during 1944-54.

1944 - J69 Nos.7338/57 were returned to the GE section from Scotland being exchanged for the lighter Class J67 Nos.7329/99, required to work the Lauder Light Railway where they ran with the tanks empty of water and coupled to ex NBR tenders. It may

be noted that No.7329 was actually a J67/2 although LNER and BR records incorrectly recorded it as a J67/1 i.e. it had 1180 gallon tanks, not 1000 gallon, and thus was only slightly lighter than a J69.

1946 - Under Thompson's general renumbering scheme the surviving J67 and J69 engines were combined in one block of numbers, 8490 to 8636. The numbers were allotted in order of building without regard to engine classification. There was one error in that 7200 became 8606 as if it had been built after 7190-8 instead of before. The scheme had been prepared in 1943 at which time it was considered that the thirteen J69s sold to the Government in 1940 might one day be returned, so they figured in the scheme. Option to repurchase by the LNER was not exercised, so the gaps in the block of numbers remained.

1946-53 - The prolongation of the life of Class J67 referred to above, caused twelve of these steam braked engines with small tanks also to receive 180lb Diagram 37 boilers during the period 1946-53. No.8587 was the first, in June 1946.

This new category was recognised in March 1950 by a separate classification, J69/2, those with the large tanks becoming J69/1. The full classification of the J67 and J69 engines can be summarised as follows:-

J67/1 - 160lb. Diag.39 boiler, small tanks.
J67/2 - 160lb. Diag.39 boiler, large tanks.
J69/1 - 180lb. Diag.37 boiler, large tanks.
J69/2 - 180lb. Diag.37 boiler, small tanks.

The twelve engines remained J69/2 to withdrawal except for No.68517 rebuilt in 1951 and changed back to J67/1 two years later.

The J69/2 conversions were recognisable by the position of the safety valves on the rear of the barrel instead of on the firebox.

1951-52 - During this period nine of the eighteen J69s remaining in the Scottish Area were sent back to the GE Section. These had been transferred to the NB section in 1927-28 and as already mentioned escaped the fitting of cast-iron chimneys and steel cab roofs initiated at Stratford during the thirties. The engines sent south were 68499, 8525, 68550/2/5/67/8, 68623/35 and when once again on Stratford maintenance some received new chimneys, but mostly the low wooden roofs were retained. The NBR shunters footboards below the bunker which had been fitted by Cowlairs soon after arrival in Scotland were left in place on some of the engines. Consequently the returned engines displayed a mixture of Stratford and Cowlairs features.

The other nine J69s stayed in Scotland until withdrawal, these being Nos.68503/4/5/24/33/5/44/51/2.

Incidentally, none of the J69s sent to Scotland were converted to J67/2, this alteration applying only to those maintained at Stratford and Gorton.

1953 - Class J67 and J69 withdrawals restarted.

1958 - Class J67 became extinct.

1962 - Class J69 extinct, including three which had been transferred to Departmental Stock in 1959.

Class J68

Following on from Holden's example, A.J.Hill produced ten engines, Nos.41 to 50, of an eventual class of thirty, which was an updated version of GER Class S56 (of 1904). They were the same, except for an improved cab and a built up chimney with cap. The cab had a high arched roof, side windows and large square front and back spectacles. They were passenger engines,

The first ten engines of what was to become LNER class J68, Nos.41 to 50, were built at Stratford between June and September 1912 for passenger work. They were fitted with ten-spoke steel, balanced, wheels, condensing apparatus, Macallan variable blastpipe, and Westinghouse brake for both the engine and for train working. Note the high cab with a wooden roof and side window, also the parallel sided chimney with a rim. The buffers had a taper shank with a solid spindle.

Forty engines, numbered 327 to 366, were built at Stratford between March 1890 and May 1892. All except Nos.330 and 336 had been rebuilt between September 1902 and May 1919 with 180lb boiler which had a longer firebox and with the safety valves moved forward onto the rear of the barrel. Widened tanks were fitted to increase water capacity to 1180 gallons (1140 gallons on the early conversions). These kept the level tops to their side tanks, a separate chamber being put on for condensing apparatus added during 1893. The LNER classified them J69. The sliding door to No.340's cab was not noted on any of the others.

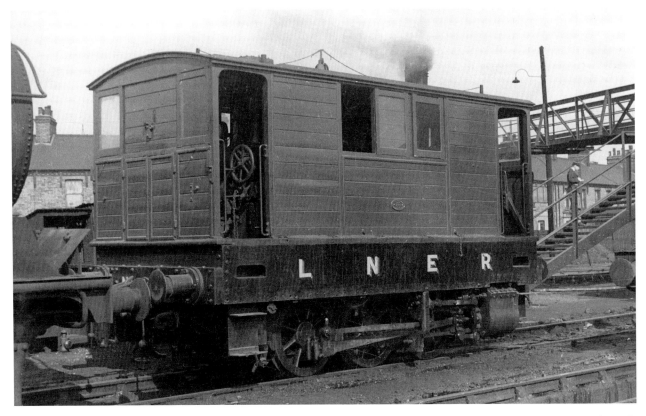

Two tram engines, Nos.135 and 136, were built at Stratford in October/November 1903 and were designed for use on public roads as at the Wisbech & Upwell tramway and to Yarmouth fish quay from Vauxhall station. They became Class J70 on the LNER.

Derived from engines originally built for the GER in 1868 by Ruston & Proctor, Lincoln, three were rebuilt in 1891/3 with cranes to serve at Stratford works. From 1st October 1894 their numbers, 204, 205 and 206, were taken off and the letters B, C and D replaced them. At first they were classified Z4 by the LNER in the miscellaneous series, but from April 1927 they became Class J92.

with Westinghouse brake, wheel reverse, condensing apparatus and ten spoke cast steel wheels with balance weights. No.47 had its condensing gear removed in 1919.

In 1913-14 ten more followed (Nos.21 to 30). These however were for goods work, with steam brake, lever reverse, and no condensing apparatus (therefore with straight topped side tanks). The sixteen spoked cast iron wheels were unbalanced. In 1923 the final ten (Nos.31 to 40), which had been ordered before Grouping, appeared under the LNER. These were also built for goods duties so were the same as Nos.21 to 30 except that they had a lower, elliptical shape, cab roof very similar to that introduced by the LNER in 1933, but still made from wood. Some of the earlier engines had been altered to this type before Grouping.

In 1923-24 vacuum ejectors were added to Nos.7041 to 7046 and 7048 (all with Westinghouse brake), and Nos.7023 and 7025 (steam brake fitted). During 1928-29 Nos.7047, 7049 and 7050 also had vacuum ejectors added. From 1935 up to 1940 all the remaining steam brake engines, except Boston based Nos.7029, 7032 and 7033, had vacuum ejectors fitted too.

The condensing apparatus was removed from Nos.7042, 7044, 7045, 7046, 7048, 7049 and 7050 during the three years 1936 to 1938. However, to further confound the observer, it was refitted to Nos.7048 and 7050 in 1940! Nos.7041 and 7043 retained the apparatus with no change. The missing engine from this list, No.7047, was reclassified J67 in 1939 when fitted with a boiler of the short firebox type with twin safety valves near the cab. In 1945 it reverted to Class J68 when given a normal boiler again.

Following a number of other exGER 0-6-0Ts, No.7041 was sold to the WD in 1940 and its ongoing history, both military and civilian, can be found in the tables.

Cast iron chimneys, as fitted to the other 0-6-0Ts, began to replace the built up type from 1930, and from 1933 steel cab roofs were fitted.

The J68 class was unique to the LNER in being the only 0-6-0T engines with side window cabs.

During 1958 a start was made to eliminate this class from British Railways but the final engine did not succumb until 1961, not quite reaching the 1962 milepost which marked the very end of Great Eastern steam.

Class J70

The first two Holden designed six-coupled Great Eastern tram engines, Nos.135 and 136, appeared in 1903 and were put to work on the docks at Ipswich. Three more came out of Stratford in 1908, Nos.137, 138 and 139, and two of these went to Yarmouth Vauxhall, the third to Wisbech. A single engine, No.130, was put into traffic in 1910 whilst another three, Nos.127, 128 and 131, were built in 1914. Finally, in 1921, three further engines, Nos.125, 126 and 129, completed what was to become LNER Class J70.

Similar in profile to the four-wheeled Y6 tram engines, they worked the same type of traffic under the same conditions and by Grouping three worked alongside the Y6 engines on the Wisbech & Upwell Tramway, three at Yarmouth and the other six at Ipswich.

Until 1926 no exchanges of boilers took place. Thereafter exchanges were made at frequent intervals, at almost every General overhaul. Like most of the GER stock, the original boiler numbers coincided with the engine numbers. Replacement boilers on Class J70 began in 1922 and took numbers 3700-3717. The final three were constructed in 1949, the last being fitted to

No.68224 in March 1950. The Diagram 46 type was also used from 1921 onwards on Class Y6.

All twelve were equipped with the Westinghouse air brake from new.

Because of their employment, which involved traversing public roads for much of their working day, the Board of Trade required that the 0-6-0s had to be fitted with cow-catchers at both ends and, that a skirt-like panel be draped over the sides beneath the footplate to cover the wheels. With the box like superstructure covering the entire engine, they appeared more like brake vans than locomotives. Nevertheless, their distinctive features became an everyday sight on the East Anglian railways for fifty years or so.

Except for one of the 1908 batch, No.7138, all of the others survived the LNER and became BR property and were numbered from 68216 to 68226 although 8218 only carried its 1946 number being condemned in September 1949. During early BR days five of the class regularly worked the Wisbech line until July 1952 when diesel shunters took over. By then the class was down to eight and in 1953 four more were withdrawn. None went in 1954 but 1955 proved to be their final year as they were picked off one at a time. The final example, No.68226 which was coincidentally the last built, was condemned in August and Class J70 became extinct.

Class J92

These three crane tanks were the oldest tank engines to work for the LNER. Built for the Great Eastern by Ruston & Proctor of Lincoln in 1868, the 204 class, as they were originally known, consisted five conventional six-coupled tank locomotives numbered 204 to 208. However, Nos.207 and 208 did not enter LNER ownership and were condemned in August 1889 and October 1892 respectively. The surviving trio were rebuilt by James Holden into crane tanks in the following order: No.205 - September 1891; Nos.204 and 206 - December 1893.

During an earlier rebuilding, by Bromley in 1881, Nos.204 and 205 acquired half cabs and steam brakes. No.206 got just a half cab and was not fitted with a steam brake until December 1893 when its crane was put on. Thereafter steam brakes sufficed throughout their lives.

These engines lost their original numbers in July 1894 and became B, C, and D, in order of their former numbers. Working continuously at Stratford works, the three crane tanks carried their 19th Century designations until June 1946 when, once again, they were given numbers: 8667, 8668 and 8669, in the same order. Renumbering by BR saw 60000 added to the numbers. Until April 1927 the LNER had classified them Z4.

The cranes carried by these engines were apparently made redundant long before the advent of the LNER but the chains and hook of the lifting gear was not removed until after WWII. The half-cab provided little shelter for the enginemen and a storm sheet, hung around a metal frame, was provided for inclement weather. However, after the cranes were no longer operated, a wooden shelter was erected to give better protection.

Having spent eighty-odd years working and most of that time at Stratford Locomotive works, the trio finally 'threw in the towel' in the following order: 68669 - October 1950; 68667 - May 1952; 68668 - November 1952 (this latter engine had become Departmental No.35 just two months previously).

No. 1 had a General repair at Stratford 24th March to 10th September 1925 from which it became LNER No 8316. The only changes of detail were replacement of the wheel on the smokebox door by a second handle and the removal of the re-railing jack.

The large MSLR number plate on the bunker was replaced by a standard LNER type plate, but apparently only after the repainting.

Built in April 1909, also by Hudswell, Clarke & Co. Leeds, MSLR No.3 was to the same dimensions as No.1, although by the takeover it had acquired a shorter chimney. The LNER decided not to spend money on further repairs so it was withdrawn on 6th August 1924 in MSLR livery.

CLASS J 64

M-SL No.1/8316

Hudswell Clarke 711.

To traffic 11/1904.

REPAIRS:
Str. 8/5—30/8/22.**G.**
Str. 24/3—10/9/25.**G.**

BOILERS:
????
1316 10/9/25.

SHEDS:
Laxfield.
Ipswich.

RENUMBERED:
8316 10/9/25.

CONDEMNED: 18/1/28.
Cut up at Stratford.

M-SL No.2/8317

Hudswell Clarke 723.

To traffic 3/1905.

REPAIRS:
Str. 18/6/20—5/5/21.**G.**
Str. 16/7/24—4/3/25.**G.**

BOILERS:
????.
1317 4/3/25.

SHEDS:
Laxfield.
Ipswich.

RENUMBERED:
8317 4/3/25.

CONDEMNED: 31/12/29.
Cut up at Stratford.

M-SL No.3

Hudswell Clarke 867.

To traffic 4/1909.

REPAIRS:
Str. 10/5—16/9/21.**G.**

BOILER:
????

SHED:
Laxfield.

RENUMBERED:
8318 *probably allocated.*

CONDEMNED: 6/8/24.
Cut up at Stratford.

MSLR No.2 was smaller than the other two as its cylinders were 13in. in diameter and its wheelbase was 11ft 6in. Built in March 1905 by Hudswell, Clarke & Co., Leeds, it had its leading sandboxes on, instead of below the running plate.

On take over No.2 went into Stratford on the 16th July 1924 and when out on the 4th March 1925 it was in unlined black as LNER 8317. The only detail difference was removal of the re-railing jack. Its withdrawal on 31st December 1929 made Class J64 extinct.

Ten more, Nos.245 to 254, were built at Stratford from February to April 1893. They differed from the first ten in having wider tanks, cab and bunker. However the height of the side tanks was less, as is apparent by comparing the position of the boiler handrails with those on No.7155 in the next illustration. The water capacity was increased to 650 gallons instead of 600 gallons in the earlier engines. Several Great Eastern 0-6-0Ts were still running in LNER days with inner fireboxes made of steel in place of the customary copper. These boilers had the safety valves placed ahead of the firebox, as shown here. No.7158 was another *see* page 24, top.

Until after Grouping all had Ramsbottom safety valves in an enclosure and with a circular casing around the base, on the right hand side of which the whistle was mounted.

New boilers built by the LNER had Ross 'pop' safety valves, and at first these were fitted on Ramsbottom mountings, with the whistle still at the side of them.

CLASS J 65

7150

Stratford .

To traffic 2/1889.

REPAIRS:
Str. 6/11/99—5/11/00.**G.**
Str. 5/9—28/11/19.**G.**
Str. 13/7—21/10/25.**G.**
Vacuum ejector fitted.
Str. ?/?—?/9/28.**G.**
Additional rails on the bunker.
Str. 30/12/30—23/1/31.**G.**
Str. 5—25/9/34.**G.**

BOILERS:
150.
150 *(new)* 5/11/00.
250 *(ex7250)* 28/11/19.
155 *(ex7155)* 21/10/25.
2840 *(ex7151)* 23/1/31.
2808 *(exJ66 7315)* 25/9/34.

SHED:
Parkeston.

RENUMBERED:
7150 21/10/25.

CONDEMNED: 2/6/37.
Cut up at Doncaster.

7151

Stratford.

To traffic 2/1889.

REPAIRS:
Str. 21/9/01—4/2/02.**G.**
Str. 13/7—18/11/21.**G.**
Str. 20/12/26—9/4/27.**G.**
Str. ?/?—?/11/29.**L.**
Additional rails on bunker.
Str. 17/6—18/7/30.**G.**
Str. ?/?—?/10/31.**L.**
Vacuum ejector fitted.
Str. 12—27/7/34.**G.**

BOILERS:
151.
151 *(new)* 4/2/02.
2840 *(new)* 18/11/21.
246 *(ex7156)* 18/7/30.
2898 *(new)* 27/7/34.

SHEDS:
Cambridge.
Stratford 16/7/30.

Colchester 8/10/31.
Norwich 18/1/35.
Parkeston 2/9/35.

RENUMBERED:
7151 ?/?/??.

CONDEMNED: 13/7/37.
Cut up at Stratford.

7152

Stratford.

To traffic 2/1889.

REPAIRS:
Str. 27/3—5/11/08.**G.**
Str. 12/1—26/4/23.**G.**
Str. ?/?—?/9/28.**G.**
Additional rails on bunker.
Str. 3—24/2/33.**G.**

BOILERS:
152.
152 *(new)* 5/11/08.
2815 *(ex7156)* 26/4/23.
252 *(exJ67 7403)* 24/2/33.

SHED:
Cambridge.
Ipswich 16/5/29.
Colchester 17/9/29.
Ipswich 11/11/29.
Parkeston 5/3/33.

RENUMBERED:
7152 ?/?/25.

CONDEMNED: 30/10/35.
Cut up at Stratford.

7153

Stratford.

To traffic 2/1889.

REPAIRS:
Str. 17/12/02—9/5/03.**G.**
Str. 12/10/23—7/3/24.**G.**
Str. ?/?—?/2/28.**G.**
Additional rails on bunker.

BOILERS:
153.
153 *(new)* 9/5/03.
152 *(ex7152)* 7/3/24.

SHEDS:
Stratford.
Ipswich 10/5/28.

RENUMBERED:
7153 7/3/24.

CONDEMNED: 25/9/31.
Cut up at Stratford.

7154

Stratford.

To traffic 2/1889.

REPAIRS:
Str. 20/4—22/11/00.**G.**
Nor. ?/?—?/9/22.**H.**
Str. ?/?—?/11/29.**G.**

BOILERS:
154.
154 *(new)* 22/11/00.

SHEDS:
Norwich.
Yarmouth 27/7/30.
Norwich 11/1/31.

RENUMBERED:
7154 ?/?/??.

CONDEMNED: 12/4/32.
Cut up at Stratford.

7155

Stratford.

To traffic 2/1889.

REPAIRS:
Str. 26/8/04—23/2/05.**G.**
Str. 9/5—22/9/22.**G.**
Str. 10/10/24—24/1/25.**G.**
Str. 20/4—6/7/29.**G.**
Additional rails on bunker.
Str. 6/7—17/8/34.**G.**
Str. 9/10/39—5/1/40.**L.**
Str. 19/4—15/5/41.**H.**
Str. 2/5—26/7/43.**G.**
Str. 25/11—21/12/45.**G.**
Str. 19/12/50—3/3/51.**G.**
Str. 13/11/53. *Not repaired.*

BOILERS:
155.
155 *(new)* 23/2/05.

2861 *(new)* 24/1/25.
2870 *(exJ67 7406)* 17/3/34.
2829 *(ex7253)* 15/5/41.
2879 *(exJ67 7360)* 21/12/45.
23903 3/3/51.

SHEDS:
Stratford.
Ipswich 18/6/37.
Cambridge 26/2/40.
Stratford 15/12/40.
Ipswich 26/2/41.
Colchester 22/7/41.
Norwich 31/12/42.
Ipswich 18/4/43.
Norwich 22/8/43.
Ipswich 4/3/45.
Yarmouth 22/7/45.
Yarmouth Beach 30/9/45.
Ipswich 2/12/45.
Yarmouth Beach 22/2/48.
Ipswich 11/6/48.

RENUMBERED:
7155 24/1/25.
8211 2/10/46.
68211 3/3/51.

CONDEMNED: 23/11/53.
Cut up at Stratford.

7156

Stratford.

To traffic 3/1889.

REPAIRS:
Str. 22/6/98—20/3/99.**G.**
Str. 20/9/17—17/6/18.**G.**
Str. 7/7—7/10/22.**G.**
Str. 22/2—7/3/30.**G.**
Additional rails on bunker.
Str. ?/?—?/10/31.**L.**
Vacuum ejector fitted.
Str. 31/12/34—16/1/35.**G.**

BOILERS:
156.
156 *(new)* 20/3/99.
2815 *(new)* 17/6/18.
246 *(ex7246)* 7/10/22.
2869 *(new)* 7/3/30.
2840 *(ex7150)* 16/1/35.

SHEDS:
Stratford.
Ipswich 22/10/31.
Parkeston 14/5/37.

After 1932 the 'pop' valves were mounted directly on to the firebox and the whistle was placed further back, just in front of the cab.

On the first ten, Nos.7150-7159, the balance weights on the wheels filled a space between adjacent spokes. Note this September 1937 photograph shows No.7150 on the scrap line at Doncaster works.

(below) On the other ten, Nos.7245 to 7254, the balance weights were the more conventional crescent shape. Ex works 2nd August 1933, No.7249 had Group Standard buffers, the only others noted so fitted were Nos.7157 (see page 24, 3rd from top) and 8215 (page 25, 2nd from top).

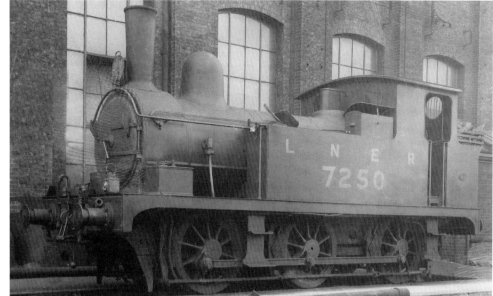

Until 1927 the standard fitting on the bunker was three open coal rails made up from flat bar iron.

Between 1927 and 1930 three extra rails were put on, filling the spaces between the existing rails.

(below) The number of coal rails on some was increased to eight, Nos.7153, 7155, 7157, 7247 and 7248 being noted so fitted. These originally had four open rails. Note No.7155 was one of those used on the Blackwall line which ran with the front coupling rod removed.

At Grouping and until the mid-1920's, a Macallan variable blast pipe was fitted with a control rod from the cab just above top of the tank. No.7246 was one with four open coal rails. Until 1927 there was no provision for carriage heating.

From 1925 the Macallan blastpipes were taken off and replaced by the plain type. Between 1927 and 1930 all were fitted for carriage heating with connections at both ends. The lagging of the pipe to the front was very noticeable; No.7155 was so fitted ex works 6th July 1929 when the additional coal rails were also put on.

For use when working from Yarmouth Beach shed, from February to June 1948, No.8211 (ex 7155) was fitted with a spark arrester. Note that it still did not have front coupling rods fitted.

Originally the handrails along the boiler ended on the side of the smokebox and there was a separate curved rail over the door. No.7248 still had this style to at least November 1932 and No.7153 kept it to its 25th September 1931 withdrawal. These were the only two so noted in LNER painting.

7156 cont./
RENUMBERED:
7156 after 22/10/24.

CONDEMNED: 25/8/37.
Cut up at Stratford.

_____

7157

Stratford.

To traffic 3/1889.

REPAIRS:
Str. 28/1—2/6/10.**G.**
Str. 20/3—12/7/24.**G.**
Str. 10/12/27—10/3/28.**G.**
Additional rails on bunker.
Str. ?/?—?/9/33.**G.**
Str. ?/?—10/3/37.**G.**
Str. ?/?—3/4/41.**G.**
Str. ?/?—?/12/44.**G.**
Str. ?/?—31/12/46.**L.**

BOILERS:
157.
157 (new) 2/6/10.
2857 (new) 12/7/24.
2866 (ex7249) ?/9/33.
2848 (exJ67 7200) 10/3/37.
2827 (exJ66 7293) 3/4/41.
2873 (exJ66 7320) ?/12/44.

SHEDS:
Stratford.
Ipswich at 5/32.
Stratford ?/?.
Norwich 1/12/41.
Ipswich ?/?.
Norwich 31/5/46.
Lowestoft 23/6/46.
Norwich 16/7/46.
Ipswich 10/9/46.

RENUMBERED:
7157 12/7/24.
8212 1/9/46.

CONDEMNED: 28/11/47.
Cut up at Darlington 4/48.

_____

7158

Stratford.

To traffic 3/1889.

REPAIRS:
Str. 14/10/02—19/3/03.**G.**
Str. 28/8/20—21/1/21.**G.**
Str. ?/?—?/4/27.**G.**
Additional rails on bunker.

BOILERS:
158.
158 (new) 19/3/03.
253 (ex7253) 21/1/21.

SHEDS:
Stratford.
Norwich 22/4/27.
Lowestoft ?/?
Yarmouth 8/7/28.
Lowestoft 27/7/30.

RENUMBERED:
7158 after 25/7/25.

CONDEMNED: 18/3/32.
Cut up at Stratford.

_____

7159

Stratford.

To traffic 6/1889.

REPAIRS:
Str. 10/9/09—17/1/10.**G.**
Nor. ?/?—?/10/20.**H.**
Str. 14/2—8/3/30.**G.**
Additional rails on bunker.
Str. 20/2—7/3/33.**G.**

BOILERS:
159.
159 (new) 17/1/10.
254 (exJ67 7012) 8/3/30.
2817 (ex7252) 7/3/33.

SHEDS:
Lowestoft.
Norwich 14/1/28.
Yarmouth 1/7/28.
Norwich 23/9/28.
Lowestoft 19/5/29.
Norwich 25/1/31.
Lowestoft 13/9/31.
Norwich 9/1/35.

RENUMBERED:
7159 ?/?/??.

CONDEMNED: 28/5/37.
Cut up at Stratford.

_____

7245

Stratford.

To traffic 2/1893.

REPAIRS:
Str. 27/5—18/12/08.**G.**
Str. 14/1—13/5/21.**G.**
Str. ?/?—31/5/24.**?.**

Str. ?/?—18/1/28.**G.**
Additional rails on bunker.

BOILERS:
245.
245 (new) 18/12/08.
2836 (new) 13/5/21.

SHED:
Ipswich.

RENUMBERED:
7245 31/5/24.

CONDEMNED: 21/1/31.
Cut up at Stratford.

_____

7246

Stratford.

To traffic 2/1893.

REPAIRS:
Str. 24/5—13/8/12.**G.**
Str. 21/3—8/7/22.**G.**
Str. 11/2—7/5/25.**G.**
Str. ?/?—?/7/28.**G.**
Additional rails on bunker.

BOILERS:
246.
246 (new) 13/8/12.
252 (ex7252) 8/7/22.
248 (ex7248) 7/5/25.

SHED:
Ipswich.

RENUMBERED:
7246 7/5/25.

CONDEMNED: 31/12/30.
Cut up at Stratford.

_____

7247

Stratford.

To traffic 2/1893.

REPAIRS:
Str. 13/1—8/5/12.**G.**
Str. 18/3—29/9/21.**G.**
Str. ?/?—?/11/27.**G.**
Additional rails on bunker.
Str. ?/?—?/4/29.**G.**
Str. 18/4—18/5/33.**G.**
Str. 19/2—11/3/36.**G.**
Str. ?/?—26/9/40.**G.**
Str. ?/?—18/11/44.**G.**

BOILERS:
247.
247 (new) 8/5/12.
245 (ex7245) 29/9/21.
2821 (exJ66 7286) ?/4/29.
2815 (ex7152) 18/5/33.
2889 (ex7253) 11/3/36.
2893 (exJ67 7192) 18/11/44.

SHEDS:
Ipswich.
Yarmouth Beach 25/11/45.
Yarmouth 3/3/46.
Yarmouth Beach 27/10/46.
Norwich 21/5/47.
Yarmouth Beach 12/10/47.

RENUMBERED:
7247 by 25/2/25.
8213 1/4/46.

CONDEMNED: 6/2/48.
Cut up at Stratford.

_____

7248

Stratford.

To traffic 3/1893.

REPAIRS:
Str. 28/1—19/5/10.**G.**
Str. 26/9/19—1/1/21.**G.**
Str. 3/1—13/6/25.**G.**
Str. ?/?—?/11/25.**L.**
Vacuum ejector fitted.
Str. 7/7—16/10/28.**G.**
Additional rails on bunker.
Str. 2—22/11/32.**G.**

BOILERS:
248.
248 (new) 19/5/10.
249 (ex7249) 13/6/25.
2829 (exJ67 7161) 16/10/28.
2811 (ex 7251) 22/11/32.

SHED:
Parkeston.
Immingham 8/4/29.
Stratford 6/3/30.
Colchester 10/9/31.
Ipswich 11/10/34.
Colchester 18/5/35.
Ipswich 7/11/35.

RENUMBERED:
7248 13/6/25.

CONDEMNED: 13/5/36.
Cut up at Stratford.

_____

(above) **By Grouping it was usual to have a continuous rail and thirteen have been checked as having this type.**

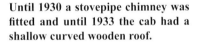

Until 1930 a stovepipe chimney was fitted and until 1933 the cab had a shallow curved wooden roof.

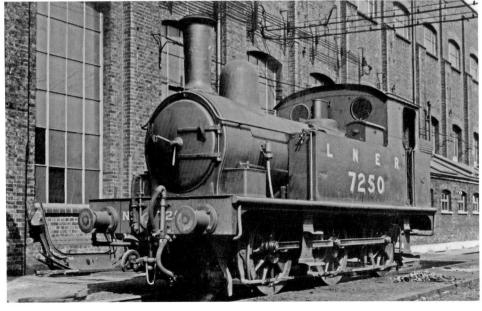

From 1930 the stovepipes were replaced by the NER pattern cast type with a lip but Nos.7153, 7154, 7158, 7245, 7246 and 7251 missed this change as they were scrapped in 1931/32. Ex works 2ⁿᵈ August 1933, No.7249 (see page 16, bottom) was the first to be changed to a steel cab roof and this made the height from rail level 11ft 10½ in. instead of 11ft 5⅞ in.

(above) **Only five, Nos.7157, 7247, 7249, 7250 and 7253 are known to have been altered to a steel roof. No.68211 (ex 7155) which survived to 23rd November 1953, kept the wooden cab roof. Ex works 3rd March 1951, it did have front coupling rods fitted but the 3rd from top illustration on page 25 shows that in service on Ipswich docks they had again been removed.**

Until after its last repair, ex works 18th November 1944, No.8213 (ex 7247) still had the usual tool box on the left hand tank in front of the cab.

During 1945 the five survivors all had this facility taken off.

7249

Stratford.

To traffic 3/1893.

REPAIRS:
Str. 4/6—6/9/12.**G.**
Str. 25/5—18/9/17.**G.**
Str. 12/6—7/10/24.**G.**
Str. 5/4—20/7/28.**G.**
Additional rails on bunker.
Str. 14/7—2/8/33.**G.**

BOILERS:
249.
249 *(new)* 6/9/12.
157 *(ex7157)* 7/10/24.
2866 *(new)* 20/7/28.
2821 *(ex7247)* 2/8/33.

SHEDS:
Stratford.
Ipswich 18/5/37.

RENUMBERED:
7249 7/10/24.

CONDEMNED: 13/7/37.
Cut up at Stratford.

7250

Stratford.

To traffic 3/1893.

REPAIRS:
Str. 21/10—30/12/10.**G.**
Str. 6/9—10/12/18.**G.**
Ips. 15/3—7/7/22.**H.**
Str. 1/9—29/11/24.**G.**
Str. 19/2—1/4/25.**L.**
Str. ?/?—?/9/25.**L.**
Vacuum ejector, and steam heating fitted.
Str. 21/7—12/11/28.**G.**
Additional rails on bunker.
Str. 7/9—20/11/30.**G.**
Str. 3/5—5/6/34.**G.**
Str. 30/6—6/8/36.**G.**
Str. 2—31/3/37.**L.**
Str. 23/6—11/7/39.**L.**
Str. 30/5—11/7/41.**G.**
Str. 12/8—8/9/45.**G.**
Str. 17/6—11/8/51.**G.**

BOILERS:
250.
250 *(new)* 30/12/10.
2814 *(new)* 10/12/18.
249 *(ex7248)* 12/11/28.
2857 *(ex7157)* 5/6/34.

2811 *(ex7248)* 6/8/36.
2870 *(ex7155)* 11/7/41.
2834 *(exJ67 7203)* 8/9/45.
23909 11/8/51.

SHEDS:
Parkeston.
South Lynn 26/2/37.
Parkeston 18/3/37.
Stratford 25/9/39.
New England 13/5/42.
Immingham 29/9/42.
Lincoln 15/2/43.
Immingham 25/11/45.
Cambridge 28/7/46.
Norwich 16/1/48.
Melton Constable 25/7/48.
Norwich 28/8/48.
Yarmouth Beach 10/4/49.
Melton Constable 24/10/54.
Yarmouth Beach 12/12/54.

RENUMBERED:
7250 29/11/24.
8214 8/6/46.
68214 11/8/51.

CONDEMNED: 22/10/56.
Cut up at Stratford.

7251

Stratford.

To traffic 3/1893.

REPAIRS:
Str. 10/12/10—27/4/11.**G.**
Str. 17/10/19—27/?/20.**G.**
Str. 11/4—21/9/21.**H.**
New cylinders.
Str. 13/9—27/11/24.**G.**
Str. ?/?—?/9/25.**L.**
Vacuum ejector fitted.
Str. ?/9—?/10/29.**G.**
Additional rails on bunker.

BOILERS:
251.
251 *(new)* 27/4/11.
2817 *(new)* 27/3/20.
2811 *(exJ66 7292)* ?/10/29.

SHED:
Parkeston.

RENUMBERED:
7251 27/11/24.

CONDEMNED: 14/12/31.
Cut up at Stratford.

7252

Stratford.

To traffic 3/1893.

REPAIRS:
Str. 5/2—17/6/10.**G.**
Str. 12/10/21—13/1/22.**G.**
Str. ?/?—?/10/25.**L.**
Vacuum ejector fitted.
Str. 31/1—9/4/27.**G.**
Additional rails on bunker.
Str. 17/12/29—29/1/30.**G.**
Str. 12/1—1/2/33.**G.**

BOILERS:
252.
252 *(new)* 17/6/10.
247 *(ex7247)* 13/1/22.
204 *(exJ67 7204)* 9/4/27.
2817 *(ex7251)* 29/1/30.
2829 *(ex7248)* 1/2/33.

SHEDS:
Ipswich.
Parkeston 3/4/29

RENUMBERED:
7252 ?/?/24.

CONDEMNED: 15/8/35.
Cut up at Stratford.

7253

Stratford.

To traffic 4/1893.

REPAIRS:
Str. 15/9/11—11/1/12.**G.**
Str. 19/4—17/7/20.**G.**
Str. ?/?—21/5/29.**G.**
Additional rails on bunker.
Str. 27/4—19/5/32.**G.**
Str. 15/12/35—16/1/36.**G.**
Str. ?/?—28/10/38.**G.**
Str. ?/?—2/4/41.**G.**
Str. ?/?—?/5/44.**G.**
Str. 8—22/2/47.**L.**

BOILERS:
253.
253 *(new)* 11/1/12.
251 *(ex7251)* 17/7/20.
2889 *(new)* 19/5/32.
2829 *(ex7252)* 16/1/36.
2836 *(exJ67 7169)* 2/4/41.
2830 *(exJ67 7399)* ?/5/44.

SHEDS:
Parkeston.

Ipswich 29/3/33.
Cambridge 26/5/40.
Ipswich 2/6/40.
Frodingham 8/1/44.
New England 7/5/44.
Barnsley 16/2/45.
New England 6/7/45.
Stratford 21/9/45.
Yarmouth Beach 2/6/48.

RENUMBERED:
7253 ?/?/??.
8215 17/11/46.

CONDEMNED: 9/5/49.
Cut up at Stratford.

7254

Stratford.

To traffic 4/1893.

REPAIRS:
Str. 24/5—21/8/12.**G.**
Str. 15/6—22/12/21.**G.**
Str. ?/?—?/9/24.**L.**
Vacuum ejector fitted.
Str. 24/6—29/9/27.**G.**
Additional rails on bunker.
Str. 13/5—26/6/30.**G.**
Str. 8—29/3/33.**G.**

BOILERS:
254.
254 *(new)* 21/8/12.
247 *(ex7252)* 29/9/27.
159 *(ex7159)* 26/6/30.
254 *(ex7159)* 29/3/33.

SHEDS:
Ipswich.
Parkeston 19/7/28.
Ipswich 6/12/28.
Colchester 14/9/31.
Parkeston 7/11/35.

RENUMBERED:
7254 ?/9/24.

CONDEMNED: 3/6/37.
Cut up at Stratford.

Until 1924 only Westinghouse brake was provided, on the engine and for train working, and twelve, No.7158 amongst them, were never altered.

During 1924/25 six Nos.7150, 7248, 7250, 7251, 7252 and 7254 (four at Parkeston and two shedded at Ipswich) had vacuum ejectors added. In October 1931 Nos.7151 and 7156 also had the vacuum brake added; No.7151 to work at Colchester and 7156 at Ipswich so that No.7251 could be withdrawn on 14th December 1931.

The first J65 to get black painting with red lining was No.152 as L&NER, ex works on 26th April 1923. The number was changed to 7152 in 1925 without alteration to the company's initials, and probably stayed that way to about June 1928. No trace has been found of any J65 getting the E suffix put on in the September 1923 to February 1924 period.

No.252 in GER grey from a January 1922 painting, changed in late 1924 to No.7252 in 19in. yellow painted figures on grey which it certainly kept to February 1927.

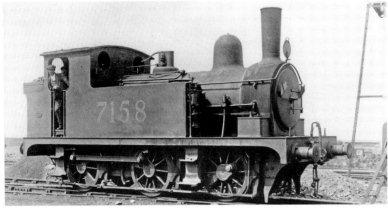

No.7158 certainly still had grey livery and 19in. painted number after its General repair in April 1927 and it probably remained so to withdrawal on 18th March 1932. Note that it had a steel firebox and although working at Yarmouth and Lowestoft, had the front coupling rods removed. Here in 1928 it is at Yarmouth docks.

Ex works 7th March 1924, No.7153 was the first to get this standard LNER livery including single red lining. It was followed by No.7245 (31st May 1924) and 7157 (12th July 1924). No.7247 was out on the 25th February 1925.

The June 1928 painting economies put an end to the red lining and only plain black was used subsequently, note Group Standard buffers and that the wheels have been changed as No.7157 had a full set with crescent shaped balance weights when ex works 10th March 1937.

From July 1942 only NE was used and none of the five survivors had LNER restored, Nos. 8212, 8213 and 8215 still being only NE when withdrawn in November 1947, February 1948, and May 1949 respectively. For five engines there were four varieties of re-numbering. No.8211 *see* page 18, 3rd from top - and 8212 got 9in. shaded transfers put on by Ipswich shed, No.7155 changed to 8211 on Wednesday 2nd October 1946 and No.7157 to 8212 on Sunday 1st September 1946.

No.7250 was at Immingham shed when re-numbered to 8214 on Saturday 8th June 1946 and, as with many on the GC section, 8in. stenciled numbers were used.

At Stratford shed on Sunday 17th November 1946, No.7253 was changed to 8215 and whilst 12in. numbers were used they were painted and without shading. No.8213 (see page 21, 2nd from top) also got 12in. figures when Yarmouth shed changed it from 7247 on Monday 1st April 1946 but they found shaded transfers to do the job properly.

Only two acquired BR painting, going straight from NE to 15½ in. emblem, smokebox number plate and with the number moved from tank to bunker and with correct Gill sans figures. No.68211 was thus when ex works 3rd March 1951 through to withdrawal on 23rd November 1953. When No.68214 was withdrawn 22nd October 1956, Class J65 became extinct.

(above) **By 1893 one of the above batch, No.281, had already become a Stratford works shunter, and at various periods had been adapted to burn oil fuel. Its short stovepipe chimney had been replaced by one of normal length well before Grouping. It remained on the same duties for a further 69 years.**

Ten further engines, Nos.307 to 316, were built at Stratford between June and August 1888. By Grouping No.307 (also 322) had the steel firebox with safety valves moved forward on to the back ring of the boiler barrel.

The final ten, Nos.317 to 326, were built as passenger engines in November and December 1888. As well as having the Westinghouse brake, they differed from the earlier engines in having a 6in. longer bunker, the cab length being reduced by a like amount. Within two years they were converted to goods engines, the Westinghouse gear transferred to new J67 class Nos.337 to 346. The longer bunker remained.

CLASS J 66

7275

Stratford.

To traffic 6/1886.

REPAIRS:
Str. 22/9/98—9/1/99.**G.**
Str. 2/2—30/4/24.**G.**
Str. ?/?—?/4/29.**G.**
Additional rails on bunker.
Str. 16/6—7/7/31.**G.**

BOILERS:
275.
275 *(new)* 9/1/99.
278 *(ex7278)* 30/4/24.
2824 *(ex7304)* 7/7/31.

SHEDS:
March.
King's Lynn 10/6/36.

RENUMBERED:
7275 30/4/24.

WITHDRAWN: 21/6/38.
Sold 11/38 to Ashington Coal
Co. as their No.18.
Scrapped 2/53.

7276

Stratford.

To traffic 5/1886.

REPAIRS:
Str. ?/?—?/5/99.**G.**
Str. 12/7—27/9/12.**G.**
Str. 18/2—29/5/24.**G.**
Str. ?/?—?/9/26.**G.**
Additional rails on bunker.
Str. 29/12/33—16/1/34.**G.**

BOILERS:
276.
276 *(new)* ?/5/99.
276 *(new)* 27/9/12.
255 *(exJ67 7255)* 29/5/24.
2892 *(new)* 16/1/34.

SHEDS:
March.
Stratford 24/2/29.
March 16/2/34.
Peterborough East 14/5/34.
New England 31/7/36.

RENUMBERED:
7276 29/5/24.

CONDEMNED: 3/7/37.
Cut up at Stratford.

7277

Stratford.

To traffic 6/1886.

REPAIRS:
Str. ?/?—?/3/98.**G.**
Str. 9/4—31/10/08.**G.**
Str. 21/2—19/12/19.**G.**
Str. 24/2—4/6/27.**G.**
Additional rails on bunker.
Str. ?/?—23/11/29.**G.**
Str. ?/?—?/9/31.**G.**

BOILERS:
277.
277 *(new)* ?/3/98.
277 *(new)* 31/10/08.
257 *(exJ67 7257* 4/6/27.
280 *(exJ67 7019)* ?/9/31.

SHEDS:
March.
King's Lynn 10/6/36.
Cambridge 16/8/36.
King's Lynn 16/5/37.

RENUMBERED:
7277 by 25/2/25.

WITHDRAWN: 29/7/38.
Sold 11/38 to Ashington Coal
Co. as their No.19.
Scrapped 12/44.

7278

Stratford.

To traffic 6/1886.

REPAIRS:
Str. ?/?—?/10/98.**G.**
Str. 8/2—23/6/10.**G.**
Str. ?/?—?/2/24.**G.**
Str. ?/?—29/4/26.**G.**
Str. ?/?—?/5/28.**G.**
Additional rails on bunker.
Str. 20/11—19/12/30.**G.**

BOILERS:
278.
278 *(new)* ?/10/98.
278 *(new)* 23/6/10.
202 *(exJ67 7202)* ?/2/24.
296 *(ex7323)* 19/12/30.

SHEDS:
March.
St Margarets 25/7/24.
March 12/11/24.
Cambridge 15/4/36.

RENUMBERED:
7278 ?/2/24 ?

WITHDRAWN: 17/10/36.
Sold 10/36 to Sir R.McAlpine &
Co. as their No.78.
Scrapped circa 1938.

7279

Stratford.

To traffic 6/1886.

REPAIRS:
Str. ?/?—?/2/99.**G.**
Str. 13/11/07—4/6/08.**G.**
Str. ?/?—?/8/25.**G.**
Str. ?/?—?/12/27.**G.**
Additional rails on bunker.
Str. 29/1—1/3/30.**G.**
Str. 18/6—11/7/34.**G.**

BOILERS:
279.
279 *(new)* ?/2/99.
279 *(new)* 4/6/08.
298 *(ex7298)* ?/8/25.
2884 *(new)* 1/3/30.
2856 *(exJ67 7259)* 11/7/34.

SHEDS:
March.
Gorton ?/7/24.
March ?/11/24.
Stratford 19/8/30.
Cambridge 11/7/34.
King's Lynn 16/8/36.

RENUMBERED:
279E ?/?/2?.
7279 ?/8/25.

CONDEMNED: 20/5/37.
Cut up at Stratford.

7280

Stratford.

To traffic 6/1886.

REPAIRS:
Str. ?/?—?/12/99.**G.**
Str. 28/6—27/9/12.**G.**
Str. ?/?—?/3/25.**G.**
Str. ?/?—?/8/27.**G.**
Additional rails on bunker.
Str. 7—23/12/31.**G.**

BOILERS:
280.
280 *(new)* ?/12/99.
280 *(new)* 27/9/12.
300 *(ex7300)* ?/3/25.
155 *(exJ65 7150)* 23/12/31.

SHEDS:
March.
New England 10/8/32.
Grantham 18/8/32.
New England 4/1/33.

RENUMBERED:
7280 ?/3/25.

CONDEMNED: 24/7/36.
Cut up at Stratford.

7281

Stratford.

To traffic 6/1886.

REPAIRS:
Str. 6/8—23/12/04.**G.**
Str. 21/12/20—4/3/21.**G.**
Str. 8/9/24—13/2/25.**G.**
Str. ?/?—10/1/29.**G.**
Str. 10—21/10/32.**G.**
Str. 14—31/1/36.**G.**
Str. ?/?—15/1/41.**G.**
Str. 28/4—12/5/45.**G.**
G.S. buffers fitted.
Str. 1/11/47.**L.**
Str. 15/12/48—1/1/49.**L.**
Str. 11—29/4/50.**G.**
Str. ?/?—14/1/54.**L.**
Str. ?/?—9/3/56.**G.**

BOILERS:
281.
281 *(new)* 23/12/04.
327 *(ex7290)* 21/10/32.

7281 cont./
  204 *(exJ67 7327)* 31/1/36.
  2885 *(exJ67 7329)* 15/1/41.
  2814 *(exJ67 7163)* 12/5/45.
  2906 *(exJ67 8532)* 29/4/50.
  2906 reno.S.B.3334 ?/5/53.
SB3343 *(23916 exJ67 68590)*
9/3/56.

SHED:
Stratford works.
(Departmental stock)

RENUMBERED:
  7281 13/2/25.
  8370 13/4/46.
  68370 30/12/48.
  DEPT'L **32** 27/9/52.

CONDEMNED: 16/9/62.
Cut up at Stratford.

_____

7282

Stratford.

To traffic 6/1886.

REPAIRS:
Str. 16/10/99—24/2/00.**G.**
Str. 18/12/22—21/3/23.**G.**
Str. 27/5—22/10/26.**G.**
Additional rails on bunker.
Str. 26/11/28—5/3/29.**G.**
Str. 28/11/31—29/1/32.**G.**
Str. 10/1—7/2/36.**G.**
Str. 26/11/39. *Not repaired.*

BOILERS:
  282.
  282 *(new)* 24/2/00.
  2845 *(new)* 21/3/23.
  2848 *(ex7302)* 5/3/29.
  2850 *(ex7285)* 29/1/32.
  2855 *(ex7295)* 7/2/36.

SHED:
Lincoln.

RENUMBERED:
7282 22/10/26.

CONDEMNED: 16/2/40.
Cut up at Stratford.

_____

7283

Stratford.

To traffic 7/1886.

REPAIRS:
Str. 21/4—22/9/99.**G.**
Str. 13/1—12/4/23.**G.**
Str. ?/?—?/6/25.**G.**
Str. ?/?—?/1/28.**G.**
Additional rails on bunker.
Str. 6—21/10/32.**G.**

BOILERS:
  283.
  283 *(new)* 22/9/99.
  2846 *(new)* 12/4/23.
  2881 *(ex7325)* 21/10/32.

SHEDS:
March.
Boston 27/12/35.
Grantham 4/1/36.
New England 3/9/36.

RENUMBERED:
7283 ?/6/25.

CONDEMNED: 27/7/39.
Cut up at Stratford.

_____

7284

Stratford.

To traffic 7/1886.

REPAIRS:
Str. 25/7—30/11/99.**G.**
Str. 19/5—22/9/16.**G.**
Str. 31/5/24.**?.**
Awaiting repair.
Str. 20/12/26—24/3/27.**G.**
Str. ?/?—?/7/29.**G.**
Additional rails on bunker.
Str. 6—27/11/31.**G.**

BOILERS:
  284.
  284 *(new)* 30/11/99.
  2805 *(new)* 22/9/16.
  259 *(exJ67 7259)* 24/3/27.
  2862 *(exJ67 7327)* 27/11/31.

SHEDS:
March.
New England 26/1/34.
Peterborough East 2/2/34.

RENUMBERED:
7284 *after* 31/5/24.

CONDEMNED: 10/5/37.
Cut up at Stratford.

_____

7285

Stratford.

To traffic 2/1887.

REPAIRS:
Str. 19/8/97—23/3/98.**G.**
Str. 31/3—22/6/23.**G.**
Str. 26/10—24/12/25.**G.**
Str. 7/9—21/11/28.**G.**
Additional rails on bunker.
Str. 29/9—13/11/31.**G.**
Str. 20/6—26/7/35.**G.**
Str. 15/8/39. *Not repaired.*

BOILERS:
  285.
  285 *(new)* 23/3/98.
  2850 *(new)* 22/6/23.
  411 *(exJ67 7015)* 13/11/31.
  2876 *(exJ67 7400)* 26/7/35.

SHEDS:
Peterborough East.
New England 30/4/39.

RENUMBERED:
7285 24/12/25.

CONDEMNED: 1/10/39.
Cut up at Stratford.

_____

7286

Stratford.

To traffic 2/1887.

REPAIRS:
Str. ?/?—?/9/98.**G.**
Str. 15/11/13—10/3/14.**G.**
Str. 20/10/23—9/1/24.**G.**
Str. 9/4—19/8/26.**G.**
Additional rails on bunker.
Str. 1/5—27/7/28.**G.**
Str. 12/11—24/12/30.**G.**
Str. 30/11—28/12/33.**G.**
Str. 24/7/39. *Not repaired.*

BOILERS:
  286.
  286 *(new)* ?/9/98.
  2821 *(ex7292)* 9/1/24.
  2841 *(exJ67 7016)* 27/7/28.
  2812 *(ex7298)* 24/12/30.
  2806 *(exJ67 7327)* 28/12/33.

SHEDS:
Stratford.
March 28/10/24.
Staveley 3/12/36.

RENUMBERED:
7286 *after* 9/1/24.

CONDEMNED: 20/9/39.
Cut up at Stratford.

_____

7287

Stratford.

To traffic 3/1887.

REPAIRS:
Str. ?/?—?/6/99.**G.**
Str. 29/11/07—29/5/08.**G.**
Str. 14/9—25/11/25.**G.**
Str. ?/?—?/9/28.**G.**
Additional rails on bunker.
Str. ?/?—?/1/31.**G.**
Str. 10—26/10/34.**G.**

BOILERS:
  287.
  287 *(new)* ?/6/99.
  287 *(new)* 29/5/08.
  279 *(ex7279)* 25/11/25.
  297 *(exJ67 7161)* ?/7/31.
  2803 *(exJ67 7398)* 26/10/34.

SHEDS:
King's Lynn.
Cambridge *by* 1932.
King's Lynn 2/12/33.
March 10/6/36.

RENUMBERED:
7287 25/11/25.

WITHDRAWN: 17/10/36.
Sold 10/36 to Sir R.McAlpine &
Co. as their No.76.
Scrapped circa 1939.

_____

7288

Stratford.

To traffic 3/1887.

REPAIRS:
Str. 2/12/99—20/4/00.**G.**
Str. 3/12/20—4/3/21.**G.**
Str. 30/11/23—14/1/24.**G.**
Str. 23/2—4/6/26.**G.**
Additional rails on bunker.
Str. 22/5—23/8/28.**G.**
Str. 8/8—1/10/30.**G.**
Str. 30/5—22/6/33.**G.**
Str. 7/9—4/10/33.**L.**
Str. 5/12/36—14/1/37.**G.**
Str. 18/5—21/6/41.**G.**
Str. 12/6—10/7/44.**G.**
Str. 18/7—12/8/44.**L.**

At Grouping No.294 was the only one with a Westinghouse brake, fitted in 1887 when this engine had been selected for trial passenger train working. Until 1925, the Macallan variable blastpipe was fitted, with a control rod from the cab.

(*below*) Ex works 25th September 1926, No.7294 was given carriage heating equipment and had its wheels changed to the 10-spoke cast steel type with crescent shaped balance weights. Additional rails were put on the bunker (*see* page 33, top).

From October 1930 No.7294 again became a shunting engine, the Westinghouse being taken off, and a steam brake put on. It was also changed from screw to lever reverse.

(above) Ex works Nos.7309 (14th April 1934) and 7295 (16th October 1935) had been fitted with 10-spoke balanced wheels, and by 14th February 1946, No.7307 (8378 later) also had that type.

During the 1930's, 12-spoke unbalanced wheels were introduced and Nos.7292, 7293, 7312 and 7315 were noted with them.

(below) The original boiler handrails ended on the side of the smokebox and there was a separate curved rail above the smokebox door. No.68375 (ex 7296) still had this style to 24th November 1952 withdrawal - *see* page 45, bottom - and Departmental No.32 kept it to 16th September 1962 when it was the last of the class *see* page 37, bottom.

7288 cont./
Str. 5/8—28/9/46.**G.**
Str. 15/6—27/8/49.**G.**
Str. 14/2—14/3/52.**C/H.**
Str. 30/10—15/11/52.**N/C.**

BOILERS:
288.
288 *(new)* 20/4/00.
2834 *(new)* 4/3/21.
204 *(exJ65 7252)* 1/10/30.
2871 *(ex7289)* 22/6/33.
2857 *(exJ65 7250)* 14/1/37.
2894 *(ex7321)* 21/6/41.
2878 *(ex7296)* 10/7/44.
2860 *(exJ67 7403)* 28/9/46.
2872 *(exJ67 8513)* 27/8/49.
23920 14/3/52.

SHEDS:
Stratford.
March 28/10/24.
Staveley 1/8/33.
Stratford 14/1/37.
Cambridge 11/8/38.
Staveley 30/5/39.

RENUMBERED:
288ᴇ 14/1/24.
7288 4/6/26.
8371 26/5/46.
68371 27/8/49.

CONDEMNED: 19/4/54.
Cut up at Stratford.

_____

7289

Stratford.

To traffic 3/1887.

REPAIRS:

Str. 19/5—12/10/99.**G.**
Str. 18/6—12/11/14.**G.**
Pbo. 5/1—29/3/23.**H.**
Str. 16/3—14/7/25.**G.**
Str. 1/8—19/10/27.**G.**
Additional rails on bunker.
Str. 21/11/29—11/1/30.**G.**
Str. 21/3—13/4/33.**G.**
Str. 24/11/36—21/1/37.**G.**
Str. 25/12/41—27/1/42.**G.**
Str. 24/9—24/10/44.**G.**
Str. 2/2—6/4/48.**G.**

BOILERS:
289.
289 *(new)* 12/10/99.
2800 *(new)* 12/11/14.
2871 *(new)* 11/1/30.
2878 *(exJ67 7334)* 13/4/33.
2831 *(exJ67 7169)* 21/1/37.
2887 *(exJ67 7015)* 27/1/42.

2886 *(exJ67 7018)* 24/10/44.
2917 *(ex8381)* 6/4/48.

SHEDS:
March.
Staveley 31/7/33.
Stratford 22/1/37.
Cambridge 18/5/37.

RENUMBERED:
7289 14/7/25.
8372 20/1/46.
68372 3/4/48.

CONDEMNED: 6/2/51.
Cut up at Stratford.

_____

7290

Stratford.

To traffic 4/1887.

REPAIRS:
Str. 28/10/03—22/5/04.**G.**
Cam. 10/4—2/8/23.**H.**
Str. 13/12/26—18/3/27.**G.**
Additional rails on bunker.
Str. 1/11—14/12/29.**G.**
Str. 3—29/9/32.**G.**
Str. 30/5—29/6/35.**G.**
Str. 1/1—8/2/40.**G.**
Str. 30/5—18/9/43.**G.**
Str. 24/10—2/11/43.**L.**
Str. 21/10—9/11/45.**G.**
Str. 11/1—15/2/49.**G.**
Str. 13/1/52. *Not repaired.*

BOILERS:
290.
290 *(new)* 22/5/04.
2805 *(ex7284)* 18/3/27.
327 *(exJ67 7016)* 14/12/29.
2818 *(exJ67 7018)* 29/9/32.
2912 *(new)* 29/6/35.
2901 *(exJ67 7333)* 8/2/40.
2812 *(exJ67 7260)* 18/9/43.
2888 *(exJ67 7169)* 9/11/45.
2869 *(ex8388)* 15/2/49.

SHEDS:
King's Lynn.
March 13/5/36.
Ipswich 5/11/36.

RENUMBERED:
290ᴇ 2/8/23.
7290 18/3/27 ?
8373 20/1/46.
68373 12/2/49.

CONDEMNED: 28/1/52.
Cut up at Stratford.

_____

7291

Stratford.

To traffic 4/1887.

REPAIRS:
Str. 6/6—28/10/03.**G.**
Str. 26/3—20/7/23.**G.**
Str. ?/?—?/2/26.**G.**
Str. ?/?—?/11/28.**G.**
Additional rails on bunker.
Str. 6—23/7/31.**G.**
Str. 8—25/5/35.**G.**

BOILERS:
291.
291 *(new)* 28/10/03.
2851 *(new)* 20/7/23.
2865 *(ex7292)* 23/7/31.
2908 *(new)* 25/5/35.

SHEDS:
Cambridge.
Colchester 25/5/35.

RENUMBERED:
291ᴇ 20/7/23.
7291 ?/2/26.

CONDEMNED: 8/2/39.
Cut up at Stratford.

_____

7292

Stratford.

To traffic 4/1887.

REPAIRS:
Str. 16/10/03—16/2/04.**G.**
Str. 27/3—30/6/20.**G.**
Str. 18/8—2/11/23.**G.**
Str. 24/10—31/12/25.**G.**
Str. 30/3—26/6/28.**G.**
Additional rails on bunker.
Str. 12—31/3/31.**G.**
Str. 12—30/4/34.**G.**

BOILERS:
292.
292 *(new)* 16/2/04.
2821 *(new)* 30/6/20.
297 *(ex7297)* 2/11/23.
2811 *(exJ67 7013)* 31/12/25.
2865 *(new)* 26/6/28.
2826 *(ex7325)* 31/3/31.
2800 *(ex7323)* 30/4/34.

SHED:
Ipswich.

RENUMBERED:
292ᴇ 2/11/23.

7292 31/12/25.

WITHDRAWN: 31/10/36.
Sold 10/36 to Guest, Keen &
Baldwins, Cardiff as their No.16.
Reno No.10 ?/52.
Cut up 1/59.

_____

7293

Stratford.

To traffic 5/1887.

REPAIRS:
Str. 25/6/02—22/1/03.**G.**
Str. 29/8—16/12/19.**G.**
Str. 27/4—19/8/22.**G.**
Str. 17/6—15/10/25.**G.**
Str. 17/11/27—15/2/28.**G.**
Additional rails on bunker.
Str. 11/4—16/5/30.**G.**
Str. 26/6—19/7/33.**G.**
Str. 11/11—11/12/36.**G.**
Str. 12/8—5/9/39.**G.**
Str. 22/12/40—3/2/41.**G.**
Str. 25/11/42—1/1/43.**G.**
Str. 15/6—21/7/45.**G.**
Str. 31/10—24/12/48.**G.**
Str. 9/9—3/11/51.**G.**
Spark arrester fitted.
Str. 30/5/54. *Not repaired.*

BOILERS:
293.
293 *(new)* 22/1/03.
2809 *(new)* 16/12/19.
403 *(exJ67 7403)* 15/10/25.
2877 *(new)* 16/5/30.
2860 *(exJ67 7400)* 19/7/33.
2827 *(exJ67 7013)* 11/12/36.
2891 *(ex7311)* 3/2/41.
2880 *(exJ67 7258)* 1/1/43.
2919 *(exJ67 7330)* 21/7/45.
2919 reno 23913 3/11/51.

SHEDS:
Colchester.
Stratford 25/9/39.
Boston 13/4/42.
New England 31/5/42.
Norwich 9/3/46.
Ipswich 27/3/46.
Staveley 26/7/53.

RENUMBERED:
7293 15/10/25.
8374 20/1/46.
68374 18/12/48.

CONDEMNED: 14/6/54.
Cut up at Stratford.

_____

(above) **Before Grouping some had been changed to a continuous handrail, but this particular modification was never completed on J66 class.**

During the 1890's all except the works shunting locomotive were fitted with coal rails on the bunker. No.7281 never did get them, or need them, because it only did short trips around Stratford works.

From 1925 the Macallan blast pipe and control gear was taken off and a plain blastpipe was substituted.

Between 1926 and 1929, three more flat coal rails were added to fill the spaces and to help avoid spillage of smaller coal.

From 1930 the chimney was changed from stovepipe to an NER cast type with a lip, but still 12ft 11in. in height from rail level.

From 1933, the original shallow curved wooden roof to the cab was replaced by a higher arched steel roof which increased the height above rail from 11ft 5⅞ in. to 11ft 10in. Some of those sold or withdrawn, pre-1939 did not get this cab alteration, but No.7291, withdrawn 8th February 1939 duly changed when ex works 25th May 1935.

Until after the LNER took over, safety valves were the Ramsbottom type, enclosed and with a circular casing around the base, on which the whistle was mounted

7294

Stratford.

To traffic 4/1887.

REPAIRS:
Str. ?/?—?/7/87.**L.**
Westinghouse brake fitted.
Str. 9/4—25/10/04.**G.**
Str. 14/2—30/4/20.**G.**
Str. 17/4—25/9/26.**G.**
Steel wheels fitted, and additional rails on bunker.
Str. ?/?—?/10/30.**G.**
West. changed for steam brake.
Str. 19—29/6/34.**G.**

BOILERS:
294.
294 (new) 25/10/04.
2819 (new) 30/4/20.
298 (ex7279) ?/10/30.
2896 (new) 29/6/34.

SHEDS:
Stratford.
Cambridge ?/?.
Stratford 21/10/30.
Cambridge 7/11/34.

RENUMBERED:
7294 25/9/26.

CONDEMNED: 3/7/37.
Cut up at Stratford.

7295

Stratford.

To traffic 5/1887.

REPAIRS:
Str. 25/5—17/10/03.**G.**
Str. 29/8/19—6/1/20.**G.**
Str. 18/5—29/7/25.**G.**
Str. 28/5—17/8/27.**G.**
Additional rails on bunker.
Str. 30/10—23/11/29.**G.**
Str. 8—24/6/32.**G.**
Str. 2—16/10/35.**L.**

BOILERS:
295.
295 (new) 17/10/03.
2810 (new) 6/1/20.
327 (exJ67 7327) 29/7/25.
277 (ex7277) 17/8/27.
2873 (new) 23/11/29.
2839 (ex7301) 16/10/35.

SHED:
Ipswich.

RENUMBERED:
7295 29/7/25.

WITHDRAWN: 1/12/38.
Sold 22/5/39 to Ocean Coal Co.,
Treorchy, Glamorgan.
Cut up ?/51.

7296

Stratford.

To traffic 10/1887.

REPAIRS:
Str. 26/5—11/11/03.**G.**
Str. 24/12/19—12/3/20.**G.**
Ips. 12/9—22/11/22.**H.**
Str. 11/4—21/8/25.**G.**
Str. 11/1—22/3/28.**G.**
Additional rails on bunker.
Str. 20/2—17/4/30.**G.**
Str. 26/11—23/12/32.**G.**
Str. 12/12/35—7/1/36.**G.**
Str. 3—5/11/37.**L.**
Str. 6/4—6/5/38.**G.**
Str. 27/1—24/2/42.**G.**
Str. 11/6—15/7/44.**G.**
Str. 20/10—19/11/46.**G.**
Str. 10/2—15/4/50.**G.**
Str. 26/10/52. *Not repaired.*

BOILERS:
296.
296 (new) 11/11/03.
2818 (new) 12/3/20.
412 (ex7316) 22/3/28.
2875 (new) 17/4/30.
2846 (ex7283) 23/12/32.
2830 (exJ67 7401) 7/1/36.
2916 (new) 6/5/38.
2878 (ex7322) 24/2/42.
2913 (exJ67 7327) 15/7/44.
2914 (exJ67 7327) 19/11/46.

SHED:
Ipswich.

RENUMBERED:
7296 21/8/25.
8375 20/1/46.
68375 15/4/50.

CONDEMNED: 24/11/52.
Cut up at Stratford.

7297

Stratford.

To traffic 6/1887.

REPAIRS:
Str. 30/4—12/9/06.**G.**
Str. 15/5—27/8/23.**G.**
Str. ?/?—?/9/24.**?.**
Additional rails on bunker.
Str. 26/5—106/32.**G.**
Str. 23/10—7/11/35.**G.**

BOILERS:
297.
297 (new) 12/9/06.
2852 (new) 27/8/23.
2883 (exJ67 7016) 10/6/32.
2828 (ex7302) 7/11/35.

SHEDS:
Ipswich.
Lincoln *by* 1/1/35.

RENUMBERED:
297E 27/8/23.
7297 ?/9/24.

WITHDRAWN: 28/5/39.
Sold 5/39 to Mersey Electric
Railway as M.E.R. No.3.
Became BR property 1/1/48.
Cut up at Stratford 6/50.

7298

Stratford.

To traffic 7/1887.

REPAIRS:
Str. 23/5—5/10/05.**G.**
Cam. 9/2—23/4/21.**H.**
Str. 16/2—7/5/25.**G.**
Str. 16/11/27—18/1/28.**G.**
Additional rails on bunker.
Str. 2/2—8/4/30.**G.**
Str. 5—29/12/33.**G.**
Str. 20/5—17/6/36.**G.**
Str. 25/4—25/5/40.**G.**
Str. 3/10—16/11/42.**G.**
Str. 3/6—14/7/45.**G.**
Str. 19/12/47—18/2/48.**G.**
Str. 28/9—9/11/49.**G.**
Str. 5/6/51. *Not repaired.*

BOILERS:
298.
298 (new) 5/10/05.
415 (exJ67 7019) 7/5/25.
2812 (exJ67 7012) 18/1/28.
2879 (new) 8/4/30.
157 (exJ67 7013) 29/12/33.
2851 (ex7313) 17/6/36.
2875 (ex7301) 25/5/40.
2899 (exJ67 7192) 16/11/42.
2896 (exJ67 7162) 14/7/45.
2874 (ex8377) 18/2/48.

SHEDS:
Cambridge.
Ebbw Vale or Ebbw Jct. ?/12/36.
Stratford 20/6/38.
New England 9/2/39.
Lincoln 5/5/44.
Frodingham 17/4/48.
Lincoln 17/11/48.

RENUMBERED:
7298 7/5/25.
8376 17/3/46.
E8376 18/2/48.

CONDEMNED: 2/7/51.
Cut up at Stratford.

7299

Stratford.

To traffic 9/1887.

REPAIRS:
Str. 3/11/04—1/3/05.**G.**
Str. 30/6—13/11/24.**G.**
Str. ?/?—?/5/28.**G.**
Additional rails on bunker.
Str. 3—26/2/31.**G.**
Str. 5—22/12/33.**G.**
Str. 17—31/12/35.**G.**

BOILERS:
299.
299 (new) 1/3/05.
2803 (exJ67 7258) 13/11/24.
326 (ex7321) 26/2/31.
2832 (exJ67 7012) 22/12/33.
2858 (exJ67 7258) 31/12/35.

SHEDS:
Lincoln.
March *by* 1/1/35.
King's Lynn 11/5/36.
March 10/6/36.
Cambridge 5/10/36.

RENUMBERED:
7299 13/11/24.

CONDEMNED: 2/6/37.
Cut up at Stratford.

7300

Stratford.

To traffic 9/1887.

REPAIRS:
Str. 24/10/06—8/2/07.**G.**
Str. 3/1—12/5/22.**G.**
Str. 14/8—23/10/24.**G.**

7300 cont./
Str. ?/?—?/10/27.**G.**
Additional rails on bunker.
Str. 17/1—12/2/30.**G.**
Str. 1—23/8/33.**G.**

BOILERS:
300.
300 (new) 8/3/07.
2859 (new) 23/10/24.
2872 (new) 12/2/30.
2890 (new) 23/8/33.

SHEDS:
Lincoln.
Cambridge *by* 1/1/35.
King's Lynn 11/8/38,

RENUMBERED:
7300 23/10/24.

CONDEMNED: 26/4/39.
Cut up at Stratford.

_____

7301

Stratford.

To traffic 9/1887.

REPAIRS:
Str. 25/11/03—28/6/04.**G.**
Str. 31/5/24—?/?/24.**?.**
Awaiting repair.
Str. 26/8—5/10/27.**G.**
Additional rails on bunker.
Str. 2—27/6/30.**G.**
Str. 5—16/12/32.**G.**
Str. 13/8—3/9/35.**G.**

BOILERS:
301.
301 (new) 28/6/04.
2867 (new) 5/10/27.
2839 (exJ67 7261) 16/12/32.
2875 (ex7320) 3/9/35.

SHEDS:
King's Lynn.
Cambridge ?/?.
King's Lynn 12/1/31.
Ebbw Vale ?/12/36.
King's Lynn ?/6/38.

RENUMBERED:
7301 ?/?/24.

CONDEMNED: 10/8/39.
Cut up at Stratford.

_____

7302

Stratford.

To traffic 9/1887.

REPAIRS:
Str. 27/11/01—25/3/02.**G.**
Str. 31/3—5/5/23.**G.**
Str. 9/7—26/9/28.**G.**
Additional rails on bunker.
Str. 10—26/11/31.**G.**
Str. 1—17/7/35.**G.**

BOILERS:
302.
302 (new) 25/3/02.
2848 (new) 5/5/23.
2809 (exJ67 7013) 26/9/28.
2828 (ex7316) 26/11/31.
2913 (new) 17/7/35.

SHEDS:
Stratford.
Cambridge ?/?.
March 15/4/36.
Staveley 3/12/36.

RENUMBERED:
7302 ?/?/??.

CONDEMNED: 4/5/39.
Cut up at Stratford.

_____

7303

Stratford.

To traffic 9/1887.

REPAIRS:
Str. 21/7—5/12/03.**G.**
Str. 18/2—30/4/21.**G.**
Str. 17/1—28/2/25.**G.**
Str. ?/?—?/3/29.**G.**
Additional rails on bunker.
Str. 21/6—12/7/32.**G.**

BOILERS:
303.
303 (new) 5/12/03.
2837 (new) 30/4/21.
276 (ex J67 7399) 12/7/32.

SHED:
Stratford.

RENUMBERED:
7303 28/2/25.

WITHDRAWN: 17/10/36.
Sold 10/36 to Sir R.McAlpine &
Co. as their No.75.
Scrapped ?/39 or ?/40.

7304

Stratford.

To traffic 9/1887.

REPAIRS:
Str. 27/6—30/12/02.**G.**
Wl. 28/11/19—14/8/20.**G.**
Str. 12/9—2/12/22.**G.**
Str. 5/12/24—30/1/25.**G.**
Str. 17/2—4/5/28.**G.**
Additional rails on bunker.
Str. 20/2—17/4/31.**G.**
Str. 18/5—20/6/35.**G.**
Str. 28/4—29/5/41.**G.**
Str. 15/5—24/6/44.**G.**
Str. 22/9—7/11/47.**G.**
Str. 29/4/51. *Not repaired.*

BOILERS:
304.
304 (new) 30/12/02.
2824 (new) 14/8/20.
2819 (ex7294) 17/4/31.
2884 (ex7279) 20/6/35.
2816 (exJ67 7327) 29/5/41.
2874 (exJ67 7206) 24/6/44.
2910 (exJ67 8628) 7/11/47.

SHEDS:
Stratford.
New England 23/6/37.
Boston 22/11/37.
Boston loaned the engine to
Cranwell 23/2/42 for one day.
New England 3/7/45.
Norwich 9/3/46.
Ipswich 29/3/46.
Norwich 26/11/47.
Melton Constable 28/4/48.

RENUMBERED:
7304 30/1/25.
8377 19/5/46.

CONDEMNED: 21/5/51.
Cut up at Stratford.

_____

7307

Stratford.

To traffic 6/1888.

REPAIRS:
Str. 5/4—12/9/07.**G.**
Str. 4/6—5/9/23.**G.**
Str. 29/1—26/3/26.**G.**
Str. 13/12/28—15/2/29.**G.**
Additional rails on bunker.
Str. 9/6—9/7/32.**G.**
Str. 3—27/2/36.**G.**
Str. 7/1—10/2/40.**G.**

Str. 9/5—7/8/43.**G.**
Str. 17/1—14/2/46.**G.**
Str. 28/6—30/7/49.**G.**
Str. 7/9—8/11/52.**G.**

BOILERS:
307.
307 (new) 12/9/07.
2810 (exJ67 7256) 15/2/29.
2852 (ex7297) 9/7/32.
2832 (ex7299) 27/2/36.
2877 (exJ67 7012) 10/2/40.
2905 (exJ67 7360) 7/8/43.
2829 (exJ65 7155) 14/2/46.
2863 (exJ67 8536) 30/7/49.
23927 (ex??) 8/11/52.
23927 reno. S.B.3336 5/53.

SHEDS:
Cambridge.
King's Lynn 21/4/34.
March 4/4/36.
Ebbw Vale ?/12/36.
Stratford 13/5/38.
Colchester 4/3/46.
Stratford 8/8/48.
Cambridge 8/1/49.
South Lynn 7/9/49.
Stratford works 15/9/52.

RENUMBERED:
7307 26/3/26.
8378 2/6/46.
68378 30/7/49.
DEPT'L 36 8/11/52.

Transfer to Serv. Stock: 15/9/52.

CONDEMNED: 9/1/59.
Cut up at Stratford.

_____

7308

Stratford.

To traffic 6/1888.

REPAIRS:
Str. 9/6—27/10/05.**G.**
Str. 3/5—19/10/21.**G.**
Str. 2/11/23—1/3/24.**G.**
Str. ?/?—?/4/29.**G.**
Additional rails on bunker.
Str. ?/?—?/11/31.**G.**
Str. 27/8—10/9/34.**G.**

BOILERS:
308.
308 (new) 27/10/05.
2843 (exJ67 7406) ?/11/31.
2804 (ex7321) 10/9/34.

SHEDS:
King's Lynn.

From 1924, Ross 'pop' safety valves were introduced and at first were put on to a Ramsbottom mounting, keeping the circular casing and whistle position.

(below) On boilers built 1932-33 and later, the 'pop' valves were mounted directly on to the firebox casing and the whistle was put on a standpipe just in front of the cab.

Until 1945 a toolbox was carried on the left hand tank top, just ahead of the cab.

From 1945 the eighteen survivors had these toolboxes taken off, and no other provision seems to have been made.

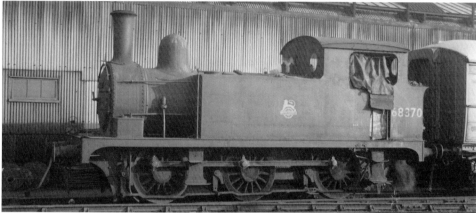

Whilst the works shunter did not have hand rail or coal rail changes, the other modifications were made to it. From 21st October 1932 it had a cast chimney and from 31st January 1936 a steel roof cab. After 15th January 1941 its boilers had 'pop' valves and ex-works 12th May 1945 Group Standard buffers had been fitted. On 13th April 1946 it was re-numbered from 7281 to 8370 and to 68370 on 30th December 1948. It got this BR livery ex works on 29th April 1950.

On 27th September 1952, in the new list, it was re-numbered 32 Departmental and had 32 put on the buffer beam, but kept the smokebox number plate showing 68370!

As late as ex-works 9th March 1956 it had a General repair and a change of boiler, with one final detail alteration, the smokebox plate was taken off and a new one showing 32 was affixed. After 2nd November 1959 it was the only J66 but it worked on to 16th September 1962, the day steam departed from the Great Eastern section of British Railways.

7308 cont./
March 13/5/36.

RENUMBERED:
7308 1/3/24.

WITHDRAWN: 17/10/36.
Sold 10/36 to Sir R.McAlpine &
Co. as their No.77.
Scrapped ?/39 or ?/40.

7309

Stratford.

To traffic 7/1888.

REPAIRS:
Str. 5/2—21/8/08.**G.**
Str. 18/2—13/7/23.**G.**
Str. 12/4—12/8/26.**G.**
Additional rails on bunker.
Str. 19/10/28—4/1/29.**G.**
Str. 24/7—8/9/31.**G.**
Str. 7/3—14/4/34.**G.**
Str. 30/8—3/10/41.**G.**
Str. 17/4—10/6/43.**L.**
Str. 31/8—12/10/44.**G.**
Str. 20/10—2/11/45.**L.**
Str. 12/8—17/9/48.**G.**
Str. 22/10/50. *Not repaired.*

BOILERS:
309.
309 *(new)* 21/8/08.
279 *(ex7287)* 8/9/31.
2893 *(new)* 14/4/34.
2869 *(exJ67 7206)* 3/10/41.
2853 *(exJ67 7398)* 12/10/44.
2909 *(exJ67 7352)* 2/11/45.
2880 *(exJ67 8498)* 17/9/48.

SHEDS:
King's Lynn.
King's Cross 14/4/34.
Stratford 10/5/34.
Cambridge 5/6/34.
March 23/6/34.
Ebbw Vale ?/12/36.
Stratford 23/6/38.
Staveley 2/10/39.

RENUMBERED:
7309 12/8/26.
8379 12/5/46.
68379 17/9/48.

CONDEMNED: 20/11/50.
Cut up at Stratford.

7310

Stratford.

To traffic 7/1888.

REPAIRS:
Str. 5/11/01—11/6/02.**G.**
Str. 17/9—30/11/20.**G.**
Str. 1/9—3/11/23.**G.**
Str. 14/1—19/3/27.**G.**
Additional rails on bunker.
Str. 13/9—19/10/29.**G.**
Str. 19/12/31—22/1/32.**G.**
Str. 6/2—6/3/36.**G.**
Str. 6/1—1/3/41.**G.**
Str. 19/1—25/2/44.**G.**
Str. 4/6—30/7/47.**G.**
Str. 3/3/52. *Not repaired.*

BOILERS:
310.
310 *(new)* 11/6/02.
2832 *(new)* 30/11/20.
2816 *(exJ67 7017)* 19/10/29.
2885 *(new)* 22/1/32.
2874 *(exJ67 7334)* 6/3/36.
204 *(ex7281)* 1/3/41.
2851 *(exJ67 7382)* 25/2/44.
2884 *(ex8386)* 30/7/47.

SHEDS:
Stratford.
Ebbw Vale ?/12/36.
Stratford ?/6/38.
New England 22/8/39.
Stratford 1/9/49.

RENUMBERED:
310E 3/11/23.
7310 19/3/27.
8380 16/6/46.

CONDEMNED: 17/3/52.
Cut up at Stratford.

7311

Stratford.

To traffic 7/1888.

REPAIRS:
Str. 26/11/02—1/4/03.**G.**
Str. 15/8—7/12/17.**G.**
Str. 11/10/22—2/3/23.**G.**
Str. 17/1/24.**?.**
In works on this date.
Str. 8/10—23/12/26.**G.**
Str. 24/8—12/10/29.**G.**
Additional rails on bunker.
Str. 29/2—19/3/32.**G.**
Str. 6/1—6/2/37.**G.**
Str. 14/7—23/8/40.**G.**

Str. 1—29/1/44.**G.**
Str. 26/11—23/12/47.**G.**
Str. 16/8/50. *Not repaired.*

BOILERS:
311.
311 *(new)* 1/4/03.
2807 *(new)* 7/12/17.
2816 *(ex7310)* 19/3/32.
2891 *(ex7319)* 6/2/37.
2837 *(exJ67 7260)* 23/8/40.
2917 *(exJ67 7011)* 29/1/44.
2838 *(ex8383)* 23/12/47.

SHEDS:
Stratford.
Parkeston 25/11/44.
Stratford 14/6/45.
Norwich 25/1/49.

RENUMBERED:
311E 17/1/24 ??.
7311 23/12/26.
8381 13/4/46.

CONDEMNED: 16/10/50.
Cut up at Stratford.

7312

Stratford.

To traffic 7/1888.

REPAIRS:
Str. 1/1—29/5/03.**G.**
Str. 7/3—5/11/19.**G.**
Str. 31/5/24—?/?/24.**?.**
Str. ?/?—?/7/27.**G.**
Additional rails on bunker.
Str. 23/1—14/2/31.**G.**
Str. ?/?—?/8/35.**G.**

BOILERS:
312.
312 *(new)* 29/5/03.
2808 *(new)* 5/11/19.
2841 *(ex7286)* 14/2/31.
2819 *(ex7304)* ?/8/35.

SHEDS:
Stratford.
Peterborough East 23/8/35.
New England 17/10/38.

RENUMBERED:
7312 by 25/2/25.

CONDEMNED: 27/1/39.

7313

Stratford.

To traffic 7/1888.

REPAIRS:
Str. 23/6—1/12/03.**G.**
Str. 28/12/22—10/3/23.**G.**
Str. 24/3—20/5/25.**G.**
Str. 22/2—16/5/28.**G.**
Additional rails on bunker.
Str. 4/8—1/9/31.**G.**
Str. 6/2—5/3/35.**G.**
Str. 4/9—22/11/39.**G.**
Str. 20/4—17/7/43.**G.**
Str. 11/11/45—16/1/46.**G.**
Str. 10/2—15/3/48.**G.**
Str. 17/3—28/5/49.**C/H.**
Str. 12/6—19/8/50.**C/H.**
Str. 13/6—29/8/52.**G.**
Str. ?/?—?/9/55.**G.**

BOILERS:
313.
313 *(new)* 1/12/03.
2847 *(new)* 10/3/23.
2851 *(ex7291)* 1/9/31.
2903 *(new)* 5/3/35.
2839 *(ex7295)* 22/11/39.
2819 *(exJ67 7016)* 17/7/43.
2881 *(exJ67 8586)* 15/3/48.
2876 *(ex8384)* 19/8/50.
23925 *(ex??)* 29/8/52.
23925 reno. S.B.3333 ?/5/53.
23910 *(ex??)* ?/9/55.
23910 reno. S.B.3340 ?/9/55.

SHEDS:
Peterborough East.
Boston 10/5/29.
Peterborough East 30/12/29.
New England 30/4/39.
Frodingham 17/10/40.
Colwick 6/10/41.
Staveley 28/8/44.
Colwick 10/11/44.
Staveley 9/2/47.
Stratford works 30/6/52.

RENUMBERED:
7313 20/5/25.
8382 27/5/46.
E**8382** 15/3/48.
68382 28/5/49.
DEPTL. 31 29/8/52.

WITHDRAWN: 13/6/52.

Transfer to Serv. Stock: 30/6/52.

CONDEMNED: 2/11/59.
Cut up at Stratford.

Two more Class J66 locomotives were transferred, in 1952, to Departmental Stock to replace the crane locomotives of Class J92. No.68382 (ex 7313) was ex works 29th August 1952 as Departmental 31 and with 31 on the buffer beam, the 68382 smokebox plate having been removed. In September 1955 it had a General repair at which smokebox plate 31 was put on, as in the following illustration. Withdrawal was on 2nd November 1959.

(above) No.68378 (ex 7307) became Departmental 36 when ex-works 8th November 1952, the 68378 smokebox plate having been taken off and 36 painted on the buffer beam. It was withdrawn 9th January 1959 and did not get a 36 smokebox plate. Note it had a boiler built in May 1930 with 'pops' on a Ramsbottom mounting and the whistle at their side.

On 28th May 1939, No.7297 was withdrawn and sold to the Mersey Electric Railway to be their service locomotive No.3. At Nationalisation, no BR number was allocated to it and in June 1950 it went back to Stratford to be withdrawn and broken up. The only Mersey alteration was a flat smokebox door with strengthening ribs.

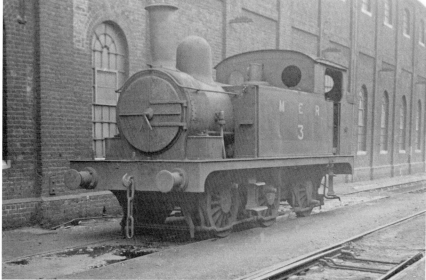

This is the original version of the stovepipe chimney, which had all been replaced by 1939. Its height from rail level was 12ft 11in. Note Load Class 2 plate fixed on the bufferbeam above the coupling hook.

During the War No.7289 (8372 later) needed a new chimney and, due to bomb damage, Stratford's foundry could not cast one. So a stovepipe was fabricated from steel sheet and fitted on the existing base. It is believed to have served to 68372's withdrawal on 6th February 1951.

No.7323 (8387 later) also needed a new chimney and had to make do with this shorter and cruder version.

Grey was the normal livery colour when the LNER took over and Stratford did not relinquish it if it could be made to serve another term. So, ex works 29th April 1926, No.7278 was still in grey with no owner's initials and with 19in. painted numbers.

7314

Stratford.

To traffic 8/1888.

REPAIRS:
Str. 20/2—24/7/07.**G.**
Str. 9/7—18/12/20.**G.**
Str. 20/4—3/7/28.**G.**
Additional rails on bunker.
Str. 17/10—3/11/32.**G.**
Str. 17/4—17/5/35.**G.**

BOILERS:
314.
314 *(new)* 24/7/07.
296 *(ex7296)* 18/12/20.
414 *(exJ67 7018)* 3/7/28.
2838 *(exJ67 7014)* 3/11/32.
2907 *(new)* 17/5/35.

SHED:
Norwich.

RENUMBERED:
7314 ?/?/?.

CONDEMNED: 13/7/37.
Cut up at Stratford.

_____

7315

Stratford.

To traffic 6/1888.

REPAIRS:
Str. 25/10/04—24/2/05.**G.**
Str. 30/4—16/7/20.**G.**
Str. 18/7—15/11/24.**G.**
Str. 25/3—2/6/27.**G.**
Additional rails on bunker.
Str. ?/?—?/4/29.**G.**
Str. ?/?—?/6/31.**G.**
Str. 20/3—7/4/34.**G.**

BOILERS:
315.
315 *(new)* 24/2/05.
2826 *(new)* 16/7/20.
2860 *(new)* 15/11/24.
290 *(ex7290)* 2/6/27.
2845 *(ex7282)* ?/4/29.
2808 *(ex7312)* ?/6/31.
2847 *(exJ67 7208)* 7/4/34.

SHED:
Ipswich.

RENUMBERED:
7315 15/11/24.

CONDEMNED: 19/2/37.
Cut up at Stratford.

_____

7316

Stratford.

To traffic 8/1888.

REPAIRS:
Str. 11/12/01—16/5/02.**G.**
Str. 23/8/18—27/2/19.**G.**
Str. 1/12/27—8/3/28.**G.**
Additional rails on bunker.
Str. ?/?—?/9/31.**G.**
Str. ?/?—?/12/35.**G.**

BOILERS:
316.
316 *(new)* 16/5/02.
412 *(exJ67 7016)* 27/2/19.
2828 *(exJ67 7336)* 8/3/28.
278 *(ex7275)* ?/9/31.
2838 *(ex7314)* ?/12/35.

SHED:
Stratford.

RENUMBERED:
7316 by 17/1/25.

CONDEMNED: 6/7/37.
Cut up at Stratford.

_____

7317

Stratford.

To traffic 11/1888.

REPAIRS:
Str. 19/8—13/12/02.**G.**
Str. 9/7—22/9/27.**G.**
Additional rails on bunker.
Str. 4—27/2/30.**G.**
Str. 31/8—19/9/32.**G.**
Str. 22/2—11/3/35.**G.**

BOILERS:
317.
317 *(new)* 13/12/02.
2860 *(ex7315)* 22/9/27.
2874 *(new)* 27/2/30.
2864 *(exJ67 7257)* 19/9/32.
2904 *(new)* 11/3/35.

SHED:
Norwich.

RENUMBERED:
7317 ?/?/?.

CONDEMNED: 4/6/37.
Cut up at Stratford.

_____

7318

Stratford.

To traffic 11/1888.

REPAIRS:
Str. 31/3—16/9/04.**G.**
Str. 28/4—14/5/15.**G.**
Str. 21/8—13/10/20.**G.**
Str. ?/?—?/10/26.**G.**
Additional rails on bunker.
Str. 13/4—4/5/33.**G.**

BOILERS:
318.
318 *(new)* 16/9/04.
2802 *(new)* 14/5/15.
314 *(ex7314)* 13/10/20.
2813 *(exJ67 7020)* 4/5/33.

SHEDS:
Cambridge.
Stratford 10/3/29.
Cambridge 28/11/34.

RENUMBERED:
7318 after 14/6/24.

CONDEMNED: 4/3/37.
Cut up at Stratford.

_____

7319

Stratford.

To traffic 11/1888.

REPAIRS:
Str. 2/6—28/10/05.**G.**
Str. 8/12/23—5/3/24.**G.**
Str. 11/6—23/9/26.**G.**
Additional rails on bunker.
Str. 28/9—7/12/28.**G.**
Str. 5/12/30—6/2/31.**G.**
Str. 13/12/33—9/1/34.**G.**
Str. 23/11—19/12/36.**G.**
Str. 28/7—5/9/40.**G.**
Str. 9/1—2/3/44.**G.**
Str. 15/8—2/10/47.**G.**
Str. 12/9—10/11/51.**G.**

BOILERS:
319.
319 *(new)* 28/10/05.
2849 *(new)* 5/3/24.
320 *(ex7320)* 6/2/31.
2891 *(new)* 9/1/34.
2845 *(exJ67 7330)* 19/12/36.
2876 *(ex7285)* 5/9/40.

2838 *(exJ67 7397)* 2/3/44.
2887 *(exJ67 7015)* 2/10/47.
23914 *(ex??)* 10/11/51.

SHEDS:
March.
Cambridge 23/6/34.
King's Lynn 20/10/34.
Cambridge 6/10/40.
March 10/2/43.
Cambridge 9/11/48.
Staveley 26/7/53.

RENUMBERED:
7319 5/3/24.
8383 13/4/46.
68383 10/11/51.

CONDEMNED: 17/10/55.
Cut up at Stratford.

_____

7320

Stratford.

To traffic 11/1888.

REPAIRS:
Str. 28/12/07—22/5/08.**G.**
Nor. 14/8—15/10/22.**H.**
Str. 27/1—16/5/25.**G.**
Str. 16/11/27—28/1/28.**G.**
Additional rails on bunker.
Str. 24/4—6/6/30.**G.**
Str. 30/1—27/2/33.**G.**
Str. 20/6—19/7/35.**G.**
Str. 11/9—28/10/39.**G.**
Str. 3/10—20/11/42.**G.**
Str. 21/10—2/12/44.**G.**
Str. 16/5—11/8/47.**G.**
Str. 21/3/50. *Not repaired.*

BOILERS:
320.
320 *(new)* 22/5/08.
2831 *(exJ67 7264)* 6/6/30.
2875 *(ex7296)* 27/2/33.
2865 *(ex7291)* 19/7/35.
2834 *(exJ67 7334)* 28/10/39.
2873 *(exJ67 7401)* 20/11/42.
2904 *(exJ67 7015)* 2/12/44.
2876 *(exJ67 8510)* 11/8/47.

SHEDS:
Norwich.

RENUMBERED:
7320 16/5/25.
8384 13/6/46.

CONDEMNED: 17/4/50.
Cut up at Stratford.

_____

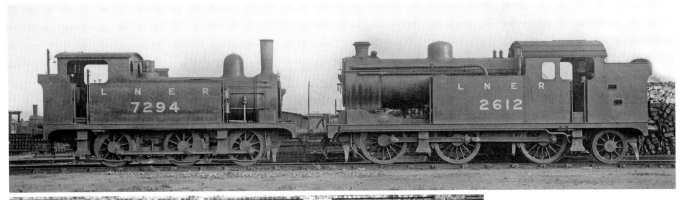

(above) Those which got black paint to June 1928 also had single red lining added.

From June 1928 only plain black was put on with no subsequent change, but until 1940 there was usually one coat of varnish applied.

Only NE was used from July 1943 to paintings done after January 1946 and by then the Thompson re-numbering had begun. No.7293 had just NE from a 21st July 1945 Stratford shopping and on Sunday 20th January 1946 at New England shed it was changed to 8374 in 12in. painted and unshaded figures.

No.8385 was at Lincoln when changed from 7321 on Sunday 26th May 1946 and like so many on the GCR section had to suffice with figures only 7in. tall.

Nine of the eighteen survivors at 1946 had LNER restored, most if not all with transfers: 8371 - 28th September 1946; 8375 19th November 1946; 8377 7th November 1947; 8380 30th July 1947; 8381 23rd December 1947; 8383 2nd October 1947; 8384 11th August 1947; 8386 4th December 1946; 8387 7th June 1946.

Whilst the BR prefix E was being applied, two J66 received it, No.E8376 being ex works 18th February 1948. Numbers were still 12in. tall but had no shading and were in Gill sans but with the LNER modified 6.

(below) When No.E8382 got its prefix ex works 15th March 1948, the style was similar but the numbers were only 10in. tall.

7321

Stratford.

To traffic 11/1888.

REPAIRS:
Str. 12/12/02—4/7/03.**G.**
Pbo. 11/11—14/12/21.**H.**
Str. 19/7—5/12/24.**G.**
Str. 28/10/27—12/1/28.**G.**
Additional rails on bunker.
Str. 11/7—10/9/30.**G.**
Str. 10/3—19/4/34.**G.**
Str. 7/4—8/6/40.**G.**
Str. 3/1—11/3/43.**G.**
Str. 23/11—?/12/45.**G.**
Str. 28/3—26/5/48.**G.**
Str. 29/4/51. *Not repaired.*

BOILERS:
321.
321 *(new)* 4/7/03.
326 *(ex7326)* 5/12/24.
2804 *(ex7322)* 10/9/30.
2894 *(new)* 19/4/34.
2832 *(ex7307)* 8/6/40.
2852 *(exJ67 7203)* 11/3/43.
2908 *(exJ67 7200)* ?/12/45.
2886 *(ex8372)* 26/5/48.

SHEDS:
Peterborough East.
Boston 11/5/29.
Peterborough East 13/11/29.
March 14/5/34.
Grantham 29/1/36.
Lincoln 22/5/39.

RENUMBERED:
7321 5/12/24.
8385 26/5/46.
68385 26/5/48.

CONDEMNED: 4/6/51.
Cut up at Stratford.

7322

Stratford.

To traffic 12/1888.

REPAIRS:
Str. 11/11/03—15/6/04.**G.**
Str. 19/4—23/8/18.**G.**
Str. 23/3—28/8/22.**G.**
Str. 17/1—16/3/25.**G.**
Str. 1/10/27—14/1/28.**G.**
Additional rails to bunker.
Str. 6/12/29—18/1/30.**G.**
Str. 17/10—8/11/32.**G.**
Str. 31/3—13/4/34.**G.**

Str. 27/8—20/9/35.**G.**
Str. 15/8—2/9/38.**G.**
Str. 5—29/11/41.**G.**
Str. 30/4—25/5/44.**G.**
Str. 6/10—4/12/46.**G.**
Str. 23/3/50. *Not repaired.*

BOILERS:
322.
322 *(new)* 15/6/04.
2813 *(new)* 23/8/18.
263 *(exJ67 7016)* 28/8/22.
2804 *(exJ67 7208)* 14/1/28.
2882 *(new)* 18/1/30.
2837 *(ex7303)* 8/11/32.
2841 *(ex7312)* 20/9/35.
2878 *(ex7289)* 2/9/38.
2914 *(exJ67 7261)* 29/11/41.
2884 *(exJ67 7403)* 25/5/44.
2846 *(exJ67 8597)* 4/12/46.

SHED:
Ipswich.

RENUMBERED:
7322 16/3/25.
8386 21/7/46.

CONDEMNED: 17/4/50.
Cut up at Stratford.

7323

Stratford.

To traffic 12/1888.

REPAIRS:
Str. 25/11/03—30/6/04.**G.**
Str. 2/7—8/8/20.**G.**
Str. 5/10—1/12/23.**G.**
Str. 25/2—28/5/26.**G.**
Additional rails on bunker.
Str. 12/5—25/7/28.**G.**
Str. 3—31/10/30.**G.**
Str. 21/11—20/12/33.**G.**
Str. 22/10—20/11/36.**G.**
Str. 13/5—8/6/40.**G.**
Str. 16/4—22/7/43.**G.**
Str. 12/5—7/6/46.**G.**
Str. 15—22/6/47.**L.**

BOILERS:
323.
323 *(new)* 30/6/04.
293 *(ex7293)* 8/9/20.
297 *(ex7292)* 28/5/26.
296 *(ex7314)* 25/7/28.
2800 *(ex7289)* 31/10/30.
2805 *(exJ67 7264)* 20/12/33.
2888 *(exJ67 7204)* 20/11/36.
2867 *(exJ67 7204)* 8/6/40.
2863 *(exJ67 7019)* 22/7/43.

2902 *(exJ67 7016)* 7/6/46.

SHEDS:
Ipswich.
New England 15/5/42.
Stratford 28/1/51.

RENUMBERED:
323E 1/12/23.
7323 28/5/26.
8387 7/6/46.

CONDEMNED: 14/2/51.
Cut up at Stratford.

7324

Stratford.

To traffic 12/1888.

REPAIRS:
Str. 29/6—23/12/04.**G.**
Str. 6/3—23/6/20.**G.**
Str. 7/2—14/4/23.**G.**
Str. 26/9—19/11/25.**G.**
Str. 28/9—23/12/28.**G.**
Additional rails on bunker.
Str. 16/1—20/2/32.**G.**
Str. 31/10—20/11/35.**G.**
Str. 23/11—23/12/39.**G.**
Str. 12/9—1/10/42.**G.**
Str. 29/11—22/12/44.**G.**
Str. 20/12/48—22/1/49.**G.**
Str. 20/4/52. *Not repaired.*

BOILERS:
324.
324 *(new)* 23/12/04.
2830 *(new)* 23/6/20.
2887 *(new)* 20/2/32.
2844 *(exJ67 7019)* 20/11/35.
2882 *(exJ67 7405)* 23/12/39.
2892 *(exJ67 7398)* 1/10/42.
2869 *(ex7309)* 22/12/44.
2916 *(exJ67 8572)* 22/1/49.

SHEDS:
Stratford.
Ebbw Vale ?/12/36.
Stratford ?/6/38.
Norwich 11//2/49.
Melton Constable 20/5/51.

RENUMBERED:
7324 19/11/25.
8388 13/4/46.
68388 22/1/49.

CONDEMNED: 28/4/52.
Cut up at Stratford.

7325

Stratford.

To traffic 12/1888.

REPAIRS:
Str. 19/2—29/8/01.**G.**
Str. 3/9/24—15/1/25.**G.**
Str. ?/?—?/10/27.**G.**
Additional rails on bunker.
Str. ?/?—?/4/30.**G.**
Str. 14/9—3/10/32.**G.**
Str. 16/4—9/5/35.**G.**

BOILERS:
325.
325 *(new)* 29/8/01.
2826 *(ex7315)* 15/1/25.
2881 *(new)* ?/4/30.
263 *(exJ67 7336)* 3/10/32.
2906 *(new)* 9/5/35.

SHED:
Norwich.

RENUMBERED:
7325 15/1/25.

CONDEMNED: 21/7/37.
Cut up at Stratford.

7326

Stratford.

To traffic 12/1888.

REPAIRS:
Str. 19/3—23/8/07.**G.**
Str. 18/8—8/11/24.**G.**
Str. ?/?—?/6/27.**G.**
Additional rails on bunker.
Str. 2—25/11/32.**G.**
Str. 16/5—6/6/35.**G.**

BOILERS:
326.
326 *(new)* 23/8/07.
299 *(ex7299)* 8/11/24.
2873 *(ex7295)* 25/11/32.
2909 *(new)* 6/6/35.

SHEDS:
Lowestoft.
Norwich 19/5/29.

RENUMBERED:
7326 8/11/24.

CONDEMNED: 21/7/37.
Cut up at Stratford.

The full BR number was used from mid-march 1948 in 10in. figures, but ex works 26th May 1948 No.68385 still had it on the tank side and front bufferbeam.

(below) No.68371 was one of the last to get BRITISH RAILWAYS; it was ex works 27th August 1949. Note Stratford using 8in. figures due to short bunker against standard 10in. by Gorton works on Class C13 No.67410.

For those shopped from September 1949 the 15½in. emblem was put on, although only five, Nos.68370, 68374, 68375, 68376 and 68383 got it.

Twenty similar engines, Nos.255 to 264, and 199 to 208, were built at Stratford between March 1899 and January 1900. By exchange, No.259 had a boiler with a steel firebox, indicated by the forward position of its two-column Ramsbottom safety valves, which it still had to October 1926.

By Grouping eight of the first ten built as passenger tanks, Nos.327, 329, 330, 331, 332, 333, 334, and 336, had been downgraded to goods work. Westinghouse was replaced by steam brake, screw coupling by three-link and 10-spoke steel wheels by 15-spoke cast iron. But only Nos.330 and 336 still had 1000 gallon tanks, the others getting wider tanks and with a chamber on top when they had been fitted with condensing apparatus until taken off in 1912. No.333 had 1180 gallon tanks.

At Grouping the fifty-one engines in Class J67 were made up by Nos.161, 164 and 169, the only three passenger tanks which had not been rebuilt with tank extension and 180 lb boiler, which would have put them into J69 class. They still had 10-spoke steel wheels, Westinghouse brake and screw couplings. Although not widened, the tank side sheets were of the built-up type masking the chamber on the tank top and they kept the vertical air vent pipe.

From March 1938, those with 1000 gallons tanks were designated Part 1 of J67 class, and by then, all had their two safety valves on the firebox, just in front of the cab, on a 160 lb boiler.

CLASS J 67

Engines 7327 to 7336.
^ *Diagram 37 boiler de-rated to 160 p.s.i.*
# *Incorrectly shown as J67/1 in official records (from 1938).*
* *Incorrectly shown as J69/2 in official records (from 1950).*

7327

Stratford.

To traffic 3/1890.
Class R24 - passenger.

REPAIRS:
Str. ?/?—?/7/04.**G.**
Rebuilt to Class J69/1.
Str. 9/3—10/6/12.**G.**
Rebuilt to Class J67/2.
Westinghouse brake replaced by steam, condensing gear removed.
Ips. 8/6—21/9/22.**H.**
At 1/1/23: Class J67 (Part 2)#
Steam brake.
Str. 26/9—30/12/24.**G.**
Str. 5/8—2/12/27.**G.**
Additional rails on bunker.
Str. 8/8—27/9/29.**G.**
Str. 13/9—23/10/31.**G.**
Str. 15/7—24/8/33.**G.**
Str. 12/12/35—9/1/36.**G.**
Str. 9/7—11/8/38.**G.**
Str. 8/1—8/2/41.**G.**
Str. 23/5—15/6/44.**G.**
Str. 18/8—22/9/46.**G.**
Str. 9/4—6/5/50.**G.**
Rebuilt to J69/1.*
Str. 18/2—14/3/53.**G.**
Str. 20/11—17/12/55.**G.**

BOILERS:
327.
327 *(new)* ?/7/04.
327 *(new)* 10/6/12.
2862 *(new)* 30/12/24.
2806 *(ex7397)* 23/10/31.
204 *(exJ66 7288)* 24/8/33.
2863 *(ex7016)* 9/1/36.
2816 *(exJ66 7311)* 11/8/38.
2913 *(exJ66 7302)* 8/2/41.
2914 *(exJ66 7322)* 15/6/44.
2857 *(ex7339)* 22/9/46.
3205 *(new)* 6/5/50.
23765 *(ex??)* 14/3/53.
23734 *(ex68581)* 17/12/55.

SHEDS:
Colchester.

Stratford 13/4/41.
Cambridge 23/3/42.
March 27/1/43.
King's Lynn 13/11/43.

RENUMBERED:
7327 30/12/24.
8490 13/9/46.
68490 6/5/50.

CONDEMNED: 7/5/58.
Cut up at Stratford.

7329

Stratford.

To traffic 3/1890.
Class R24 - passenger.

REPAIRS:
Str. 28/4—17/10/02.**G.**
Rebuilt to Class J69/1.
Str. ?/?—?/11/12.**G.**
Rebuilt to Class J67/2 (Diag.37 boiler, de-rated). Westinghouse brake replaced by steam, condensing gear removed.
Str. 28/2—19/5/20.**G.**
At 1/1/23: J67/2. # *Steam brake.*
Str. 7/5—25/8/25.**G.**
Str. ?/?—?/8/28.**G.**
Additional rails on bunker.
Str. 16/9—2/10/31.**G.**
Diagram 39 boiler.
Str. 11—26/3/36.**G.**
Str. ?/?—3/10/40.**G.**
Str. ?/?—16/4/42.**G.**
Str. 20/11—13/12/43.**G.**
Cow. ?/?—15/4/44.**L.**
NBR tender No.9741 attached.
Cow. ?/?—18/8/45.**L.**
Inv. 19/4—3/5/47.**H.**
Cow. 17/5—17/6/50.**G.**
Cow. 15/10—17/11/51.**N/C.**
Cow. 23—28/6/52.**C/L.**
Cow. 15—16/7/52.**N/C.**
Cow. 27/8—11/9/52.**C/L.**
Cow. 26/1—7/2/53.**C/L.**
Cow. 1—10/2/55.**N/C.**
Cow. 11/6/56. *Not repaired.*

BOILERS:
329.
329 *(new)* 17/10/02 ^(11/12).
268 *(ex268)* 19/5/20 ^.
2820 *(ex7330)* 2/10/31.
2885 *(exJ66 7310)* 26/3/36.
2883 *(ex7203)* 3/10/40.
2831 *(exJ66 7289)* 16/4/42.

2901 *(exJ66 7290)* 13/12/43.
2901 reno.23961 28/6/52.

SHEDS:
Stratford.
Cambridge 3/11/39.
Stratford 14/4/40.
Colchester 13/4/41.
Stratford 6/6/42.
St Margarets 29/3/44
(Galashiels).

RENUMBERED:
7329 25/8/25.
8492 24/3/46.
68492 17/6/50.

CONDEMNED: 22/6/56.
Cut up at Cowlairs.

7330

Stratford.

To traffic 3/1890.
Class R24 - passenger.

REPAIRS:
Str. 18/11/01—6/3/02.**G.**
Str. ?/?—?/10/12.**G.**
Westinghouse brake replaced by steam, condensing gear removed.
Str. 28/2—11/6/20.**G.**
Str. 28/6—29/9/22.**G.**
At 1/1/23: J67 (Part 1)
Steam brake.
Str. 9/2—27/3/25.**G.**
Str. 18/11/27—17/2/28.**G.**
Additional rails on bunker.
Str. 4/7—20/8/31.**G.**
Str. 7/10—4/11/36.**G.**
Str. 3/1—23/2/40.**G.**
Str. 28/1—27/5/43.**G.**
Str. 3—28/6/45.**G.**
Str. 27/8—6/10/48.**G.**
Str. 17/5—3/6/49.**C/L.**
Str. 6—26/1/52.**G.**
Str. 12—24/10/53.**N/C.**
Str. 14/4—5/5/54.**C/L.**
Str. 7/10/54. *Not repaired.*

BOILERS:
330.
330 *(new)* 6/3/02.
2820 *(new)* 11/6/20.
2845 *(exJ66 7315)* 20/8/31.
2852 *(exJ66 7307)* 4/11/36.
2859 *(ex7336)* 23/2/40.
2919 *(ex7207)* 27/5/43.

2885 *(exJ66 7281)* 28/6/45.
2870 *(ex8606)* 6/10/48.
23918 *(ex??)* 26/1/52.

SHEDS:
Cambridge.
Stratford 17/5/24.
King's Lynn 13/5/37.
Ipswich 26/7/53.

RENUMBERED:
7330 27/3/25.
8493 15/9/46.
68493 2/10/48.

CONDEMNED: 25/10/54.
Cut up at Stratford.

7331

Stratford.

To traffic 3/1890.
Class R24 - passenger.

REPAIRS:
Str. 9/7—28/10/04.**G.**
Rebuilt to Class J69/1.
Str. ?/?—?/11/12.**G.**
Rebuilt to Class J67/2 (Diag.37 boiler de-rated). Westinghouse brake replaced by steam, condensing gear removed.
Str. 17/11/19—13/2/20.**G.**
Str. 17/1—31/3/22.**G.**
At 1/1/23: J67/2. # *Steam brake.*
Str. 19/11/24—17/1/25.**G.**
Str. 1/2—2/5/28.**G.**
Additional rails on bunker.
Str. 13/12/30—6/2/31.**G.**
Str. 12/12/35—9/1/36.**G.**
Str. 7/3—4/5/40.**G.**
Diagram 39 boiler.
Str. 20/12/42—19/2/43.**G.**
Str. 11/6—13/7/45.**G.**
Rebuilt to J69/1.*
Str. 18/11/47—2/1/48.**G.**
Str. 25/2—21/3/51.**G.**
Str. 21/4—22/5/53.**C/L.**
Str. 30/5—1/7/54.**G.**

BOILERS:
331.
331 *(new)* 28/10/04^(11/12).
2985 *(new)* 13/2/20^.
2989 *(exJ69 7266)* 6/2/31^.
3047 *(exJ69 7335)* 9/1/36^.
2890 *(exJ66 7300)* 4/5/40.
2881 *(ex7163)* 19/2/43.
32 *(exJ69 7366)* 13/7/45.

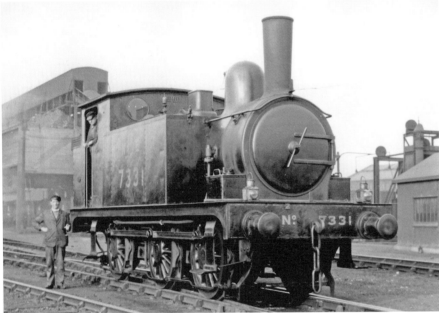

(above) **Part 2 was introduced in March 1938 to cover those which had larger capacity tanks but with 160 lb. pressure Diagram 39 boilers. By 7th April 1944 when No.7371 was converted there were twenty-six in J67 Part 2, six 1912 conversions to J67, nineteen 1938-44 from J69 and one from J68. From December 1940 to May 1954 fifteen reverted to 180 lb boiler, the eleven still in Part 2 to withdrawal being Nos.7333 (28th September 1939), and 68492, 68496, 68531, 68536, 68540, 68547, 68572, 68597, 68610 and 68628, withdrawn between 29th November 1954 and 24th February 1958. No.7082 was Part 2 from 5th August 1938 to 24th February 1958 when withdrawn as No.68628.**

(left) Those which were running with 180lb Diagram 37 boiler, although de-rated to 160lb, had four-column Ramsbottom safety valves mounted forward of the firebox. No.7331 carried this boiler from February 1920 to 7th March 1940.

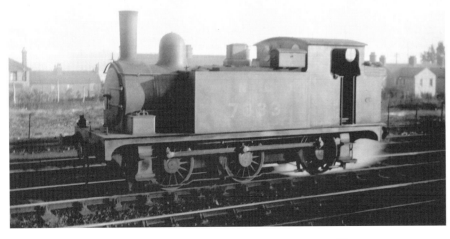

At Grouping No.7333 had a Diagram 39 boiler with two-column Ramsbottom valves on the firebox (*see* page 46, 2nd from top). From 11th May 1928 to 22nd May 1930 it carried this Diagram 37 boiler with four safety valves. Out from the shops on 25th July 1930, it had Ross 'pops' on a new Diagram 39 boiler, then from 29th January 1935 to withdrawal on 28th September 1939, another new boiler with Ross 'pop' valves.

No.8531 was ex 7354 which had become Part 2 on 23rd October 1943. When rebuilt in October 1903 its tanks had been made 4 in. wider, increasing the water capacity to 1140 gallons. No.7360 was the only other with 1140 gallons tanks to become J67 class. Note that Group Standard buffers are fitted.

In Part 2 there were also two which had been built in 1904 with 1200 gallons tanks and 5cwt extra coal capacity. On these the cab and bunker were the same width as the side tanks. No.7086 was only J67 (Part 2) from the 13th January 1940 to 8th February 1944 but No.7082 (8628 from 1st September 1946) was Part 2 from 5th August 1938 to its withdrawal on 24th February 1958. Note the extension to the lower footstep at the front.

Originally the smokebox door was a plain dished pattern and flush fitting. Although these began to be discarded from 1915, No. 403 still carried one to 2nd April 1925. The spark arrester was for use on the dock lines at King's Lynn.

7331 cont./
23802 *(new)* 21/3/51.
23814 *(ex68522)* 1/7/54.

SHEDS:
Stratford.
Cambridge 13/5/37.
King's Lynn 4/5/39.
Cambridge 21/3/43.
King's Lynn 28/3/43.
Norwich. 8/6/52.
South Lynn 26/7/53.

RENUMBERED:
7331 17/1/25.
8494 15/9/46.
68494 21/3/51.

CONDEMNED: 8/4/58.
Cut up at Stratford.

_____

7332

Stratford.

To traffic 4/1890.
Class R24 - passenger.

REPAIRS:
Str. 26/2—2/9/02.**G**.
Rebuilt to Class J69/1.
Str. ?/?—?/9/12.**G**.
*Rebuilt to Class J67/2 (Diag.37
boiler de-rated). Westinghouse
brake replaced by steam,
condensing gear removed.*
Str. 21/3—4/12/19.**G**.
At 1/1/23: J67/2. Steam brake.
Str. 31/1—15/3/24.
Str. 22/10—24/12/26.**G**.
Str. 26/1—23/2/27.**L**.
Str. 7/4—21/6/29.**G**.
*Diagram 39 boiler. Additional
rails on bunker.*
Str. 26/2—7/4/32.**G**.
Diagram 37 boiler de-rated.
Str. 12/4—31/5/35.**G**.
Str. 25/10—10/12/40.**G**.
Rebuilt to J69/1.
Str. 2/2—26/3/43.**G**.
Str. 14/12/47—13/2/48.**G**.
Str. 22/2—1/3/48.**N/C**.
Str. 3—30/12/50.**G**.
Str. 17/3—2/4/53.**G**.
Str. 23/4—7/6/56.**G**.

BOILERS:
  332.
  332 *(new)* 2/9/02^(9/12).
  2984 *(new)* 4/12/19^.
  245 *(exJ65 7247)* 21/6/29.
  3054 *(exJ69 7396)* 7/4/32^.
  3038 *(exJ68 7033)* 31/5/35^.
  38 *(ex7349)* 10/12/40.

3087 *(ex7367)* 26/3/43.
3064 *(exJ68 8645)* 13/2/48.
23709 *(ex??)* 30/12/50.
23767 *(ex??)* 2/4/53.
23721 *(exJ68 68654)* 7/6/56.

SHEDS:
Stratford.
Ipswich 26/2/27.
Colchester ?/?.
Stratford 31/5/35.
Cambridge 11/10/37.
Lincoln 28/2/38.
Frodingham 16/2/40.
Colwick 6/10/41.
Annesley 11/10/45.
Staveley 21/10/45.
Colwick 18/11/45.
Staveley ?/12/45.
Annesley 10/2/46.
Gorton 2/6/46.
Norwich 28/7/46.
King's Lynn 26/7/53.

RENUMBERED:
7332 15/3/24.
8495 8/9/46.
ᴇ8495 13/2/48.
68495 30/12/50.

CONDEMNED: 7/5/58.
Cut up at Stratford.

_____

7333

Stratford.

To traffic 4/1890.
Class R24 - passenger.

REPAIRS:
Str. 27/2—18/9/08.**G**.
Rebuilt to Class J69/1.
Str. ?/?—?/5/12.**G**.
*Rebuilt to Class J67/2 (Diag.37
boiler de-rated). Westinghouse
brake replaced by steam,
condensing gear removed.*
Str. 17/9—16/12/20.**G**.
Diagram 39 boiler.
At 1/1/23: J67/2. Steam brake.
Ips. 29/5—9/8/23.**H**.
Str. 15/8—9/10/25.**G**.
Str. 27/1—11/5/28.**G**.
*Diagram 37 boiler de-rated.
Additional rails on bunker.*
Str. 22/5—25/7/30.**G**.
Diagram 39 boiler.
Str. 20/2—18/3/33.**G**.
Str. 1—29/1/35.**G**.
Str. 24/7/39. *Not repaired.*

BOILERS:
  333.

333 *(new)* 18/9/08^(5/12).
2833 *(new)* 16/12/20.
3013 *(ex7089)* 11/5/28^.
2876 *(new)* 25/7/30.
  253 *(exJ65 7152)* 18/3/33.
2901 *(new)* 29/1/35.

SHEDS:
Ipswich.
Stratford 29/1/35.

RENUMBERED:
7333 9/10/25.

CONDEMNED: 28/9/39.
Cut up at Stratford.

_____

7334

Stratford.

To traffic 4/1890.
Class R24 - passenger.

REPAIRS:
Str. 20/10/02—20/3/03.**G**.
Rebuilt to Class J69/1.
Str. ?/?—?/9/12.**G**.
*Rebuilt to Class J67/2 (Diag.37
boiler de-rated). Westinghouse
brake replaced by steam,
condensing gear removed.*
At 1/1/23: J67/2. # Steam brake.
Str. 21/2—25/9/23.**G**.
Str. 19/10/25—5/1/26.**G**.
Str. 19/6—17/9/28.**G**.
Additional rails on bunker.
Str. 6/2—5/4/30.**G**.
Diagram 39 boiler.
Str. 16/2—16/3/33.**G**.
Str. 12—29/11/35.**G**.
Str. 17/6—10/7/37.**G**.
After collision.
Str. 9/7—28/9/39.**G**.
Str. 20/8—9/9/42.**G**.
Str. 20/5—15/6/45.**G**.
Str. 14/1—28/2/49.**G**.
Str. 28/4—18/5/53.**G**.

BOILERS:
  334.
  334 *(new)* 20/3/03^(9/12).
  3029 *(new)* 25/9/23^.
  2878 *(new)* 5/4/30.
  2874 *(exJ66 7317)* 16/3/33.
  2834 *(ex7161)* 29/11/35.
  2895 *(ex7398)* 28/9/39.
  2871 *(ex7193)* 9/9/42.
  2889 *(exJ65 7247)* 15/6/45.
  2903 *(ex8516)* 28/2/49.
  23929 *(ex??)* 18/5/53.

SHEDS:
Colchester.

Stratford 25/9/39.
Hitchin 30/5/54.
New England 26/9/54.
Hitchin 30/1/55.

RENUMBERED:
7334 5/1/26.
8496 18/10/46.
68496 26/2/49.

CONDEMNED: 14/5/56.
Cut up at Stratford.

_____

7336

Stratford.

To traffic 4/1890.
Class R24 - passenger.

REPAIRS:
Str. 24/6/01—15/1/02.**G**.
Str. ?/?—?/12/12.**G**.
*Westinghouse brake replaced by
steam, condensing gear removed.*
Str. 31/8—1/12/20.**G**.
At 1/1/23: J67/1. Steam brake.
Ips. 23/11/22—8/2/23.**H**.
Str. 12/3—10/7/25.**G**.
Str. 17/11/27—3/3/28.**G**.
Additional rails on bunker.
Str. 24/1—7/3/30.**G**.
Str. 7/2—24/3/32.**G**.
Str. 18/1—11/2/35.**G**.
Str. 23/10—24/11/39.**G**.
Str. 20/10—6/11/41.**L**.
Str. 15/4—23/7/43.**G**.
Str. 9—29/9/45.**G**.
Str. 12/7—17/8/48.**G**.
Str. 22/7—18/8/51.**G**.
Rebuilt to J69/2.
Str. 13/11—19/12/53.**G**.
Str. 19/1—23/2/57.**G**.
Str. 31/7—3/8/59.**N/C**.

BOILERS:
  336.
  336 *(new)* 15/1/02.
  2838 *(new)* 1/12/20.
  263 *(exJ66 7322)* 3/3/28.
  256 *(ex7206)* 24/3/32.
  2859 *(ex7207)* 11/2/35.
  2846 *(ex7013)* 24/11/39.
  2845 *(ex7396)* 23/7/43.
  2880 *(exJ66 7293)* 29/9/45.
  2908 *(exJ66 8385)* 17/8/48.
  23806 *(new)* 18/8/51.
  23787 *(ex??)* 19/12/53.
  23828 *(new)* 23/2/57.
  23828 reno S.B.3385 3/8/59.

SHEDS:
Ipswich.

The heavier replacement smokebox doors put on from 1915 were more dished with beveled edge and a surrounding rim.

(below) As built, there were hand rails along the boiler, ending on the sides of the smokebox with a separate curved rail above the smokebox door.

From 1904 there was a gradual change to a continuous rail as fitted on J69 class built in that year. Note stepped shanks to buffers which are not Group Standard as they have a circular flange.

By no means all got this change of handrail. No.7017 still had separate rails when it was withdrawn 2nd June 1937 and No.7015 even kept them to its 17th August 1959 withdrawal as No.68520, although it was J69 Part 2 class from 4th February 1950 (*see* page 46, bottom).

At Grouping, the Macallan variable blastpipe, with control rod from the cab, was fitted and No.12 had it when it went for its first LNER repair 28th February 1925.

(below) From 1925 the variable blastpipes were taken off and replaced by plain type which did not need control gear.

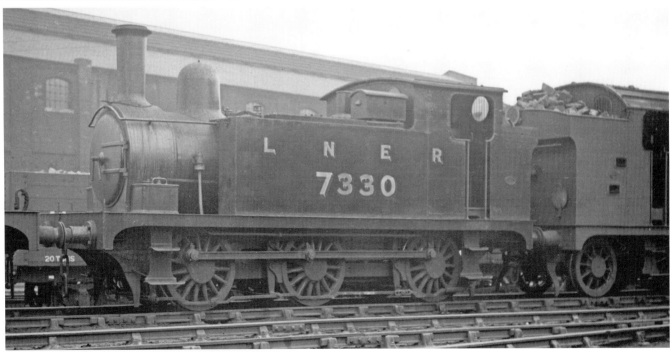

7336 cont./
King's Lynn 26/7/53.
Retford 27/7/58.
Doncaster 9/11/58.
Stratford works 3/8/59.

RENUMBERED:
7336 10/7/25.
8498 17/3/46.
68498 14/8/48.
DEPT'L 44 21/8/59.

To Service Stock: 3/8/59.
CONDEMNED: 16/9/62.
Cut up at Stratford.

___

7397

Stratford.

To traffic 11/1890.
Class R24 - goods.

REPAIRS:
Str. 11/7—15/11/05.**G.**
Cam. 14/8—7/12/22.**H.**
At 1/1/23: J67. Steam brake.
Cam. 6/7—25/9/25.**H.**
Str. 28/2—6/6/28.**G.**
Additional rails on bunker.
Str. 4/7—13/8/31.**G.**
Str. 23/10—16/11/34.**G.**
Str. 26/6—23/9/39.**G.**
Str. 6/8—3/9/42.**L.**
Str. 19/12/43—18/1/44.**G.**
Str. 13/4—7/5/46.**L.**
Str. 8/10—18/11/47.**G.**
Str. 14—23/2/48.**L.**
Jay-Gee smoke eliminator fitted.
Str. 4—29/6/51.**G.**
Jay-Gee removed.
Str. 7/3/54. *Not repaired.*

BOILERS:
397.
397 *(new)* 15/11/05.
2806 *(ex7260)* 6/6/28.
2825 *(ex7203)* 13/8/31.
2822 *(ex7199)* 16/11/34.
2838 *(exJ66 7316)* 23/9/39.
2855 *(ex7208)* 18/1/44.
2904 *(exJ66 8384)* 18/11/47.
23908 *(ex??)* 29/6/51.

SHEDS:
Cambridge.
King's Lynn 5/7/28.
Cambridge 23/8/31.
Stratford 17/11/34.
Parkeston 25/9/39.
Stratford 15/8/42.
Parkeston 2/1/43.
Stratford 8/6/46.
Cambridge 26/2/48.

South Lynn ?/11/48.
Cambridge ?/1/49.
Ipswich 26/7/53.

RENUMBERED:
7397 25/9/25.
8509 28/9/46.
68509 29/6/51.

CONDEMNED: 22/3/54.
Cut up at Stratford.

___

7398

Stratford.

To traffic 11/1890.
Class R24 - goods.

REPAIRS:
Str. 3/11/04—7/3/05.**G.**
Cam. 7/9—16/11/22.**H.**
At 1/1/23: J67. Steam brake.
Str. 29/8—23/10/25.**G.**
Str. 15/3—14/6/28.**G.**
Additional rails on bunker.
Str. 15/4—27/5/31.**G.**
Str. 16/4—31/5/34.**G.**
Str. 26/2—12/8/39.**G.**
Str. 4/4—8/5/42.**G.**
Str. 30/7—28/8/44.**G.**
Str. 29/12/46—28/1/47.**G.**
Str. 29/1—10/3/50.**G.**
Rebuilt to J69/2.
Str. 16/10—21/11/52.**G.**
Str. 4/3—16/4/57.**G.**
Str. 16/9/59. *Not repaired.*

BOILERS:
398.
398 *(new)* 7/3/05.
2803 *(exJ66 7299)* 27/5/31.
2895 *(new)* 31/5/34.
2892 *(exJ66 7276)* 12/8/39.
2853 *(ex7164)* 8/5/42.
2876 *(exJ66 7319)* 28/8/44.
2831 *(ex8558)* 28/1/47.
3201 *(new)* 10/3/50.
23716 *(ex68599)* 21/11/52.
23818 *(ex68633)* 16/4/57.

SHEDS:
King's Lynn.
Cambridge 5/7/28.
Stratford 31/5/34.
Parkeston 25/9/39.
Colchester 20/7/41.
Parkeston 10/8/41.
Colchester 2/11/41.
Stratford 23/5/42.
Parkeston 15/8/42.
Ipswich 29/11/42.
Stratford 29/2/48.
Lincoln 1/6/58.

RENUMBERED:
7398 23/10/25.
8510 29/9/46.
68510 10/3/50.

CONDEMNED: 28/9/59.
Cut up at Stratford.

___

7399

Stratford.

To traffic 11/1890.
Class R24 - goods.

REPAIRS:
Str. ?/?—?/6/04.**G.**
At 1/1/23: J67. Steam brake.
Str. 4/4—22/8/24.**G.**
Str. ?/?—?/8/29.**G.**
Additional rails on bunker.
Str. 30/12/31—15/1/32.**G.**
Str. 11—27/2/35.**G.**
Str. ?/?—21/9/39.**G.**
Str. 29/1—11/3/44.**G.**
Cow. ?/?—13/7/44.**L.**
NBR tender attached.
Cow. 5/3—20/5/49.**G.**
Cow. 9—13/1/51.**N/C.**
Cow. 22—25/5/51.**C/L.**
Cow. 14—21/11/51.**N/C.**
Cow. 23/6—12/7/52.**C/L.**
Cow. 21—29/10/52.**C/L.**
Cow. 20/1—12/2/53.**H/I.**
Cow. 26/1—5/2/55.**N/C.**

BOILERS:
399.
399 *(new)* ?/6/04.
276 *(exJ66 7276)* 22/8/24.
2835 *(ex7208)* 15/1/32.
2902 *(new)* 27/2/35
2830 *(exJ66 7296)* 21/9/39.
2837 *(exJ66 7311)* 11/3/44.
2837 reno.23960 12/7/52.

SHEDS:
Cambridge.
Stratford 27/2/35.
Parkeston 25/9/39.
Stratford 2/2/41.
St Margarets 18/6/44
(Galashiels).

RENUMBERED:
7399 22/8/24.
8511 14/9/46.
68511 20/5/49.

CONDEMNED: 14/12/56.
Cut up at Cowlairs.

___

7400

Stratford.

To traffic 11/1890.
Class R24 - goods.

REPAIRS:
Str. ?/?—?/12/01.**G.**
Str. 25/7—28/11/22.**G.**
At 1/1/23: J67. Steam brake.
Str. 27/1—10/3/25.**G.**
Str. 12/10—8/12/27.**G.**
Additional rails on bunker.
Str. 18/2—17/4/30.**G.**
Str. 29/3—25/4/33.**G.**
Str. 27/5—14/6/35.**H.**
Str. 15/10—6/11/36.**G.**
Str. 4/12/39—6/1/40.**G.**
Str. 9/10/40—1/2/41.**L.**
Str. 8/3—22/3/42.**H.**
Str. 28/4—14/8/43.**G.**
Str. 14/12/47—21/1/48.**G.**
Str. 30/1—24/2/51.**G.**
Rebuilt to J69/2.
Str. 27/3—23/4/54.**G.**
Str. 23/3/57. *Not repaired.*

BOILERS:
400.
400 *(new)* ?/12/01.
2813 *(exJ66 7322)* 28/11/22.
2860 *(exJ66 7317)* 17/4/30.
2876 *(ex7333)* 25/4/33.
2910 *(new)* 14/6/35.
2833 *(ex7015)* 6/11/36.
2903 *(exJ66 7313)* 6/1/40.
2835 *(ex7256)* 14/8/43.
???? 21/1/48.
23710 *(ex??)* 24/2/51.
23790 *(ex??)* 23/4/54.

SHEDS:
Peterborough East.
New England 30/4/39.
Gorton 7/10/40.
Trafford Park 24/2/41.
Frodingham 15/1/42.
New England 9/10/43.
Hitchin 6/2/44.
New England 2/10/52.
Hitchin 26/10/52.
Lincoln 26/7/53.
Staveley 1/8/54.
Lincoln 29/8/54.
Darnall 28/9/54.
Lincoln 5/10/54.
Staveley 3/4/55.

RENUMBERED:
7400 10/3/25.
8512 7/9/46.
E8512 21/1/48.
68512 24/2/51.

Three open flat bar type coal rails had been put on from 1895 and were un-altered until after the LNER took over.

Between June 1926 (No.7404) and May 1930 (No.7201), all fifty-one had three extra rails added to close the spaces and stop spillage of small coal. Note the Load Class 2 tablet fixed on the buffer beam.

(below) The Diagram 39 boiler had two Ramsbottom safety valves in a casing with round ends just in front of the cab with the whistle on the right hand side.

When a steel firebox was fitted, the safety valves were further forward on the rear ring of the boiler with the whistle still alongside. No.7330 was the only one of the 7327 to 7336 batch to keep the 1000 gallons tanks to withdrawal. Note the chamber put on the tank top from when it had condensing apparatus 1893 to 1912 and which it kept to withdrawal.

On boilers built by the LNER, Ross 'pop' safety valves were used, at first fitted on a Ramsbottom mounting, and still with the whistle on their right hand side.

Later boilers had the 'pops' mounted directly on to the firebox casing and the whistle was then put on a standpipe between the rear valve and the front of the cab.

7400 cont./
CONDEMNED: 1/4/57.
Cut up at Stratford.

7401

Stratford.

To traffic 11/1890.
Class R24 - goods.

REPAIRS:
Str. ?/?—?/6/05.**G.**
At 1/1/23: J67. Steam brake.
Str. 1/1—13/3/24.**G.**
Str. 12/1—10/3/27.**G.**
Additional rails on bunker.
Str. 13/6—24/8/29.**G.**
Str. 20/3—29/4/32.**G.**
Str. 23/7—30/8/35.**G.**
Str. 10/9—28/10/39.**G.**
Str. 13/9—9/10/42.**G.**
Str. 12/5—13/6/44.**G.**
Str. 11—24/11/45.**G.**
Str. 13/5—4/6/49.**G.**
Str. 19/5—12/6/52.**G.**
Rebuilt to J69/2.
Str. 19/3—9/6/56.**C/L.**
Str. 12/8—14/9/57.**G.**

BOILERS:
401.
401 (new) ?/6/05.
2855 (new) 13/3/24.
2830 (exJ66 7324) 29/4/32.
2818 (exJ66 7290) 30/8/35.
2873 (ex7019) 28/10/39.
2916 (exJ66 7296) 9/10/42.
2872 (ex7208) 24/11/45.
2912 (ex8592) 4/6/49.
23746 (ex??) 12/6/52.
23756 (ex68623) 14/9/57.

SHEDS:
Peterborough East.
Stratford 29/7/35.
Cambridge 2/11/39.
Stratford 15/4/40.
Parkeston 28/11/42.
Stratford 2/1/43.

RENUMBERED:
7401 13/3/24.
8513 20/10/46.
68513 4/6/49.

CONDEMNED: 18/10/60.
Cut up at Stratford.

7402

Stratford.

To traffic 11/1890.
Class R24 - goods.

REPAIRS:
Str. ?/?—?/6/08.**G.**
At 1/1/23: J67. Steam brake.
Str. 26/11/25—2/3/26.**G.**
Str. ?/?—?/8/28.**G.**
Additional rails on bunker.
Str. 3—19/1/34.**G.**

BOILERS:
402.
402 (new) ?/6/08.
287 (exJ66 7287) 2/3/26.
326 (exJ66 7299) 19/1/34.

SHED:
King's Lynn.

RENUMBERED:
7402 2/3/26.

CONDEMNED: 15/5/37.

7403

Stratford.

To traffic 12/1890.
Class R24 - goods.

REPAIRS:
Str. ?/?—?/6/05.**G.**
Str. 27/3—23/6/22.**G.**
At 1/1/23: J67. Steam brake.
Str. 2/4—17/6/25.**G.**
Str. 16/9—9/12/27.**G.**
Additional rails on bunker.
Str. 10/4—23/5/30.**G.**
Str. 22/12/32—23/1/33.**G.**
Str. 24/10—18/11/35.**G.**
Str. 31/8—30/9/38.**G.**
Str. 8/6—9/7/41.**G.**
Str. 26/3—2/4/44.**G.**
Str. 23/6—11/8/46.**G.**
Str. 18/9—5/11/49.**G.**
Str. 9—28/6/52.**G.**

BOILERS:
403.
403 (new) ?/6/05.
252 (exJ65 7246) 17/6/25.
2867 (exJ66 7301) 23/1/33.
2854 (ex7255) 18/11/35.
2904 (exJ66 7317) 30/9/38.
2884 (exJ66 7304) 9/7/41.
2860 (ex7261) 29/4/44.
2844 (ex8588) 11/8/46.
2852 (ex8608) 5/11/49.

23923 (ex??) 28/6/52.

SHEDS:
King's Lynn.
Norwich 26/7/53.

RENUMBERED:
7403 17/6/25.
8514 20/10/46.
68514 5/11/49.

CONDEMNED: 25/7/55.
Cut up at Stratford.

7404

Stratford.

To traffic 12/1890.
Class R24 - goods.

REPAIRS:
Str. 25/10/07—13/2/08.**G.**
Str. 30/4—21/7/20.**G.**
At 1/1/23: J69. Steam brake.
Str. ?/?—?/6/26.**G.**
Additional rails on bunker.
Str. ?/?—?/11/28.**G.**
Str. ?/?—?/12/31.**G.**
Str. 12/12/34—3/1/35.**G.**

BOILERS:
404.
404 (new) 13/2/08.
2814 (exJ65 7250) ?/11/28.
2809 (exJ66 7302) ?/12/31.
2861 (exJ65 7155) 3/1/35.

SHED:
Cambridge.

RENUMBERED:
7404 ?/?/?.

CONDEMNED: 26/5/37.

7405

Stratford.

To traffic 12/1890.
Class R24 - goods.

REPAIRS:
Str. ?/?—?/12/01.**G.**
Str. 8/5—12/8/22.**G.**
At 1/1/23: J67. Steam brake.
Str. 11/5—3/7/25.**G.**
Str. 28/4—30/7/28.**G.**
Additional rails on bunker.
Str. 23/4—3/6/31.**G.**
Str. 17/6—29/7/31.**L.**
Str. 25/1—23/2/34.**G.**

Str. 14/9—8/10/36.**G.**
Str. 8/10—18/11/39.**G.**
Str. 29/11/42—13/1/43.**G.**
Str. 10/12/43—29/1/44.**G.**
Str. 3—25/2/46.**G.**
Str. 19/5—11/6/49.**G.**
Str. 30/3—24/4/52.**G.**

BOILERS:
405.
405 (new) ?/12/01.
2844 (new) 12/8/22.
402 (ex7259) 3/6/31.
2812 (exJ66 7286) 23/2/34.
2882 (ex7263) 8/10/36.
2902 (ex7399) 18/11/39.
2875 (exJ66 7298) 13/1/43.
2841 (ex7256) 29/1/44.
2907 (ex7011) 25/2/46.
2890 (ex8583) 11/6/49.
23921 (ex??) 24/4/52.

SHEDS:
Cambridge.
King's Lynn 4/5/39.
South Lynn 28/9/52.
Melton Constable 26/7/53.

RENUMBERED:
7405 3/7/25.
8515 3/11/46.
68515 11/6/49.

CONDEMNED: 9/1/57.
Cut up at Stratford.

7406

Stratford.

To traffic 12/1890.
Class R24 - goods.

REPAIRS:
Str. ?/?—?/6/05.**G.**
Str. 1/4—27/7/22.**G.**
At 1/1/23: J67. Steam brake.
Str. ?/?—?/3/27.**G.**
Additional rails on bunker.
Str. ?/?—?/7/31.**G.**
Str. 5—21/2/34.**G.**

BOILERS:
406.
406 (new) ?/6/05.
2843 (new) 27/7/22.
2870 (ex7013) ?/7/31.
287 (ex7402) 21/2/34.

SHEDS:
March.
Stratford 16/2/34.

Standard buffers were parallel shank type with hollow spindle and circular flange behind which a wood packing was fitted. At least five were equipped with Group Standard type buffers during the period 1932-35: Nos.7011, 7012, 7205, 7403 and 7404 being noted.

Until 1930 the standard chimney was the stovepipe which had a beaded rim at the top and was 12ft 11in. above rail level.

(below) From June 1930 the chimney was gradually replaced by an NER pattern cast type which reduced height from rail level to 12ft 8 ½ in. Seen here ex-works 3rd February 1932, No.7011 had also been fitted with Group Standard buffers.

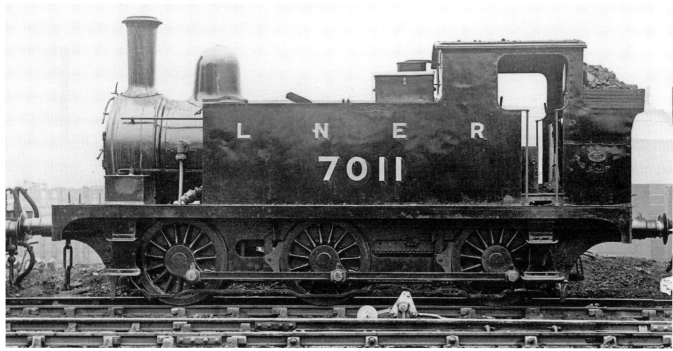

Until 1933 the cab roof was made of wood with a relatively shallow curve and a straight rain strip at each edge.

(centre) From 1933, a steel cab roof was introduced and this had a higher arch, with sliding ventilator and curved rain strips. By 1939 the wood roof seems to have been cleared from J67 class.

(below) On 29th March 1944 No.7329 was transferred to Scottish Area to work the Lauder Light Railway from Galashiels shed. Being one of the heavier ones with wide tanks, it was a curious choice because weight restrictions required it to work with empty tanks, the water being carried in a 3500 gallons ex North British tender permanently coupled to it. Cowlairs recorded this tender as ex D36 class No.9695 which was withdrawn in 1943. No.7329 was renumbered 8492 on 24th march 1946.

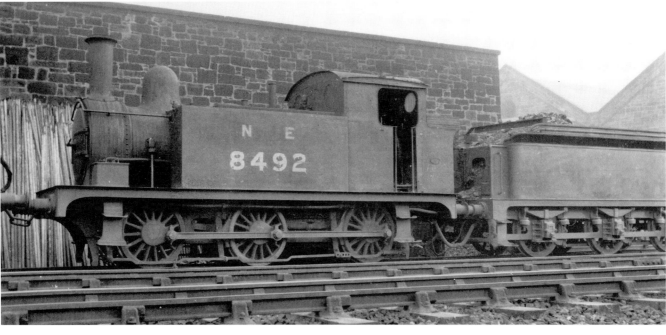

RENUMBERED:
7406 ?/?/??.

CONDEMNED: 3/7/37.

_____

7011

Stratford.

To traffic 12/1890.
Class R24 - goods.

REPAIRS:
Str. 5/10/01—25/4/02.**G.**
Str. 20/9—23/12/21.**G.**
At 1/1/23: J67. Steam brake.
Str. 20/10—13/12/24.**G.**
Str. 19/8—23/11/27.**G.**
Additional rails on bunker.
Str. 26/2—5/4/30.**G.**
Str. 1/1—3/2/32.**G.**
Str. 4/10—1/11/34.**G.**
Str. 9—19/11/34.**H.**
Str. 1—26/5/38.**G.**
Str. 1/8—6/10/43.**G.**
Str. 13/1—7/2/46.**G.**
Str. 10/12/48—22/1/49.**G.**
Str. 28/5—19/7/51.**G.**
Str. 20/3—15/5/54.**G.**

BOILERS:
  407.
  407 (new) 25/4/02.
  295 (exJ66 295) 23/12/21.
  2814 (ex7404) 3/2/32.
  2880 (ex7201) 1/11/34.
  2917 (new) 26/5/38.
  2907 (ex7161) 6/10/43.
  2903 (ex7256) 7/2/46.
  2877 (ex8595) 22/1/49.
  23907 (ex??) 19/7/51.

SHEDS:
Cambridge.
Stratford 3/11/34.
Cambridge 3/11/39.
Norwich 26/7/53.
Stratford 2/12/56.

RENUMBERED:
11 from **407** 1/1/20.
  7011 13/12/24.
  8516 12/1/47.
68516 22/1/49.

CONDEMNED: 29/4/57.
Cut up at Stratford.

_____

7012

Stratford.

To traffic 12/1890.
Class R24 - goods.

REPAIRS:
Str. 24/1—16/9/01.**G.**
Str. ?/?—?/2/20.**G.**
Pbo. 11/9—6/10/22.**H.**
At 1/1/23: J67. Steam brake.
Str. 28/2—8/5/25.**G.**
Str. 26/8—15/12/27.**G.**
Additional rails on bunker.
Str. 23/11/29—25/1/30.**G.**
Str. 22/8—22/9/33.**G.**
Str. 19/11—21/12/39.**G.**
Str. 9/10—20/11/42.**G.**
Str. 4—27/2/45.**G.**
Str. 20/9—11/11/47.**G.**
Str. 7/1—10/2/51.**G.**
Rebuilt to J69/2.
Str. 31/8—19/9/53.**G.**
Rebuilt to J67/1.

BOILERS:
  408.
  408 (new) 16/9/01.
  2812 (new) ?/2/20.
  254 (exJ65 7254) 15/12/27.
  2832 (exJ66 7310) 25/1/30.
  2877 (exJ66 7293) 22/9/33.
  2825 (ex7258) 21/12/39.
  2883 (ex7329) 20/11/42.
  2892 (exJ66 7324) 27/2/45.
  2894 (ex8522) 11/11/47.
  23707 (ex??) 10/2/51.
  23932 (ex??) 19/9/53.

SHEDS:
Cambridge.
Stratford 15/8/30.
Cambridge 25/6/37.
King's Lynn 7/3/43.
Cambridge 27/6/43.
Stratford 29/2/48.

RENUMBERED:
12 from **408** 1/1/20.
  7012 8/5/25.
  8517 4/1/47.
68517 10/2/51.

CONDEMNED: 1/3/56.
Cut up at Stratford.

_____

7013

Stratford.

To traffic 12/1890.
Class R24 - goods.

REPAIRS:
Str. ?/?—?/6/02.**G.**
Str. ?/?—?/12/19.**G.**
At 1/1/23: J67. Steam brake.
Str. 13/12/22—27/3/23.**G.**
Str. 14/9—12/11/25.**G.**
Str. 26/4—25/7/28.**G.**
Additional rails on bunker.
Str. 23/3—1/5/31.**G.**
Str. 19/10—15/11/33.**G.**
Str. 18/6—20/7/36.**G.**
Str. 22/6—26/9/39.**G.**
Str. 19/2—14/5/43.**G.**
Str. 22/6—28/7/45.**G.**
Str. 25/7—2/9/48.**G.**
Str. 19/8—15/9/51.**G.**
Str. 23/5—17/6/54.**G.**

BOILERS:
  409.
  409 (new) ?/6/02.
  2811 (new) ?/12/19.
  2809 (exJ66 7293) 12/11/25.
  2870 (new) 25/7/28.
  157 (ex7256) 1/5/31.
  2827 (ex7164) 15/11/33.
  2846 (exJ66 7296) 20/7/36.
  2908 (exJ66 7291) 26/9/39.
  2859 (ex7330) 14/5/43.
  2825 (exJ67 7047) 28/7/45.
  2893 (exJ65 8213) 2/9/48.
  23910 (ex??) 15/9/51.
  23908 (ex68509) 17/6/54.

SHED:
Ipswich

RENUMBERED:
13 from **409** 1/1/20.
  7013 12/11/25.
  8518 8/9/46.
68518 28/8/48.

CONDEMNED: 18/2/58.
Cut up at Stratford.

_____

7014

Stratford.

To traffic 1/1891.
Class R24 - goods.

REPAIRS:
Str. ?/?—?/6/04.**G.**
Str. 11/2—14/5/21.**G.**
At 1/1/23: J67. Steam brake.
Str. 13/8—29/10/26.**G.**
Str. 23/3—1/6/29.**G.**
Additional rails on bunker.
Str. 12/9—6/10/32.**G.**
Str. 4—28/10/36.**G.**
Str. 3—30/3/40.**G.**
Str. 28/12/42—20/2/43.**G.**

Str. 29/7—28/9/45.**G.**
Str. 19/4—2/5/48.**L.**
Str. 20/3—22/4/50.**G.**
Rebuilt to J69/2.
Str. 15/1—12/2/54.**G.**

BOILERS:
  410.
  410 (new) ?/6/04.
  2838 (new) 14/5/21.
  2807 (exJ66 7311) 6/10/32.
  2812 (ex7405) 28/10/36.
  2844 (exJ66 7324) 30/3/40.
  2891 (exJ66 7293) 20/2/43.
  3204 (new) 22/4/50.
  23707 (ex68517) 12/2/54.

SHEDS:
Stratford.
Parkeston 8/6/46.
Stratford 16/5/48.
New England 6/11/55.
Retford 4/12/55.

RENUMBERED:
14 from **410** 1/1/20.
  7014 29/10/26.
  8519 24/11/46.
68519 22/4/50.

CONDEMNED: 6/8/58.
Cut up at Stratford.

_____

7015

Stratford.

To traffic 1/1891.
Class R24 - goods.

REPAIRS:
Str. ?/?—?/9/05.**G.**
Str. 20/10—17/12/21.**G.**
At 1/1/23: J67. Steam brake.
Str. 2/1—18/4/25.**G.**
Str. 28/4—15/8/28.**G.**
Additional rails on bunker.
Str. 22/8—3/10/31.**G.**
Str. 6/7—12/8/36.**G.**
Str. 7/11—6/12/41.**G.**
Str. 15/10—3/11/44.**G.**
Str. 30/10—5/12/46.**G.**
Str. 6—26/12/48.**L.**
Str. 28/12/49—4/2/50.**G.**
Rebuilt to J69/2.
Str. 2—28/2/53.**G.**
Str. 30/1—17/3/56.**L/I.**
Str. 26/3—12/4/56.**N/C.**

BOILERS:
  411.
  411 (new) ?/9/05.
  2833 (ex7260) 3/10/31.
  2887 (exJ66 7324) 12/8/36.

7015 cont./
2904 (ex7403) 6/12/41.
2887 (exJ66 7289) 3/11/44.
2854 (ex7377) 5/12/46.
3198 (new) 4/2/50.
23761 (ex??) 28/2/53.

SHEDS:
Stratford.
Mexborough 21/3/54.
Doncaster 4/12/55.
Retford 18/12/55.
Doncaster 17/2/57.

RENUMBERED:
15 *from* **411** 1/1/20.
7015 18/4/25.
8520 29/8/46.
68520 24/12/48.

CONDEMNED: 17/8/59.
Cut up at Stratford.

_____

7016

Stratford.

To traffic 1/1891.
Class R24 - goods.

REPAIRS:
Str. ?/?—?/6/07.**G.**
Str. ?/?—?/10/18.**G.**
Str. 12/12/21—25/2/22.**G.**
At 1/1/23: J67. Steam brake.
Str. 6/3—1/5/25.**G.**
Str. 18/6—16/9/27.**G.**
Additional rails on bunker.
Str. 20/9—19/10/29.**G.**
Str. 4/4—12/5/32.**G.**
Str. 12/2—23/3/35.**G.**
Str. 29/1—21/3/40.**G.**
Str. 31/1—30/3/43.**G.**
Str. 7/3—7/4/44.**G.**
Str. 17/2—15/3/46.**G.**
Str. 11—20/3/48.**L.**
Str. 4/9—21/10/49.**G.**
Str. 24/6—8/8/52.**G.**

BOILERS:
412.
412 (new) ?/6/07.
263 (ex7263) ?/10/18.
2841 (new) 25/2/22.
327 (exJ66 7295) 16/9/27.
2883 (new) 19/10/29.
2863 (ex7204) 12/5/32.
2905 (new) 23/3/35.
2819 (exJ66 7312) 21/3/40.
2902 (exJ66 7405) 30/3/43.
2905 (exJ66 7307) 15/3/46.
23924 (ex??) 8/8/52.

SHEDS:
Ipswich.
Norwich 16/6/37.
Stratford 9/4/40.
Parkeston 25/11/44.
Stratford 16/5/48.
Ipswich 4/4/54.

RENUMBERED:
16 *from* **412** 1/1/20.
7016 1/5/25.
8521 17/11/46.
68521 21/10/49.

CONDEMNED: 17/8/56.
Cut up at Stratford.

_____

7017

Stratford.

To traffic 1/1891.
Class R24 - goods.

REPAIRS:
Str. ?/?—?/10/02.**G.**
At 1/1/23: J67. Steam brake.
Str. ?/?—?/3/26.**G.**
Str. ?/?—?/7/29.**G.**
Additional rails on bunker.
Str. 1—17/2/33.**G.**

BOILERS:
413.
413 (new) ?/10/02.
2816 (ex7206) ?/3/26
2868 (new) ?/7/29.
2842 (ex7263) 17/2/33.

SHED:
Stratford.

RENUMBERED:
17 *from* **413** 1/1/20.
7017 ?/3/26.

CONDEMNED: 2/6/37.
Cut up at Stratford.

_____

7018

Stratford.

To traffic 1/1891.
Class R24 - goods.

REPAIRS:
Str. ?/?—?/8/01.**G.**
Str. ?/?—?/12/13.**G.**
At 1/1/23: J67. Steam brake.
Str. 11/12/22—14/4/23.**G.**
Str. 2/3—18/4/25.**G.**
Str. 18/2—12/6/28.**G.**

Additional rails on bunker.
Str. 14/11—18/12/31.**G.**
Str. 19/2—6/3/36.**G.**
Str. 24/5—26/6/41.**G.**
Str. 27/8—6/10/44.**G.**
Str. 30/12/46—23/1/47.**G.**
Str. 9/2—22/3/50.**G.**
Rebuilt to J69/2.
Str. 31/3—3/5/52.**G.**
Str. 31/5—25/6/54.**G.**
Str. 29/8—12/10/56.**G.**

BOILERS:
414.
414 (new) ?/8/01.
414 (new) ?/12/13.
2818 (exJ66 7296) 12/6/28.
309 (exJ66 7309) 18/12/31.
327 (exJ66 7281) 6/3/36.
2886 (ex7263) 26/6/41.
2894 (exJ66 7288) 6/10/44.
2906 (ex8536) 23/1/47.
3068 (ex8570) 22/3/50.
23814 (new) 3/5/52.
23791 (ex??) 25/6/54.

SHEDS:
Stratford.
Colchester 6/6/42.
Stratford 8/1/44.
Colchester 20/10/45.
Stratford 7/12/46.
Colchester 14/5/50.
Stratford 25/5/58.
Colwick 27/7/58.
Boston 8/11/59.

RENUMBERED:
18 *from* **414** 1/1/20.
7018 18/4/25.
8522 8/12/46.
68522 22/3/50.

CONDEMNED: 17/3/61.
Into Don. for c/u 17/3/61.

_____

7019

Stratford.

To traffic 1/1891.
Class R24 - goods.

REPAIRS:
Str. 7/9/06—15/1/07.**G.**
Str. 30/5—29/8/22.**G.**
At 1/1/23: J67. Steam brake.
Str. 2/2—4/4/25.**G.**
Str. 1/2—5/4/28.**G.**
Additional rails on bunker.
Str. 2—29/7/31.**G.**
Str. 21/6—19/7/35.**G.**
Str. 16/4—29/8/39.**G.**
Str. 14/3—15/5/43.**G.**

Str. 26/8—22/9/45.**G.**
Str. 21/4—14/5/49.**G.**
Str. 4/4—16/5/52.**G.**
Str. 14/11/55. *Not repaired.*

BOILERS:
415.
415 (new) 15/1/07.
280 (exJ66 7280) 4/4/25.
2844 (ex7405) 29/7/31.
2873 (exJ66 7326) 19/7/35.
2863 (ex7327) 29/8/39.
2911 (exJ67 7047) 15/5/43.
2897 (ex7260) 22/9/45.
2888 (exJ66 8373) 14/5/49.
23922 (ex??) 16/5/52.

SHEDS:
Stratford.
Colchester 8/1/44.
Stratford 25/11/44.
Staveley 25/1/53.
Darnall 5/7/53.
Staveley 26/7/53.
Ipswich 16/8/53.
Norwich 13/9/53.

RENUMBERED:
19 *from* **415** 1/1/20.
7019 4/4/25.
8523 1/9/46.
68523 14/5/49.

CONDEMNED: 5/12/55.
Cut up at Stratford.

_____

7020

Stratford.

To traffic 1/1891.
Class R24 - goods.

REPAIRS:
Str. ?/?—?/11/07.**G.**
At 1/1/23: J67. Steam brake.
Str. 3/3—8/5/24.**G.**
Str. ?/?--?/10/27.**G.**
Additional rails on bunker.
Str. 17/4—21/5/30.**G.**
Str. 6—22/3/33.**G.**

BOILERS:
416.
416 (new) ?/11/07.
2856 (new) 8/5/24.
2813 (ex7400) 21/5/30.
2868 (ex7017) 22/3/33.

SHED:
Stratford.

RENUMBERED:
20 *from* **416** 1/1/20.

(above) No.7329 having been proven satisfactory, No.7399 was also transferred to Scottish Area on 18th June 1944 and Cowlairs attached a tender of only 2500 gallons capacity, taken from a J36 class engine, two of which (Nos.9674 and 9741) had been withdrawn in 1943.

(right) From a heavy repair, No.68511 (ex7399) was ex Cowlairs on 12th February 1953 with their version of a stovepipe chimney which it then kept to its 14th December 1956 withdrawal.

(below) Ex works 22nd September 1933, No.7012 had been fitted for grease lubrication to its coupling rods and to the big ends. It reverted to oil lubrication at a date which was not recorded.

In 1944/45 Stratford had only limited foundry capacity due to bomb damage, and some engines got stovepipes riveted to the base of the existing chimney. No.7013 was ex works 28th July 1945.

(above) No.7019 was ex works 22nd September 1945 and had lost the toolbox from its tank top. Compare with the previous illustration of No.7013, ex works 28th July 1945, which kept its toolbox.

From 1945 Stratford took off the toolbox from the top of the left hand tank.

7020 8/5/24.

CONDEMNED: 2/6/37.
Cut up at Stratford.

7255

Stratford.

To traffic 3/1899.
Class R24 - goods.

REPAIRS:
Str. 31/8—12/12/11.**G.**
At 1/1/23: *J67. Steam brake.*
Str. 27/11/23—22/2/24.**G.**
Str. ?/?—?/8/27.**G.**
Additional rails on bunker.
Str. ?/?—?/9/29.**G.**
Ross 'pop' safety valves fitted.
Str. 31/12/34—16/1/35.**G.**

BOILERS:
 255.
 255 (new) 12/12/11.
2854 (new) 22/2/24.
2849 (ex7202) 16/1/35.

SHED:
Stratford.

RENUMBERED:
7255 *after* 22/2/24.

CONDEMNED: 15/5/37.
Cut up at Stratford.

7256

Stratford.

To traffic 3/1899.
Class R24 - goods.

REPAIRS:
Str. 22/1—6/8/09.**G.**
At 1/1/23: *J67. Steam brake.*
Str. 19/3—12/5/23.**G.**
Str. 29/8—13/11/25.**G.**
Str. 15/6—31/8/28.**G.**
Additional rails on bunker.
Str. 6/12/30—23/1/31.**G.**
Str. 4—31/7/35.**G.**
Str. 4/6—13/9/39.**G.**
Str. 29/8—10/11/43.**G.**
Str. 9/12/45—11/1/46.**G.**
Str. 27/4—28/5/49.**G.**
Gor. 21/5—18/6/55.**C/L.**
Gor. 18—25/5/57.**C/L.**
Gor. 25/4/58. *Not repaired.*

BOILERS:
 256.

256 (new) 6/8/09.
2810 (exJ66 7295) 13/11/25.
 157 (exJ65 7249) 31/8/28.
 403 (exJ66 7293) 23/1/31.
2835 (ex7399) 31/7/35.
2841 (exJ66 7322) 13/9/39.
2903 (ex7400) 10/11/43.
2890 (ex7384) 11/1/46.
2899 (ex8589) 28/5/49.
2899 reno 23956 18/6/55.

SHEDS:
Stratford.
Cambridge 2/10/39.
King's Lynn 7/3/43.
Cambridge 18/4/43.
Gorton 21/10/49.
Trafford Park 30/10/49.
Wrexham 19/5/56.
Bidston ?/2/57.

RENUMBERED:
 7256 13/11/25.
 8583 22/12/46.
68583 28/5/49.

CONDEMNED: 25/4/58.
Cut up at Gorton 23/8/58.

7257

Stratford.

To traffic 3/1899.
Class R24 - goods.

REPAIRS:
Str. ?/?—?/4/11.**G.**
Str. 28/5—20/7/21.**G.**
At 1/1/23: *J67. Steam brake.*
Str. 28/8—3/12/24.**G.**
Str. 6/1—1/4/27.**G.**
Str. 19/10—7/12/29.**G.**
Additional rails on bunker.
Str. 29/3—22/4/32.**G.**
Str. 21/2—2/4/37.**G.**
Str. 8/2—18/3/41.**G.**
Gor. 8/7—12/8/44.**G.**
Gor. 10/4—7/6/47.**G.**
Gor. 23/12/50—20/1/51.**H/I.**
Gor. 17/5—14/6/52.**G.**
Gor. 2—9/10/54.**C/L.**

BOILERS:
 257.
 257 (new) ?/4/11.
2864 (new) 1/4/27.
2823 (ex7200) 22/4/32.
2910 (ex7400) 2/4/37.
2915 (ex7396) 18/3/41.
2915 reno.23953 20/1/51.
23954 (ex??) 14/6/52.

SHEDS:
Stratford.
Northwich 11/12/42.
Trafford Park 11/3/43.
Bidston 25/4/43.
Trafford Park 25/7/43.
Walton-on-the-Hill 4/9/47.
Wrexham ?/12/51.

RENUMBERED:
 7257 3/12/24.
 8584 20/7/46.
68584 19/3/49.

CONDEMNED: 8/8/55.
Into Gorton for c/u 13/8/55, c/u 17/9/55.

7258

Stratford.

To traffic 3/1899.
Class R24 - goods.

REPAIRS:
Str. 14/1—16/5/16.**G.**
Str. 15/7—17/9/21.**G.**
At 1/1/23: *J67. Steam brake.*
Str. 13/5—23/8/24.**G.**
Str. 26/8—1/12/27.**G.**
Additional rails on bunker.
Str. 2/8—3/10/30.**G.**
Str. 9/6—6/7/35.**G.**
Str. 2/4—4/9/39.**G.**
Str. 25/4—11/6/42.**G.**
Gor. 25/2—7/4/45.**G.**
Gor. 18/4—1/9/47.**G.**
Rebuilt to J69/2.
Gor. 5/8—2/9/50.**G.**
Gor. 18/9—30/10/54.**G.**
Gor. 30/6/58. *Not repaired.*

BOILERS:
 258.
2803 (new) 16/5/16.
2858 (new) 23/8/24.
2825 (ex7397) 6/7/35.
2880 (ex7011) 4/9/39.
2866 (ex7082) 11/6/42.
2983 (ex7086) 1/9/47.
23840 (ex??) 2/9/50.
23843 (ex??) 30/10/54.

SHEDS:
Stratford.
Northwich 11/12/42.
Trafford Park 23/2/43.
Walton-on-the-Hill ?/?/49.
Chester ?/5/56.
On loan to Wrexham (WR) when withdrawn.

RENUMBERED:
 7258 23/8/24.
 8585 16/1/46.
68585 19/3/49.

CONDEMNED: 5/7/58.
Cut up at Gorton 23/8/58.

7259

Stratford.

To traffic 3/1899.
Class R24 - goods.

REPAIRS:
Str. 26/4—31/7/11.**G.**
At 1/1/23: *J67. Steam brake.*
Str. ?/?—?/10/26.**G.**
Str. ?/?—?/2/30.**G.**
Additional rails on bunker.
Str. ?/?—?/1/31.**G.**
Str. 15/5—8/6/34.**G.**

BOILERS:
 259.
 259 (new) 31/7/11.
 402 (ex7402) ?/10/26.
2856 (ex7020) ?/1/31.
2826 (exJ66 7292) 8/6/34.

SHED:
Stratford.

RENUMBERED:
7259 ?/10/26?

CONDEMNED: 20/5/37.
Cut up at Stratford.

7260

Stratford.

To traffic 3/1899.
Class R24 - goods.

REPAIRS:
Str. 25/5—3/9/17.**G.**
Str. 16/3—13/5/21.**G.**
At 1/1/23: *J67. Steam brake.*
Str. 20/8—30/10/24.**G.**
Str. 1/2—24/5/28.**G.**
Additional rails on bunker.
Str. 27/6—29/7/31.**G.**
Str. 23/12/35—17/1/36.**G.**
Str. 8/4—15/5/40.**G.**
Str. 4/4—30/7/43.**G.**
Str. 15/7—18/8/45.**G.**
Str. 2/1—16/2/48.**G.**
Jay-Gee smoke eliminator fitted.
Str. 18/6—22/7/50.**G.**
Smoke eliminator removed.

7260 cont./
Str. 23/12/52—8/1/53.**N/C.**
Str. 21/6—1/8/53.**G.**

BOILERS:
   260.
   2806 *(new)* 3/9/17.
   2833 *(ex7333)* 24/5/28.
   2853 *(ex7202)* 29/7/31.
   2837 *(exJ66 7322)* 17/1/36.
   2812 *(ex7014)* 15/5/40.
   2897 *(ex7384)* 30/7/43.
   2881 *(ex7331)* 18/8/45.
   2892 *(ex8517)* 16/2/48.
   2857 *(ex8490)* 22/7/50.
23930 *(ex??)* 1/8/53.

SHEDS:
Stratford.
Norwich 23/6/37.
Ipswich 24/2/52.
Norwich 8/6/52.
Ipswich 13/9/53.

RENUMBERED:
   7260 30/10/24.
   8586 17/3/46.
   E8586 16/2/48.
68586 22/7/50.

CONDEMNED: 21/5/56.
Cut up at Stratford.

_____

7261

Stratford.

To traffic 4/1899.
Class R24 - goods.

REPAIRS:
Str. 25/5—26/9/17.**G.**
Str. 29/3—9/7/21.**G.**
At 1/1/23: J67. Steam brake.
Str. 26/2—9/5/24.**G.**
Str. 22/4—25/6/27.**G.**
Additional rails on bunker.
Str. 8/3—17/4/30.**G.**
Str. 25/10—17/11/32.**G.**
Str. 7/4—18/5/37.**G.**
Str. 21/3—17/4/41.**G.**
Str. 14/1—10/2/44.**G.**
Don. 18/2—1/5/44.**L.**
Str. 5/5—7/6/46.**G.**
Rebuilt to J69/2.
Str. 12/6—13/8/49.**G.**
Str. 24/8—18/9/52.**G.**
Str. 10/9—14/10/55.**G.**

BOILERS:
   261.
   260 *(new)* 26/9/17.
   2839 *(new)* 9/7/21.
   2810 *(exJ66 7307)* 17/11/32.

2914 *(new)* 18/5/37.
2860 *(ex7262)* 17/4/41.
2875 *(ex7405)* 10/2/44.
3169 *(new)* 7/6/46.
23733 *(ex68573)* 18/9/52.
23732 *(ex68545)* 14/10/55.

SHEDS:
Stratford.
N.E.Area 2/10/24.
Stratford 11/11/24.
New England 17/10/39.
Hatfield 19/3/41.
Lincoln 17/5/41.
Doncaster 24/3/57.

RENUMBERED:
   7261 9/5/24.
   8587 22/1/46.
68587 13/8/49.

CONDEMNED: 1/10/59.
Cut up at Stratford.

_____

7262

Stratford.

To traffic 4/1899.
Class R24 - goods.

REPAIRS:
Str. 8/11/17—9/4/18.**G.**
At 1/1/23: J67. Steam brake.
Str. 16/4—21/6/23.**G.**
Str. 14/9—4/12/25.**G.**
Str. 14/9—15/11/28.**G.**
Additional rails on bunker.
Str. 2/1—5/2/32.**G.**
Str. 11/4—1/6/37.**G.**
Str. 25/1—26/3/41.**G.**
Str. 19/2—17/4/43.**G.**
Str. 9/4—1/6/46.**G.**
Str. 2—24/10/48.**C/L.**
Str. 14/11—9/12/50.**G.**
Str. 15/5—27/6/53.**G.**
Rebuilt to J69/2.
Str. 17/10—25/11/55.**G.**
Str. 13/9—12/10/56.**C/L.**
Str. 25/4—7/5/57.**C/L.**

BOILERS:
   262.
   311 *(exJ66 311)* 9/4/18.
   250 *(exJ65 7150)* 4/12/25.
   308 *(exJ66 7308)* 5/2/32.
   2860 *(exJ66 7293)* 1/6/37.
   2879 *(ex7208)* 26/3/41.
   2844 *(ex7014)* 17/4/43.
   2867 *(ex7161)* 1/6/46.
23902 *(ex??)* 9/12/50.
23740 *(ex68661)* 27/6/53.
23725 *(ex68618)* 25/11/55.

SHEDS:
Stratford.
Lincoln 9/6/39.
Frodingham 29/8/40.
Hitchin 30/6/43.
Frodingham 22/8/43.
Gorton 4/6/46.
Bidston *by* 9/46.
New England 2/3/47.
Stratford 1/9/49.

RENUMBERED:
   7262 4/12/25.
   8588 17/3/46.
68588 9/12/50.

CONDEMNED: 1/5/58.
Cut up at Stratford.

_____

7263

Stratford.

To traffic 4/1899.
Class R24 - goods.

REPAIRS:
Str. 26/1—4/6/12.**G.**
Str. 21/12/17—30/4/18.**G.**
Str. 11/4—21/7/22.**G.**
At 1/1/23: J67. Steam brake.
Str. 16/1—7/2/25.**G.**
Str. 15/7—9/11/27.**G.**
Additional rails on bunker.
Str. 10/5—11/7/30.**G.**
Str. 18/11—22/12/32.**G.**
Str. 9/8—2/9/36.**G.**
Str. 12/5—7/6/40.**G.**
Str. 25/7—6/9/43.**G.**
Str. 26/8—15/9/45.**G.**
Str. 22/2—28/3/49.**G.**
Str. 17/9—27/10/51.**G.**

BOILERS:
   263.
   263 *(new)* 4/6/12.
   262 *(ex7262)* 30/4/18.
   2842 *(new)* 21/7/22.
   2882 *(exJ66 7322)* 22/12/32.
   2886 *(ex7206)* 2/9/36.
   2872 *(ex7200)* 7/6/40.
   2877 *(exJ66 7307)* 6/9/43.
   2899 *(exJ66 7298)* 15/9/45.
   2889 *(ex8496)* 28/3/49.
   2889 *reno* 23912 27/10/51.

SHEDS:
Stratford.
Colchester 16/10/43.
Stratford 20/10/45.
Staveley 2/5/54.

RENUMBERED:
   7263 7/2/25.

   8589 16/3/46.
68589 26/3/49.

CONDEMNED: 30/1/56.
Cut up at Stratford.

_____

7264

Stratford.

To traffic 4/1899.
Class R24 - goods.

REPAIRS:
Str. ?/?—?/6/09.**G.**
Str. 26/8—9/11/20.**G.**
At 1/1/23: J67. Steam brake.
Str. 6/6—15/9/23.**G.**
Str. 1/10—15/12/26.**G.**
Str. 5/12/29—25/1/30.**G.**
Additional rails on bunker.
Str. 7—29/9/33.**G.**
Str. 24/11—29/12/39.**G.**
Str. 1/12/42—7/1/43.**G.**
Str. 16/5—8/6/43.**L.**
Str. 19/8—1/9/45.**G.**
Str. 5/9—19/10/48.**G.**
Special sandboxes fitted.
Str. 17/10—24/11/51.**G.**

BOILERS:
   264.
   264 *(new)* ?/6/09.
   2831 *(new)* 9/11/20.
   2805 *(exJ66 7290)* 25/1/30.
   2801 *(ex7169)* 29/9/33.
   2865 *(exJ66 7320)* 29/12/39.
   2882 *(exJ66 7324)* 7/1/43.
   2895 *(ex7207)* 1/9/45.
   2885 *(ex8493)* 19/10/48.
23916 *(ex??)* 24/11/51.

SHEDS:
Stratford.
Staveley 14/11/54.
Stratford 19/12/54.

RENUMBERED:
   7264 15/12/26.
   8590 16/3/46.
68590 16/10/48.

CONDEMNED: 29/9/55.
Cut up at Stratford.

_____

7199

Stratford.

To traffic 12/1899.
Class R24 - goods.

The three which kept their Westinghouse brakes, Nos.7161, 7164 and 7169, had vacuum ejectors fitted in 1939 as follows: No.7161 – 21st December; Nos.7164 and 7169 both 11th November.

Apart from the above three, J67 class only had steam brake, and no facility for train braking.

(below) At Grouping, the class was in grey without lining and many changed to the 1924 LNER numbering on grey and with 19in. yellow painted figures. Only No.199E (29th November 1923) is known as in black and with area suffix. No.7014 was painted as this 29th October 1926.

Apart from the passenger engines, Nos.7161, 7164 and 7169, it seems doubtful if any other J67 got black with red lining - *see* page 46, 3rd from top. Certainly from June 1928, they were only in plain black to withdrawal, and it was into 1929 before the grey disappeared.

From July 1942 only NE was put on, those repaired at Stratford still getting 7½ in. lettering, but at Gorton 12 in. transfers were used – *see* page 49, top. Only six got 12 in.: Nos.7257 – 12th August 1944; 7258 – 7th April 1945; 7352 – 20th October 1945; 7354 – 23rd October 1943; 7363 – 30th December 1944; 7371 – 7th April 1944.

Whilst the two engines working the Lauder Light Railway went from Stratford in 1944 with 7½ in. NE on the tanks, the tenders which Cowlairs attached were lettered differently. The ex J36 tender put with No.7399 (8511) had 12in. NE but the D36 tender with 7329 (8492) – *see* page 58, bottom – still had 7½ in. LNER from its last Cowlairs repair of 23rd March 1940.

7199 cont./
REPAIRS:
Str. ?/?—?/12/19.**G.**
At 1/1/23: J67. Steam brake.
Str. 28/6—29/11/23.**G.**
Str. ?/?—?/10/26.**G.**
Additional rails on bunker.
Str. 26/5—30/6/31.**G.**
Str. 18/6—9/7/34.**G.**

BOILERS:
199.
199 *(new)* ?/12/19.
2822 *(ex7207)* 30/6/31.
2897 *(new)* 9/7/34.

SHEDS:
Cambridge.
King's Lynn 23/8/31.
Stratford 9/7/34.

RENUMBERED:
199E 29/11/23.
7199 ?/10/26.

CONDEMNED: 3/7/37.
Cut up at Stratford.

7200

Stratford.

To traffic 12/1899.
Class R24 - passenger.

REPAIRS:
Str. 4/8—31/12/17.**G.**
Woolwich Arsenal. 31/12/19—
8/6/20.**G.**
At 1/1/23: J67. Steam brake.
Str. 10/3—28/4/23.**G.**
Str. 28/8—16/10/26.**G.**
Str. 16/6—28/9/28.**G.**
Additional rails on bunker.
Str. 13/2—18/3/32.**G.**
Str. 29/11—31/12/36.**G.**
Str. 16/6—15/7/37.**G.**
Str. 10/3—30/4/40.**G.**
Str. 4/4—25/6/43.**G.**
Str. 16/9—6/10/45.**G.**
Str. 22/9—3/10/47.**L.**
Str. 25/11—13/12/47.**L.**
Str. 5/7—3/8/48.**G.**
Str. 26/4—23/5/51.**G.**

BOILERS:
200.
261 *(ex7261)* 31/12/17.
2823 *(new)* 8/6/20.
2848 *(exJ66 7282)* 18/3/32.
2872 *(ex7164)* 31/12/36.
2833 *(ex7400)* 30/4/40.
2908 *(ex7013)* 25/6/43.
2870 *(exJ65 7250)* 6/10/45.

2911 *(ex8529)* 3/8/48.
23905 *(ex??)* 23/5/51.

SHEDS:
Stratford.
Colchester 17/10/48.
Stratford 14/5/50.
Ipswich 26/7/53.

RENUMBERED:
7200 16/10/25.
8606 14/9/46.
68606 31/7/48.

CONDEMNED: 7/3/55.
Cut up at Stratford.

7201

Stratford.

To traffic 12/1899.
Class R24 - goods.

REPAIRS:
Str. 26/1—26/5/15.**G.**
Str. 17/1—1/7/21.**G.**
At 1/1/23: J67. Steam brake.
Str. 22/12/26—28/5/27.**G.**
Str. 1/4—2/5/30.**G.**
Additional rails on bunker.
Str. 6—23/7/34.**G.**

BOILERS:
201.
2801 *(new)* 26/5/15.
293 *(exJ66 7328)* 28/5/27.
2880 *(new)* 2/5/30.
2899 *(new)* 23/7/34.

SHED:
Stratford.

RENUMBERED:
7201 by 25/2/25.

CONDEMNED: 3/7/37.
Cut up at Stratford.

7202

Stratford.

To traffic 12/1899.
Class R24 - goods.

REPAIRS:
Str. ?/?—?/1/14.**G.**
Str. 10/1—17/3/21.**G.**
At 1/1/23: J67. Steam brake.
Str. ?/?—?/8/23.**G.**
Str. ?/?—?/6/26.**G.**
Additional rails on bunker.

Str. ?/?—?/4/31.**G.**
Str. 20/9—9/10/34.**G.**

BOILERS:
202.
202 *(new)* ?/1/14.
2853 *(new)* ?/8/23.
2849 *(exJ66 7319)* ?/4/31.
2900 *(new)* 9/10/34.

SHED:
Stratford.

RENUMBERED:
7202 ?/6/26.

CONDEMNED: 3/7/37.
Cut up at Stratford.

7203

Stratford.

To traffic 12/1899.
Class R24 - goods.

EPAIRS:
Woolwich Arsenal. 26/1—
26/6/20.**G.**
At 1/1/23: J67. Steam brake.
Str. 30/1—24/3/23.**G.**
Str. 12/6—28/8/25.**G.**
Str. 17/2—5/5/28.**G.**
Additional rails on bunker.
Str. 18/5—2/7/31.**G.**
Str. 18/11—12/12/35.**G.**
Str. 26/2—6/4/40.**G.**
Str. 20/12/42—9/1/43.**G.**
Str. 10/6—9/7/45.**G.**
Str. 5/10—9/11/48.**G.**
Rebuilt to J69/2.
Str. 21/1—16/2/52.**G.**
Str. 12/6—28/7/56.**G.**

BOILERS:
203.
2825 *(new)* 26/6/20.
2836 *(exJ65 7245)* 2/7/31.
2883 *(exJ66 7297)* 12/12/35.
2852 *(ex7330)* 6/4/40.
2834 *(exJ66 7320)* 29/1/43.
2883 *(ex7012)* 9/7/45.
3077 *(ex8581)* 9/11/48.
23735 *(ex??)* 16/2/52.
23767 *(ex68495)* 28/7/56.

SHEDS:
Stratford.
Staveley 1/6/58.
Langwith Jct. 6/10/59.

RENUMBERED:
7203 28/8/25.
8591 14/9/46.

68591 6/11/48.

CONDEMNED: 4/1/60.
Cut up at Stratford.

7204

Stratford.

To traffic 12/1899.
Class R24 - goods.

REPAIRS:
Str. ?/?—?/4/13.**G.**
At 1/1/23: J67. Steam brake.
Str. 12/12/23—9/2/24.**G.**
Str. 24/12/26—25/3/27.**G.**
Str. 30/8—19/10/29.**G.**
Additional rails on bunker.
Str. 10/3—4/4/32.**G.**
Str. 12/6—6/7/36.**G.**
Str. 17/3—30/4/40.**G.**
Str. 14/2 9/4/43.**G.**
Str. 13/1—7/2/46.**G.**
Str. 23/1—7/3/49.**G.**
Str. 5/5—16/6/51.**G.**

BOILERS:
204.
204 *(new)* ?/4/13.
2863 *(new)* 25/3/27.
2888 *(new)* 4/4/32.
2867 *(ex7403)* 6/7/36.
2912 *(exJ66 7290)* 30/4/40.
2865 *(ex7264)* 9/4/43.
2912 *(ex7396)* 7/2/46.
2883 *(ex8591)* 7/3/49.
23906 *(ex??)* 16/6/51.

SHEDS:
Stratford.
Staveley 13/7/52.
Norwich 26/7/53.

RENUMBERED:
204E 9/2/24.
7204 25/3/27.
8592 27/4/46.
68592 5/3/49.

CONDEMNED: 28/7/55.
Cut up at Stratford.

7205

Stratford.

To traffic 12/1899.
Class R24 - goods.

REPAIRS:
Str. 24/12/18—30/5/19.**G.**
At 1/1/23: J67. Steam brake.

7205 cont./
Str. 17/12/23—20/3/24.**G.**
Str. ?/?—?/7/27.**G.**
Additional rails on bunker.
Str. 8—23/10/34.**G.**

BOILERS:
205.
316 *(exJ66 7316)* 30/5/19.
286 *(exJ66 7286)* 20/3/24.
2843 *(exJ66 7308)* 23/10/34.

SHED:
Stratford.

RENUMBERED:
7205 20/3/24.

CONDEMNED: 15/5/37.
Cut up at Stratford.

_____

7206

Stratford.

To traffic 12/1899.
Class R24 - goods.

REPAIRS:
Str. 16/5—21/11/19.**G.**
At 1/1/23: *J67. Steam brake.*
Str. 27/7—27/9/23.**G.**
Str. 3/10—23/12/25.**G.**
Str. 18/8—31/10/28.**G.**
Additional rails on bunker.
Str. 19/12/31—22/1/32.**G.**
Str. 8—30/3/36.**G.**
Str. 26/5—28/6/41.**G.**
Str. 30/4—20/5/44.**G.**
Str. 15/9—13/10/47.**G.**
Str. 14—23/2/48.**L.**
Jay-Gee smoke eliminator fitted.
Str. 1/10—4/11/50.**G.**
Smoke eliminator removed.
Str. 9/8—4/9/53.**G.**
Str. 13/1/58. *Not repaired.*

BOILERS:
206.
2816 *(new)* 21/11/19.
256 *(ex7256)* 23/12/25.
2886 *(new)* 22/1/32.
2869 *(exJ65 7156)* 30/3/36.
2874 *(exJ66 7310)* 28/6/41.
2848 *(ex7082)* 20/5/44.
2851 *(ex8380)* 13/10/47.
23901 *(ex??)* 4/11/50.
23931 *(ex??)* 4/9/53.

SHEDS:
Stratford.
Colchester 23/5/42.
Stratford 25/11/44.
Ipswich 26/2/48.

RENUMBERED:
206ᴇ 27/9/23.
7206 23/12/25.
8593 11/9/46.
68593 4/11/50.

CONDEMNED: 20/1/58.
Cut up at Stratford.

_____

7207

Stratford.

To traffic 1/1900.
Class R24 - goods.

REPAIRS:
Str. 15/6—25/8/20.**G.**
Str. 23/8—26/10/22.**G.**
At 1/1/23: *J67, Steam brake.*
Str. 19/2—9/4/25.**G.**
Str. 24/2—18/5/28.**G.**
Additional rails on bunker.
Str. 10/1—27/2/31.**G.**
Str. 5—28/11/34.**G.**
Str. 6—24/6/38.**G.**
Str. 13/12/42—25/1/43.**G.**
Str. 24/6—27/7/45.**G.**
Str. 15/9—6/11/48.**G.**
Str. 25/5—16/6/50.**G.**
Str. 29/10—24/11/51.**G.**

BOILERS:
207.
2822 *(new)* 25/8/20.
2859 *(exJ66 7300)* 27/2/31.
2814 *(ex7011)* 28/11/34.
2919 *(new)* 24/6/38.
2895 *(ex7334)* 25/1/43.
2871 *(ex7334)* 27/7/45.
2909 *(exJ66 8379)* 6/11/48.
2909 reno. 23917 24/11/51.

SHEDS:
Stratford.
Ipswich 7/11/54.

RENUMBERED:
7207 9/4/25.
8594 14/9/46.
68594 6/11/48.

CONDEMNED: 18/11/55.
Cut up at Stratford.

_____

7208

Stratford.

To traffic 1/1900.
Class R24 - goods.

REPAIRS:
Str. 26/4—3/8/16.**G.**
Str. 4/4—15/7/22.**G.**
At 1/1/23: *J67. Steam brake.*
Str. 11/7—16/10/24.**G.**
Variable blast pipe removed.
Str. 14/9—23/11/27.**G.**
Additional rails on bunker.
Str. 12/9—17/10/31.**G.**
Str. 23/1—12/2/34.**G.**
Str. 13/5—11/6/40.**G.**
Str. 20/10—6/11/40.**L.**
After collision.
Str. 8—18/3/41.**L.**
Str. 29/8—22/10/43.**G.**
Str. 23/9—12/10/45.**G.**
Str. 25/9—11/11/48.**G.**
Gor. 17/6—1/7/50.**G.**
Gor. 13/12/52—10/1/53.**G.**
Gor. 3/3/56.**C/L.**
Back plate welded.

BOILERS:
208.
2804 *(new)* 3/8/16.
2835 *(ex7169)* 23/11/27.
2847 *(exJ66 7313)* 17/10/31.
2879 *(exJ66 7298)* 12/2/34.
2855 *(exJ66 7282)* 11/6/40.
2872 *(ex7263)* 22/10/43.
2877 *(ex7263)* 12/10/45.
2895 *(ex8590)* 11/11/48.
2900 *(ex68531)* 1/7/50.
23950 *(ex68540)* 10/1/53.

SHEDS:
Stratford.
Norwich 25/6/37.
Gorton 18/10/49.
Trafford Park 21/10/49.
Wrexham ?/8/54.
Trafford Park ?/11/54.
Wrexham ?/12/54.

RENUMBERED:
7208 16/10/24.
8595 5/5/46.
68595 6/11/48.

CONDEMNED: 8/1/57.
*Into Gorton for c/u 16/2/57 but
c/u at Doncaster.*

_____

7161

Stratford.

To traffic 6/1901.
Class R24 - passenger.

REPAIRS:
Str. 15/9—10/12/20.**G.**
Nor. 17/10/22—7/3/23.**H.**

At 1/1/23: *J67. Westinghouse
brake. Non condensing.*
Str. 27/3—9/7/25.**G.**
Str. 8/6—15/9/28.**G.**
*Steam heat and additional rails
on bunker.*
Str. 23/12/30—13/2/31.**G.**
Str. 20/5—29/6/35.**G.**
Str. 23/9/38—10/6/39.**G.**
Str. 20—21/12/39.**L.**
Vacuum ejector fitted.
Str. 28/4—2/9/43.**G.**
Str. 28/12/45—25/1/46.**G.**
Str. 18/8—1/10/49.**G.**
Str. 19/3—6/5/54.**G.**

BOILERS:
161.
2829 *(new)* 10/12/20.
297 *(exJ66 7323)* 15/9/28.
2834 *(exJ66 7288)* 13/2/31.
2911 *(new)* 29/6/35.
2907 *(exJ66 7314)* 10/6/39.
2867 *(exJ66 7323)* 2/9/43.
2852 *(exJ66 7321)* 25/1/46.
2875 *(ex8597)* 1/10/49.
23933 *(ex??)* 6/5/54.

SHEDS:
Norwich.
Lowestoft 26/9/28.
Norwich ?/?/?
Lowestoft 10/4/32.
Norwich 7/4/33.
Colchester 2/12/35.
Stratford 26/3/39.
Colchester 3/12/39.
Stratford 8/9/40.
Colchester 13/4/41.
Stratford 20/7/41.
Colchester 9/5/42.
Stratford 8/1/44.
Colchester 25/11/44.
Stratford 8/6/46.
Colchester 21/11/48.
Stratford 10/4/49.
Colchester 28/8/49.
Stratford 2/7/50.
Colchester 17/9/50.
Stratford 6/1/52.
Norwich 26/7/53.
Staveley 4/3/56.

RENUMBERED:
7161 9/7/25.
8608 8/9/46.
68608 1/10/49.

CONDEMNED: 15/10/58.
Cut up at Stratford.

_____

LNER was restored from January 1946 and overlapped the renumbering which began in that month. Part 2 No.7352 changed to 8529 at Lincoln shed on Sunday 1st September 1946 and got the 7½ in. stenciled figures used by ex GC sheds.

No.7327 was undergoing a General repair 18th August to 22nd September 1946 in Stratford when it was renumbered 8490 on 13th September. This was done in normal shaded transfers and with LNER restored.

No.7397 became 8509 on 28th September 1946 and then got these shaded transfers ex works 18th November 1947. It went back to Stratford 14th to 23rd February 1948 to be fitted with this Jay-Gee smoke eliminating device which it then carried to 4th June 1951. Nos.8586 and 8593 were similarly fitted from February 1948 to June and October 1950 respectively.

First BRITISH RAILWAYS painting left the number on the tank but changed the style from shaded transfers to plain painted Gill sans although with LNER modified figure 6. Five got the regional prefix E in 1948: Nos.8512 – 21st January; 8586 – 16th February at Stratford, and Nos.8531 – 22nd January; 8540 – 11th March; 8547 – 16th February, at Gorton.

(below) A light repair did not usually include a repaint but did provide opportunity to renumber. LNER 8520 went to Stratford 6th December 1948 and when out 26th December, had got its BR number in the previously normal shaded transfers and on the tank.

From June 1948 it became standard to put the number on the bunker and for its height to match that of the lettering at 10in. No.68594 was ex Stratford 6th November 1948 and by then smokebox plates were being fitted using the correct Gill sans 6 and 9.

7164

Stratford.

To traffic 6/1901.
Class R24 - passenger.

REPAIRS:
Str. 25/6—23/9/20.**G.**
At 1/1/23: J67. Westinghouse
brake. Condensing.
Nor. 8/2—20/7/23.**H.**
Str. 4/10—14/12/27.**G.**
*Seam heat fitted and additional
rails on bunker.*
Str. 29/9—28/11/30.**G.**
Str. 14/9—10/10/33.**G.**
Str. 29/6—24/7/36.**G.**
Condensing gear removed.
Str. ?/?—11/11/39.**?.**
Vacuum ejector fitted.
Str. 6/7—19/8/41.**G.**
Str. 26/11/44—4/1/45.**G.**
Str. 21/6—11/8/48.**G.**
Str. 11/5—13/6/52.**G.**
Str. 14/7/55. *Not repaired.*

BOILERS:
  164.
  2827 *(new)* 23/9/20.
  2872 *(exJ66 7300)* 10/10/33.
  2853 *(ex7260)* 24/7/36.
  2918 *(ex7382)* 19/8/41.
  2827 *(exJ65 7157)* 4/1/45.
  2896 *(exJ66 8376)* 11/8/48.
  23919 *(ex??)* 13/6/52.

SHEDS:
Norwich.
Lowestoft ?/?/?.
Norwich 10/4/32.
Colchester 5/10/35.
Stratford 26/3/39.
Colchester 8/9/40.
Stratford 13/4/41.
Norwich 1/12/41.
Lowestoft 13/12/41.

RENUMBERED:
  7164 14/12/27?
  8611 1/9/46.
  68611 11/8/48.

CONDEMNED: 25/7/55.
Cut up at Stratford.

_____

7169

Stratford.

To traffic 8/1901.
Class R24 - passenger.

REPAIRS:
Str. 10/1—28/4/21.**G.**
At 1/1/23: J67. Westinghouse
brake. Condensing.
Str. 25/8—25/10/24.**G.**
Str. 1/8—14/10/27.**G.**
Additional rails on bunker.
Str. 13/2—22/3/30.**G.**
Str. 4—28/7/33.**G.**

Str. 12—22/2/35.**L.**
Str. 3—29/7/36.**G.**
Condensing gear removed.
Str. ?/? 11/11/39.**N/C.**
Vacuum ejector fitted.
Str. 8/9—2/11/40.**G.**
Str. 12/5—30/7/42.**G.**
Cow. 23/6—9/7/43.**L.**
Str. 9/9—20/10/45.**G.**
Str. 23/10—19/11/49.**G.**
Str. 25/1—5/2/54.**C/L.**
Str. 15/5—11/6/54.**G.**

BOILERS:
  169.
  2835 *(new)* 28/4/21.
  2801 *(ex7201)* 14/10/27.
  2831 *(exJ66 7320)* 28/7/33.
  2836 *(ex7203)* 29/7/36.
  2888 *(exJ66 7323)* 2/11/40.
  2882 *(ex7264)* 20/10/45.
  2844 *(ex8514)* 19/11/49.
  23911 *(ex68529)* 11/6/54.

SHEDS:
King's Lynn.
Cambridge 4/10/30.
Colchester 31/12/35.
Stratford 3/12/39.
Colchester 24/12/39.
Stratford 10/3/40.
Colchester 13/4/41.
Stratford 2/11/41.
Colchester 22/2/42.
Stratford 9/5/42.
W.D. 30/7/42.

Stratford 29/5/45.
Colchester 8/6/46.
Stratford 4/12/49.
Colchester 9/7/50.
Stratford 6/1/52.
Norwich 26/7/53.
Staveley 30/10/55.

RENUMBERED:
  7169 25/10/24.
  8616 8/9/46.
  68616 19/11/49.

CONDEMNED: 27/11/58.
Cut up at Stratford.

_____

No.68572, ex Stratford 28th November 1948, was a curiosity. Its 6 was true Gill sans and numbers and letters matched for height but were smaller at no more than 7in. Note that BRITISH RAILWAYS was also centred on the widened tank side only, which appreciably cut the length available.

Ex Cowlairs on 20th May 1949, No.68511 had ownership displayed on the tank and the tender. The smokebox plate had the correct 6 but the paint shop were not yet including it.

No.68509, ex works 29th June 1951, had lost the smoke eliminator but retained evidence of its fitting by the plugs on the smokebox front plate. BRITISH RAILWAYS ceased to be used from September 1949, being superseded by the 15½ in. size emblem, and this was the last livery change on J67 class.

The BR emblem was handed to face the front on both sides and because the class was extinct from 24th February 1958 when No.68628 was withdrawn, none got the BR crest used from 1957.

(above) **Ten more engines, Nos.21 to 30, were built at Stratford during the period December 1913 to February 1914. These ten were for shunting so had fifteen-spoke, unbalanced, cast iron wheels. Because they were not fitted with condensing gear, the tank tops were straight. The blastpipe was of the plain variety and only 3-link couplings were required. A steam brake sufficed the engine. Note that the cab roof was still the high wooden variety and that the buffers also had taper shanks.**

(centre) **In March 1923 the LNER built ten similar shunters that were on order and from 6th October to 22nd November 1923, Nos.31 to 40 were turned out from Stratford. They differed from the previous ten in having lower cab roofs with the front ventilator now level with the top of the windows. Their buffers had stepped parallel shanks with hollow spindle.**

By Grouping, a start had been made on altering the high cab roof on the first twenty engines to the lower profile used for the ten built in 1923.

CLASS J 68

7041

Stratford.

To traffic 6/1912.

REPAIRS:
Str. 10/1—23/2/24.**G.**
Vacuum ejector fitted.
Str. 14/12/25—16/3/26.**G.**
Str. 28/4—30/8/28.**G.**
Additional rails on bunker.
Str. 12/11—12/12/32.**G.**
Str. 7—29/11/35.**G.**
Str. 18/9—18/10/38.**G.**
Str. 21/10/39.**L.** *Vacuum ejector removed before entering HMG service at Longmoor.*
Cow. ?/?—9/10/42.**L.**
(as WD 85).

BOILERS:
41.
44 *(ex7044)* 16/3/26.
3046 *(new)* 30/8/28.
3017 *(ex7043)* 12/12/32.
2999 *(exJ69 7350)* 29/11/35.
3013 *(exJ69 7335)* 18/10/38.

SHEDS:
Stratford.
WD Longmoor 21/10/39.
WD Bicester ?/3/42.
WD Faslane ?/5/42

RENUMBERED:
7041 23/2/24.
WD 70085 *after* 9/10/42.

SOLD:
To WD 19/10/40.
To Metal Industries Ltd., Faslane 1946. Cut up by 1952.

7042

Stratford.

To traffic 6/1912.

REPAIRS:
Str. 11/1—20/6/18.**G.**
Str. 1/5—2/8/22.**G.**
Str. 23/1—20/3/24.**G.**
Vacuum ejector fitted.
Str. 23/10—30/12/25.**G.**
Str. 1/9—10/12/27.**G.**
Additional rails on bunker & GS buffers fitted.
Str. 18/4—6/6/31.**G.**

Str. 1/8—15/9/33.**G.**
Str. 15/2—22/3/37.**G.**
Condensing gear removed.
Str. 21/2—30/3/40.**G.**
Str. 27/10—20/11/43.**G.**
Str. 12/1—13/2/47.**G.**
Str. 16/8—16/9/50.**G.**
Str. 2—27/2/54.**G.**

BOILERS:
42.
305 *(exJ69 7305)* 20/6/18.
3016 *(new)* 2/8/22.
391 *(ex7023)* 6/6/31.
3031 *(exJ69 7197)* 15/9/33.
3040 *(ex7037)* 22/3/37.
3049 *(ex7058)* 30/3/40.
3007 *(ex7025)* 20/11/43.
3082 *(exJ69 8617)* 13/2/47.
23700 *(ex?)* 16/9/50.
23788 *(ex?)* 27/2/54.

SHEDS:
Stratford.
Norwich 11/9/31.
Stratford 15/9/33.
Parkeston 21/5/37.
Stratford 25/9/39.
Colchester 8/9/40.
Stratford 20/7/41.
Colchester 6/6/42.
Startford 25/11/44.
Parkeston 12/4/47.
Stratford 10/4/49.
Colchester 8/10/50.
Stratford 12/2/56.
Hitchin 10/6/56.
Grantham 13/4/58.

RENUMBERED:
7042 20/3/24.
8638 12/1/47.
68638 16/9/50.

CONDEMNED: 24/2/59.
Cut up at Stratford.

7043

Stratford.

To traffic 6/1912.

REPAIRS:
Str. 28/11/22—3/2/23.**G.**
Vacuum ejector fitted 5/23.
Str. 18/12/24—2/4/25.**G.**
Str. 21/12/26—19/3/27.**G.**
Str. 16/8—9/10/30.**G.**
Additional rails on bunker.

Str. 29/9—2/11/32.**G.**
Str. 6/12/35—9/1/36.**G.**
Str. 26/2—19/7/39.**G.**
Str. 22—30/5/40.**L.**
Trip Cock gear fitted.
Str. 1/3—17/4/42.**G.**
Str. 8/5—22/6/44.**G.**
Str. 2—22/9/45.**G.**
Str. 21—24/3/47.**N/C.**
Trip Cock gear refitted.
Str. 18/8—24/9/49.**G.**
Str. 11/8—10/9/53.**G.**
Str. 11/6—9/8/57.**C/L.**

BOILERS:
43.
384 *(exJ69 7384)* 19/3/27.
3017 *(exJ69 7344)* 9/10/30.
269 *(exJ69 7168)* 2/11/32.
3066 *(exJ69 7273)* 9/1/36.
3017 *(exJ69 7165)* 19/7/39.
3058 *(exJ69 7160)* 17/4/42.
3101 *(ex7025)* 22/6/44.
3041 *(exJ69 7196)* 22/9/45.
3094 *(exJ69 8599)* 24/9/49.
23780 *(ex?)* 10/9/53.

SHEDS:
Stratford.
King's Cross 4/9/24.
Stratford 27/10/24.

RENUMBERED:
7043 2/4/25.
8639 10/1/47.
68639 24/9/49.

CONDEMNED: 17/4/59.
Cut up at Stratford.

7044

Stratford.

To traffic 6/1912.

REPAIRS:
Str. 9/2—4/4/24.**G.**
Vacuum ejector fitted.
Str. 30/10/25—20/2/26.**G.**
Str. 22/7—7/9/26.**L.**
Str. 28/4—18/7/28.**G.**
Additional rails on bunker.
Str. 2/5—1/7/31.**G.**
Str. 29/6—1/8/34.**G.**
Grease lubrication for side rods.
Str. 20/7—20/8/37.**G.**
Condensing gear removed.
Str. 25/8—18/10/40.**G.**
Str. 12/9—30/10/43.**G.**

Str. 11/11—1/12/45.**G.**
Str. 2/1—16/2/49.**G.**
Str. 30/7—2/9/50.**C/L.**
Str. 4—24/5/52.**G.**
Str. 22/5—1/7/55.**G.**

BOILERS:
44.
3035 *(new)* 20/2/26.
3033 *(ex7029)* 1/7/31.
45 *(ex7046)* 1/8/34.
3043 *(exJ69 7394)* 20/8/37.
3050 *(ex7022)* 18/10/40.
3066 *(exJ69 7266)* 30/10/43.
3027 *(ex7026)* 1/12/45.
3058 *(exJ69 8633)* 16/12/49.
23744 *(ex?)* 24/5/52.
23813 *(exJ69 68643)* 1/7/55.

SHEDS:
Stratford.
Yarmouth 12/11/31.
Norwich 2/6/34.
Lowestoft 8/12/40.
Norwich 13/11/55.

RENUMBERED:
7044 4/4/24.
8640 1/9/46.
68640 12/2/49.

CONDEMNED: 22/4/59.
Cut up at Stratford.

7045

Stratford.

To traffic 7/1912.

REPAIRS:
Str. 8/2—30/7/18.**G.**
Str. 31/10/23—10/1/24.**G.**
Vacuum ejector fitted.
Str. 11/3—15/5/24.**L.**
Str. 9/12/26—25/3/27.**G.**
Str. 2/2—25/4/29.**G.**
Additional rails on bunker.
Str. 15/9—13/11/31.**G.**
Str. 27/11—19/12/34.**G.**
Grease lubrication for side rods.
Str. 18/10—10/11/37.**G.**
Condensing gear removed.
Str. 21/3—1/5/41.**G.**
Str. 28/5—18/7/44.**G.**
Str. 3—22/2/46.**L.**
Str. 18/7—4/9/48.**G.**
Str. 25/9—1/11/51.**G.**
Str. 25/8—31/10/53.**C/H.**
Str. 25/6—18/8/55.**G.**

The lower wood roof was applied to the shunters as well as to those used for passenger work. Note that by February 1927 No.7030 had changed from taper to parallel shank buffers with hollow spindle, but see also page 89, 3rd from top. Note no mechanical lubricator was fitted, also that allocation plate P'BORO can be seen under the rear window in the cab.

From 1933, steel cab roof superseded the wood type, to very similar height and profile, but rain strips were curved instead of straight. Note change of buffer type also applied to the passenger engines.

From 1925 the Macallan variable type was taken off Nos.7041 to 7050. When ex works 16th March 1926, No.7041 had been changed to plain blast pipe.

Until 1926 all had three open coal rails of flat bar iron above the bunker.

Between 2nd September 1926 (No.7023) and 9th October 1930 (No.7043) all had three extra rails put on to fill the spaces between and to help stop spillage of small coal.

The condensing apparatus was taken off No.47 in November 1919 and the LNER removed it from Nos.7042, 7044, 7045, 7046, 7048, 7049, and 7050 between 23rd June 1936 (No.7049) and 15th July 1938 (No.7050); the other five losing the apparatus during 1937. That left only Nos.7041 and 7043 still fitted, but all kept the stepped top to the tank side plate.

For war emergency working on London Transport's East London line, three were fitted in 1940 with trip cock gear, No.7043 (30th May), No.7048 (22nd June), and No.7050 (8th June). The absent condensing gear was put back on Nos.7048 and 7050. In March 1947 these three, by then Nos.8639, 8644 and 8646, had the trip cock gear re-fitted and they continued to work from Stratford shed.

There was some changing of wheel types from the 1930's. From June 1935 No.7050 had twelve-spoke wheels which were not balanced but by April 1949 *see* previous illustration ten-spoke balanced wheels had been regained.

7045 cont./
BOILERS:
  45.
  2973 *(new)* 30/7/18.
    38 *(new)* 10/1/24.
  2977 *(exJ69 7393)* 25/3/27.
    267 *(exJ69 7168)* 25/4/29.
  3034 *(exJ69 7363)* 13/11/31.
  3021 *(exJ69 7166)* 19/12/34.
  3099 *(new)* 10/11/37.
  3048 *(exJ69 7394)* 1/5/41.
  3062 *(exJ69 7385)* 18/7/44.
  3097 *(exJ69 8602)* 4/9/48.
  23720 *(ex?)* 1/11/51.
  23705 *(exJ69 68636)* 18/8/55.

SHEDS:
Stratford.
Norwich 25/4/29.
Stratford 13/11/31.
Colchester 30/1/35.
Norwich 5/12/35.
Lowestoft 3/2/41.
Yarmouth Beach 28/1/45.
Lowestoft 22/3/45.
Yarmouth Beach 23/6/46.
Lowestoft 16/7/46.
Norwich 11/9/46.
Melton Constable 26/3/47.
Norwich 4/5/47.

RENUMBERED:
  7045 15/5/24.
  8641 2/9/46.
  68641 4/9/48.

CONDEMNED: 6/11/59.
Cut up at Stratford.

7046

Stratford.

To traffic 8/1912.

REPAIRS:
Str. 5/10/17—8/3/18.**G.**
Str. 13/11/22—20/1/23.**G.**
Vacuum ejector fitted 4/23.
Str. 9/2—24/4/25.**G.**
Str. 29/4—8/7/27.**G.**
Additional rails on bunker.
Str. 15/11/30—16/1/31.**G.**
Heating apparatus fitted.
Str. 18/12/33—18/1/34.**G.**
Grease lubrication for side rods.
Str. 5/7—10/8/37.**G.**
Condensing gear removed.
Str. 10/4—17/5/41.**G.**
Str. 23/1—11/3/44.**G.**
Str. 28/4—3/6/46.**G.**
Str. 18/12/49—11/2/50.**G.**
Str. 11/5—12/6/53.**G.**
Str. 6/1—9/2/57.**G.**

BOILERS:
  46.
  2968 *(new)* 8/3/18.
  2972 *(exJ69 7383)* 24/4/25.
    45 *(exJ69 7274)* 16/1/31.
  3053 *(exJ69 7056)* 18/1/34.
  3031 *(ex7042)* 10/8/37.
  3093 *(ex7037)* 17/5/41.
  3045 *(ex7038)* 11/3/44.
  3072 *(ex spare)* 3/6/46.
  23771 *(ex?)* 12/6/53.
  23741 *(exJ69 68542)* 9/2/57.

SHEDS:
Stratford.
King's Cross 4/9/24.
Stratford 10/11/24.
Norwich 9/4/34.
Yarmouth 2/6/34.
Norwich 17/5/36.
Yarmouth 3/10/37.
Norwich 23/3/39.
Yarmouth 17/5/39.
Yarmouth Beach 17/12/39.
Yarmouth 15/1/40.
Norwich 19/5/40.
Stratford 20/6/46.
Parkeston 7/12/46.
Stratford 18/1/48.
Norwich 14/8/55.
Lowestoft 17/8/58.
Startford 1/11/59.

RENUMBERED:
  7046 24/4/25.
  8642 31/5/46.
  68642 11/2/50.

CONDEMNED: 10/9/61.
Cut up at Stratford.

7047

Stratford.

To traffic 8/1912.

REPAIRS:
Str. 28/2—14/11/19.**G.**
Str. 10/1—29/2/24.**G.**
Str. 25/10/26—12/2/27.**G.**
*Additional rails on bunker &
heating apparatus fitted.*
Vacuum ejector fitted 13/3/29.
Str. 19/7—12/9/30.**G.**
Str. 10—30/10/33.**G.**
Str. 13/7—28/8/36.**G.**
Str. 31/7—16/9/39.**G.**
Rebuilt to Class J67.
Str. 10/7—9/8/40.**G.**
Str. 4/12/42—29/1/43.**G.**
Str. 27/5—13/7/45.**G.**
Rebuilt to J68.
Str. 5/9—26/10/48.**G.**

Str. 27/3—19/4/52.**G.**
Str. 16/5—25/6/55.**G.**
Str. 31/8—8/9/55.**N/C.**

BOILERS:
  47.
    387 *(exJ69 7387)* 14/11/19.
  3036 *(new)* 12/2/27.
  2974 *(exJ69 7361)* 12/9/30.
  3049 *(exJ69 7165)* 30/10/33.
  2981 *(exJ69 7395)* 28/8/36.
  2911 *(exJ67 7161)* 16/9/39.
  2825 *(exJ67 7012)* 29/1/43.
  3099 *(exJ69 7393)* 13/7/45.
  3193 *(new)* 26/10/48.
  23813 *(new)* 19/4/52.
  23712 *(ex68645)* 25/6/55.

SHEDS:
Stratford.
Colchester 2/9/35.
Norwich 2/12/35.
Yarmouth 3/6/37.
Norwich 3/10/37.
Stratford 24/9/39.
Norwich 16/10/39.
Yarmouth 25/10/39.
Norwich 19/5/40.
Stratford 25/7/47.
Parkeston 18/1/48.

RENUMBERED:
  7047 29/2/24.
  8643 1/9/46.
  68643 23/10/48.

CONDEMNED: 16/11/59.
Cut up at Stratford.

7048

Stratford.

To traffic 9/1912.

REPAIRS:
Str. 13/6—9/9/22.**G.**
Str. 28/5—9/9/24.**G.**
Vacuum ejector fitted.
Str. 8/1—14/5/27.**G.**
Str. 20/1—4/5/29.**G.**
Additional rails on bunker.
Str. 27/7—1/9/33.**G.**
Str. 27/1—6/3/37.**G.**
Condensing gear removed.
Str. 10—22/6/40.**L.**
*Trip cock gear fitted &
condensing apparatus refitted.*
Str. 7/7—15/8/40.**G.**
Str. 16/7—26/8/44.**G.**
Str. 4/10—15/11/46.**G.**
Str. 1—2/4/47.**N/C.**
Trip cock refitted.
Str. 25/11—30/12/49.**C/L.**

Str. 20/7—26/8/50.**G.**
Str. 7/11—3/12/55.**G.**

BOILERS:
  48.
    43 *(ex7043)* 14/5/27.
  3009 *(exJ69 7353)* 4/5/29.
  2997 *(exJ69 7394)* 1/9/33.
  3060 *(ex7022)* 6/3/37.
  2994 *(exJ69 7271)* 15/8/40.
  3048 *(ex7045)* 26/8/44.
  3083 *(ex7035)* 15/11/46.
  3207 *(new)* 26/8/50.
  23733 *(exJ69 68587)* 3/12/55.

SHEDS:
Stratford.
Colchester 21/8/29.
Parkeston 29/1/36.
Stratford 25/9/39.
Colchester 15/2/47.
Stratford 12/4/47.

RENUMBERED:
  7048 9/9/24.
  8644 8/11/46.
  68644 30/12/49.

CONDEMNED: 28/11/60.
Cut up at Stratford.

7049

Stratford.

To traffic 9/1912.

REPAIRS:
Str. 7/6—13/12/18.**G.**
Str. 1/5—17/11/23.**G.**
Str. 18/8—11/11/25.**G.**
Heating app. fitted 21/12/26.
Str. 10/6—8/7/27.**L.**
Str. 8/6—21/9/28.**G.**
Additional rails on bunker.
Str. 8—10/5/29.**N/C.**
Vacuum ejector fitted.
Str. 27/10—17/12/30.**G.**
Str. 12/2—8/3/34.**G.**
Grease lubrication for side rods.
Str. 27/5—23/6/36.**G.**
Condensing apparatus removed.
Str. 29/6—1/8/40.**G.**
Str. 13/2—23/3/44.**G.**
GS buffers fitted.
Str. 27/8—3/11/47.**G.**
Str. 4/6—28/7/51.**G.**
Str. 27/2—26/3/55.**G.**

BOILERS:
  49.
    42 *(ex7042)* 13/12/18.
  3011 *(exJ69 7370)* 11/11/25.
  3045 *(new)* 21/9/28.

Two shunting engines also changed to twelve-spoke wheels, No.8658, ex works 8th December 1947 being so fitted.

No.68663 was the other shunter to get twelve-spoke wheels, by April 1956 and which it kept to withdrawal. The illustration on page 94, top, shows No.8661 as ex works 9th September 1946 fitted with ten-spoke balanced wheels.

(below) Ex works 30th April 1937, shunter No.7025 had a set of ten-spoke balanced wheels which it had acquired by 19th May 1928 as shown on page 89, top.

When new, all thirty were fitted with 4-column Ramsbottom safety valves in a rectangular casing and their 180 lb. boilers had the valves on the rear ring of the barrel ahead of the firebox, with the whistle on a standpipe just in front of the cab. The only change of position was on No.7047 from 16th September 1939 to 27th May 1945 when it had a 160 lb. Diagram 39 boiler which transferred it to Class J67. Ex works 13th July 1945 *see* page 77, 2nd from top it was J68 again.

Boilers built 1926 and later had two Ross 'pop' safety valves mounted directly on the boiler barrel but in the same position ahead of the firebox.

(below) Some boilers fitted with Ramsbottom valves were still being used by J68 class at the end of the LNER.

7049 cont./
  38 *(exJ69 7367)* 17/12/30.
  3056 *(exJ69 7372)* 8/3/34.
  2968 *(exJ69 7197)* 23/6/36.
  3081 *(exJ69 7335)* 1/8/40.
  3064 *(ex7034)* 23/3/44.
  3187 *(new)* 3/11/47.
  23712 *(ex?)* 28/7/51.
  23821 *(new)* 26/3/55.

SHEDS:
Stratford.
Cambridge 12/4/34.
King's Lynn 7/3/43.
Cambridge 21/3/43.
Norwich 26/7/53.
Lowestoft 17/8/58.
Norwich 16/11/58.

RENUMBERED:
  49ᴇ 17/11/23.
  7049 11/11/25.
  8645 22/12/46.
  68645 28/7/51.

CONDEMNED: 6/11/59.
Cut up at Stratford.

_____

7050

Stratford.

To traffic 9/1912.

REPAIRS:
Str. 20/6—30/11/17.**G.**
Str. 24/10/21—7/2/22.**G.**
Str. 21/7—1/11/23.**G.**
Str. 15/8—6/11/25.**G.**
Str. ?/?—6/1/27.**N/C.**
Heating apparatus fitted.
Str. 28/7—8/11/28.**G.**
Vacuum ejector fitted &
additional rails on bunker.
Str. 11/11—18/12/31.**G.**
Str. 18/5—28/6/35.**G.**
Str. 29/6—15/7/38.**G.**
Condensing gear removed.
Str. 31/5—8/6/40.**L.**
Trip cock gear fitted &
condenser refitted.
Str. 28/6—16/8/41.**G.**
Str. 14—25/9/42.**L.**
Str. 26/11—23/12/44.**G.**
Str. 15—18/3/47.**N/C.**
Trip cock gear refitted.
Str. 9/3—23/4/49.**G.**
Str. 2/9—11/10/52.**G.**
Str. 13/8—14/9/57.**G.**

BOILERS:
  50.
  82 *(exJ69 7082)* 30/11/17.
  45 *(exJ69 7052)* 7/2/22.

2967 *(ex7029)* 6/11/25.
2990 *(exJ69 7090)* 18/12/31.
3019 *(exJ69 7362)* 28/6/35.
3039 *(exJ69 7353)* 15/7/38.
3098 *(ex7025)* 16/8/41.
3069 *(exJ69 7328)* 23/12/44.
3040 *(ex8655)* 23/4/49.
23753 *(ex?)* 11/10/52.
23701 *(exJ69 68554)* 14/9/57.

SHEDS:
Stratford.
Parkeston 28/6/35.
Cambridge 21/12/35.
Stratford 2/10/39.

RENUMBERED:
  50ᴇ 1/11/23.
  7050 6/11/25.
  8646 11/1/47.
  68646 23/4/49.

CONDEMNED: 10/9/61.
Cut up at Stratford.

_____

7021

Stratford.

To traffic 12/1913.

REPAIRS:
Str. 5/1—4/4/22.**G.**
Str. 17/3—11/7/24.**G.**
Str. 20/8—10/11/26.**G.**
Additional rails on bunker.
Str. 27/4—9/8/29.**G.**
Str. 21/3—19/4/33.**G.**
Str. 9/8—2/9/37.**G.**
Vacuum ejector fitted.
Str. 1/3—16/4/40.**G.**
Str. 10/4—6/5/44.**G.**
Str. 12—25/10/44.**L.**
GS buffers fitted.
Str. 2/11—11/12/47.**G.**
Str. 29/3—22/4/50.**C/H.**
Str. 2—29/9/51.**G.**
Str. 13/8—21/9/56.**G.**

BOILERS:
  21.
  22 *(ex7022)* 11/7/24.
  29 *(exJ69 7051)* 19/4/33.
  2993 *(exJ69 7270)* 2/9/37.
  3054 *(exJ69 7168)* 16/4/40.
  3032 *(exJ69 7380)* 6/5/44.
  23718 *(ex?)* 29/9/51.
  23816 *(exJ69 68543)* 21/9/56.

SHED:
Stratford.

RENUMBERED:
  7021 11/7/24.

8647 23/12/46.
68647 22/4/50.

CONDEMNED: 4/12/60.
Cut up at Stratford.

_____

7022

Stratford.

To traffic 12/1913.

REPAIRS:
Str. 9/2—9/4/24.**G.**
Str. 18/3—21/5/27.**G.**
Additional rails on bunker.
Str. 27/5—16/8/29.**G.**
Str. 9/9—23/10/31.**G.**
Str. 6/12/33—10/1/34.**G.**
Str. 28/11/36—1/1/37.**G.**
Vacuum ejector fitted.
Str. 1/4—10/5/40.**G.**
Str. 4/6—19/7/44.**G.**
Str. 24/3—9/6/48.**G.**
Str. 22/7—25/8/51.**G.**
Str. 10/5—11/6/55.**C/L.**
Str. 24/7—8/9/56.**G.**
Str. 21/8/59. *Not repaired.*

BOILERS:
  22.
  23 *(ex7023)* 9/4/24.
  3060 *(new)* 23/10/31.
  3050 *(exJ69 7160)* 1/1/37.
  2984 *(exJ69 7090)* 10/5/40.
  3065 *(ex7036)* 19/7/44.
  3189 *(new)* 9/6/48.
  23805 *(new)* 25/8/51.
  23735 *(exJ69 68591)* 8/9/56.

SHEDS:
Stratford.
Cambridge 15/8/27.
March ?/?.
Stratford 10/1/34.
Plaistow 22/5/52.
Stratford 19/4/53.

RENUMBERED:
  7022 9/4/24.
  8648 8/9/46.
  68648 5/6/48.

CONDEMNED: 24/8/59.
Cut up at Stratford.

_____

7023

Stratford.

To traffic 12/1913.

REPAIRS:
Str. 30/11/23—27/2/24.**G.**
Vacuum ejector fitted.
Str. 24/4—2/9/26.**G.**
Additional rails on bunker.
Str. 29/10/28—7/2/29.**G.**
Str. 7/2—17/4/31.**G.**
Str. 1—22/1/35.**G.**
Str. 17/4—11/5/38.**G.**
Str. 5—30/10/41.**G.**
Str. 4—27/3/45.**G.**
Str. 1/5—24/6/47.**G.**
Str. 23/5—10/6/50.**G.**
Str. 4—29/8/53.**G.**
Str. 19/11/56—5/1/57.**C/L.**
Str. 21/4—9/5/58.**G.**

BOILERS:
  23.
  391 *(exJ69 7387)* 27/2/24.
  2971 *(exJ69 7052)* 17/4/31.
  3083 *(new)* 22/1/35.
  3086 *(ex7026)* 11/5/38.
  2979 *(exJ69 7390)* 30/10/41.
  3103 *(exJ69 7085)* 27/3/45.
  3182 *(new)* 24/6/47.
  3045 *(exJ69 8625)* 10/6/50.
  23778 *(ex?)* 29/8/53.
  23789 *(exJ69 68566)* 9/5/58.

SHEDS:
Stratford.
Parkeston 28/1/51.
Stratford 8/3/53.

RENUMBERED:
  7023 *after* 27/2/24.
  8649 22/12/46.
  68649 10/6/50.

CONDEMNED: 10/9/61.
Cut up at Stratford.

_____

7024

Stratford.

To traffic 12/1913.

REPAIRS:
Str. 5/1—1/4/22.**G.**
Str. 9/6—1/10/24.**G.**
Str. 30/4—9/6/26.**G.**
Str. 18/8—26/11/27.**G.**
Additional rails on bunker.
Str. 26/7—19/9/30.**G.**
Str. 5/12/33—2/1/34.**G.**
Str. 17/7—12/8/38.**G.**
Str. 21—25/5/40.**L.**
Vacuum ejector fitted.
Str. 8/3—24/4/42.**G.**
Str. 13/8—20/9/44.**G.**
Str. 3/11—13/12/47.**G.**
GS buffers fitted.

Ex works 30th December 1925, No.7042 still had its original taper shank buffers as shown in the photograph on page 76, bottom. By August 1927 it had acquired the later type with parallel shank and hollow spindle. Note the Load Class 3 collar fixed on the vacuum standpipe. On the shunters it was fixed on the bufferbeam *see* page 76, top.

When No.7042 needed replacement buffers in December 1927 it was the first J68 to get the Group Standard type. These resembled buffers fitted on the 1923 built engines but had square instead of circular flange.

Because the toolbox on the top of the left hand tank obstructed the fireman's view, it was taken off, usually just after the war *see* page 85, 3rd from top. However, No.7037 had it removed when this 20th August 1939 photograph was taken.

Ex works 30th September 1931, No.7027 was fitted for grease lubrication of the coupling pins and the connecting rod big ends. This facility was extended during 1934 to four of the passenger type engines, Nos.7044 (1st August), 7045 (19th December), 7046 (18th January), and 7049 (8th March). It was not recorded if and when - they reverted to oil lubrication.

Somewhat strangely for shunting engines, a mechanical lubricator was provided.

7024 cont./
Str. 21/6—4/8/51.**G.**
Str. 30/9—21/10/54.**C/L.**
Str. 6/7—18/8/56.**G.**

BOILERS:
24.
21 *(ex7021)* 1/10/24.
2979 *(exJ69 7305)* 19/9/30.
33 *(exJ69 7190)* 2/1/34.
3083 *(ex7023)* 12/8/38.
3080 *(ex7033)* 24/4/42.
3060 *(exJ69 7267)* 20/9/44.
3014 *(exJ69 8497)* 13/12/47.
23715 *(ex?)* 4/8/51.
23751 *(exJ69 68599)* 18/8/56.

SHEDS:
Stratford.
Parkeston 18/1/48.
Stratford 28/8/49.

RENUMBERED:
7024 1/10/24.
8650 22/12/46.
68650 4/8/51.

CONDEMNED: 11/10/60.
Cut up at Stratford.

7025

Stratford.

To traffic 12/1913.

REPAIRS:
Str. 5/3—28/4/23.**G.**
Vacuum ejector fitted 7/23.
Str. 2/4—15/7/25.**G.**
Str. 10/2—19/5/28.**G.**
Additional rails on bunker.
Str. 17/8—23/10/30.**G.**
Str. 8/5—7/6/33.**G.**
Str. 1—30/4/37.**G.**
Str. 7/6—24/7/41.**G.**
Str. 28/4—28/5/43.**G.**
Str. 7/5—7/6/44.**G.**
Str. 6/9—12/10/46.**G.**
Str. 12/2—25/3/50.**G.**
Str. 23/8—26/9/53.**G.**

BOILERS:
25.
3043 *(new)* 19/5/28.
3025 *(exJ69 7383)* 7/6/33.
3098 *(new)* 30/4/37.
3007 *(exJ69 7360)* 24/7/41.
3101 *(exJ69 7361)* 28/5/43.
3054 *(ex7021)* 7/6/44.
3061 *(exJ69 7389)* 12/10/46.
3202 *(new)* 25/3/50.
23781 *(ex?)* 26/9/53.

SHEDS:
Stratford.
Peterborough E. 3/8/25.
Stratford 2/1/26.
Lowestoft 11/10/34.
Norwich 17/8/41.
Ipswich 10/11/46.
Yarmouth Beach 16/2/47.

RENUMBERED:
7025 15/7/25.
8651 1/9/46.
68651 25/3/50.

CONDEMNED: 19/5/58.
Cut up at Stratford.

7026

Stratford.

To traffic 12/1913.

REPAIRS:
Str. 16/6—11/8/21.**G.**
Str. 31/5—12/7/24.**G.**
Str. 12/5—13/8/27.**G.**
Additional rails on bunker.
Str. 17/5—18/7/30.**G.**
Str. 21/2—27/3/35.**G.**
Vacuum ejector & heating apparatus fitted.
Str. 5/3—2/4/38.**G.**
Str. 8/3—24/4/42.**G.**
Str. 15/7—4/8/45.**G.**
Str. 8/5—25/6/49.**G.**
Str. 14/5—5/6/52.**G.**
Str. 24/7—1/9/56.**G.**
Str. 24/9/59. *Not repaired.*

BOILERS:
26.
3039 *(new)* 13/8/27.
3086 *(new)* 27/3/35.
3021 *(ex7045)* 2/4/38.
3027 *(exJ69 7165)* 24/4/42.
3100 *(exJ69 7160)* 4/8/45.
3098 *(exJ69 8596)* 25/6/49.
23745 *(ex?)* 5/6/52.
23747 *(exJ69 68609)* 1/9/56.

SHEDS:
Stratford.
Parkeston 25/9/39.
Stratford 25/11/44.

RENUMBERED:
7026 12/7/24.
8652 5/1/47.
68652 25/6/49.

CONDEMNED: 28/9/59.
Cut up at Stratford.

7027

Stratford.

To traffic 12/1913.

REPAIRS:
Str. 28/11/22—2/2/23.**G.**
Str. 14/4—20/8/25.**G.**
Cab roof altered.
Str. 21/7—9/10/28.**G.**
Additional rails on bunker.
Str. 14/8—30/9/31.**G.**
Special grease lubrication to coupling & connecting rods.
Str. 7/6—7/7/36.**G.**
Vacuum ejector fitted.
Str. 29/4—7/9/39.**G.**
Str. 3—26/9/41.**G.**
Str. 1/8—11/9/43.**G.**
Str. 22/10—17/11/45.**G.**
Str. 23/10—23/12/49.**G.**
Str. 24/2—20/3/53.**G.**

BOILERS:
27.
2964 *(exJ69 7366)* 30/9/31.
3045 *(exJ69 7383)* 7/7/36.
3024 *(exJ69 7162)* 7/9/39.
3037 *(exJ69 7059)* 26/9/41.
3068 *(exJ69 7083)* 11/9/43.
3101 *(ex7043)* 17/11/45.
3104 *(exJ69 8629)* 23/12/49.
23764 *(ex?)* 20/3/53.

SHEDS:
Cambridge.
Stratford 15/8/27
Parkeston 8/1/50.
Stratford 24/6/51.

RENUMBERED:
7027 20/8/25.
8653 4/1/47.
68653 23/12/49.

CONDEMNED: 28/7/58.
Cut up at Stratford.

7028

Stratford.

To traffic 1/1914.

REPAIRS:
Str. 18/10—27/11/22.**G.**
Str. 20/1—18/4/25.**G.**
Cab roof altered.
Str. 19/7—1/10/27.**G.**
Additional rails on bunker.
Str. 7/8—5/10/29.**G.**
Str. 26/8—8/10/31.**G.**
Str. 19/7—8/9/33.**H.**
Str. 7/2—8/3/35.**G.**
Vacuum ejector fitted.
Str. 2/11—10/12/37.**L.**
Str. 11/5—18/9/39.**G.**
Str. 9/9—24/12/43.**G.**
Str. 14/7—8/9/47.**G.**
Str. 21/11—18/12/47.**L.**
Str. 17/7—31/8/49.**C/L.**
Str. 25/9—20/10/51.**G.**
Str. 26/3—5/5/56.**G.**

BOILERS:
28.
344 *(exJ69 7344)* 18/4/25.
3016 *(ex7042)* 8/10/31.
3033 *(ex7044)* 8/3/35.
3085 *(exJ69 7083)* 18/9/39.
3023 *(exJ69 7350)* 24/12/43.
23721 *(ex?)* 20/10/51.
23795 *(ex?)* 5/5/56.

SHEDS:
March.
Stratford 4/2/51.
Hitchin 16/12/56.
Doncaster 15/6/58.

RENUMBERED:
7028 18/4/25.
8654 5/1/47.
68654 20/10/51.

CONDEMNED: 11/3/60.
Cut up at Stratford.

7029

Stratford.

To traffic 1/1914.

REPAIRS:
Str. 2/6—19/10/23.**G.**
Str. 17/8—23/10/25.**G.**
Str. 10/5—30/7/28.**G.**
Additional rails on bunker.
Str. 16/3—15/5/31.**G.**
Str. 5/2—9/3/34.**G.**
Str. 2/12/36—19/1/37.**G.**
Str. 26/1—2/2/38.**L.**
Spark arrestor fitted.
Str. 30/6—8/9/40.**G.**
Str. 4/10—1/12/43.**G.**
Str. 6/1—24/2/47.**G.**
Str. 1/12/48—9/1/49.**C/H.**
Str. 30/7—26/8/50.**G.**
Str. 15/8—17/9/55.**G.**

BOILERS:
29.
2967 *(exJ69 7057)* 19/10/23.
356 *(exJ69 7379)* 23/10/25.
3033 *(exJ69 7355)* 30/7/28.
3030 *(exJ69 7390)* 15/5/31.

Unlike the other four classes of Great Eastern 0-6-0 tanks (which had stovepipes), J68 were built with a parallel sided chimney with a wide rim at the top.

From June 1930, as on the other classes, a North Eastern cast tapered chimney was substituted, No.7028 having this change ex works 8th October 1931. Note it also changed then to Group Standard buffers.

In this 6th October 1946 photograph, No.7028's chimney appears to have had an emergency repair recently. It had last been shopped 24th December 1943 as borne out by the poor condition of its painting. Ex works again, 8th September 1947 a normal chimney was fitted.

No reason for this short stovepipe being fitted on No.8641 in 1947 has been discovered, and none of its normal duties needed reduced height above rail level.

(above) The ten built for passenger workings were fitted at both ends to carry GER type destination plates as shown in photograph on page 88, centre. This indication was banned during the war and rarely used afterwards but the brackets generally survived. Here they are on a shunter due to a transferred door on the smokebox.

No.68654's final exit from Stratford works was on 5th May 1956 when action had been taken to remove the redundant brackets.

Until after they became LNER property, the passenger engines had only Westinghouse brakes on the engine, and for the train. No carriage heating gear was fitted.

7029 cont./
2979 *(ex7024)* 9/3/34.
40 *(exJ69 7190)* 19/1/37.
2993 *(ex7021)* 8/9/40.
38 *(exJ69 7332)* 1/12/43.
3040 *(exJ69 8599)* 24/2/47.
3024 *(exJ69 8607)* 9/1/49.
3182 *(ex8649)* 26/8/50.
23792 *(ex?)* 17/9/55.

SHEDS:
Peterborough East.
Boston 4/1/30.
Stratford 26/7/53.

RENUMBERED:
7029 23/10/25.
8655 31/8/46.
68655 9/1/49.

CONDEMNED: 24/11/59.
Cut up at Stratford.

_____

7030

Stratford.

To traffic 2/1914.

REPAIRS:
Str. 6/10—12/12/23.**G.**
Str. 27/11/26—9/2/27.**G.**
Additional rails on bunker.
Str. 23/8—28/9/29.**G.**
Str. 8/9—29/10/31.**G.**
Str. 19/2—1/4/35.**G.**
Vacuum ejector fitted.
Str. 14—29/1/38.**G.**
Str. 21/5—6/10/39.**G.**
Str. 3/1—6/3/43.**G.**
Str. 3/4—5/5/44.**L.**
Str. 27/1—25/2/46.**G.**
Str. 1/3—8/4/49.**G.**
Str. 8/3—3/4/52.**G.**
Str. 4/12/55—14/1/56.**G.**

BOILERS:
30.
40 *(new)* 12/12/23.
3008 *(exJ69 7385)* 28/9/29.
2980 *(exJ69 7194)* 29/10/31.
3090 *(new)* 1/4/35.
3091 *(exJ69 7054)* 29/1/38.
2974 *(exJ69 7346)* 6/10/39.
2998 *(exJ69 7387)* 6/3/43.
3066 *(ex7044)* 25/2/46.
3052 *(exJ69 8631)* 8/4/49.
23811 *(new)* 3/4/52.
23704 *(exJ69 68532)* 14/1/56.

SHEDS:
Peterborough East.
March 2/9/30.
King's Lynn 4/5/40.

Yarmouth 26/7/53.
Lowestoft 25/10/59.

RENUMBERED:
7030 9/2/27.
8656 7/10/46.
68656 8/4/49.

CONDEMNED: 4/4/60.
Cut up at Stratford.

_____

7031

Stratford.

To traffic 6/10/1923.

REPAIRS:
Str. 22/4—3/9/26.**G.**
Additional rails on bunker.
Str. 8/11/28—15/2/29.**G.**
Str. 1/12/31—29/1/32.**G.**
Str. 13/8—17/9/34.**G.**
Str. 16/7—25/8/37.**G.**
Vacuum ejector fitted.
Str. 9—16/2/38.**L.**
Spark arrestor fitted.
Str. 17/3—19/4/41.**G.**
Str. 28/2—5/4/44.**G.**
Str. 10/3—8/5/47.**G.**
Str. 29/12/49—11/2/50.**G.**
Str. 7/6—25/7/53.**G.**

BOILERS:
3024.
25 *(ex7025)* 15/2/29.
3024 *(exJ69 7378)* 29/1/32.
36 *(exJ69 7390)* 17/9/34.
3071 *(ex7040)* 25/8/37.
2968 *(ex7049)* 19/4/41.
3067 *(exJ69 7090)* 5/4/44.
3179 *(new)* 8/5/47.
23776 *(ex?)* 25/7/53.

SHEDS:
Peterborough East.
New England 24/10/29.
Boston 24/10/29.
Stratford 26/7/53.

RENUMBERED:
7031 3/9/26.
8657 1/9/46.
68657 11/2/50.

CONDEMNED: 18/8/58.
Cut up at Stratford.

_____

7032

Stratford.

To traffic 11/10/1923.

REPAIRS:
Str. 24/7—27/10/26.**G.**
Str. 3/4—22/6/29.**G.**
Additional rails on bunker.
Str. 27/2—6/4/32.**G.**
Str. 10/12/34—10/1/35.**G.**
Str. 17/11—11/12/37.**G.**
Spark arrestor fitted.
Str. 6/6—23/7/41.**G.**
Str. 1/8—6/9/44.**G.**
Gor. 26/10—8/12/47.**G.**
Str. 17/3—14/4/51.**G.**
Str. 2/1—4/2/56.**G.**

BOILERS:
3025.
3057 *(new)* 22/6/29.
25 *(ex7031)* 6/4/32.
2996 *(exJ69 7370)* 10/1/35.
3100 *(new)* 11/12/37.
3014 *(exJ69 7194)* 23/7/41.
3073 *(exJ69 7340)* 6/9/44.
3049 *(ex8665)* 8/12/47.
23804 *(new)* 14/4/51.
23765 *(exJ69 68490)* 4/2/56.

SHEDS:
Peterborough East.
Stratford 22/6/29.
Peterborough East 11/9/29.
Boston 20/9/29.
Stratford 26/7/53.

RENUMBERED:
7032 27/10/26.
8658 1/9/46.
68658 14/4/51.

CONDEMNED: 17/4/59.
Cut up at Stratford.

_____

7033

Stratford.

To traffic 16/10/1923.

REPAIRS:
Str. 21/1—17/3/27.**G.**
Additional rails on bunker.
Str. 9/10—23/11/29.**G.**
Str. 15/6—20/7/32.**G.**
Str. 14/2—27/3/35.**G.**
Str. 28/3—4/5/38.**G.**
Spark arrestor fitted.
Str. 26/10—5/12/41.**G.**
Str. 2/2—20/3/44.**G.**
GS buffers fitted.
Str. 15/6—3/8/47.**G.**
Str. 17/9—21/10/50.**G.**
Str. 31/8—2/10/53.**G.**

BOILERS:
3026.

3038 *(exJ69 7350)* 20/7/32.
3087 *(new)* 27/3/35.
3080 *(exJ69 7354)* 4/5/38.
3030 *(exJ69 7195)* 5/12/41.
35 *(exJ69 7195)* 20/3/44.
3184 *(new)* 3/8/47.
3184 *reno.*23703 21/10/50.
23783 *(ex?)* 2/10/53.

SHEDS:
Stratford.
York 5/8/27.
Ardsley 20/3/28.
New England 11/3/31.
Boston 14/3/31.
Stratford 26/7/53.

RENUMBERED:
7033 by 27/4/26.
8659 2/9/46.
68659 21/10/50.

CONDEMNED: 18/8/58.
Cut up at Stratford.

_____

7034

Stratford.

To traffic 20/10/1923.

REPAIRS:
Str. 22/6—27/8/25.**G.**
Str. 7/9—2/11/28.**G.**
Additional rails on bunker.
Str. 14/11—22/12/31.**G.**
Str. 9/8—3/9/36.**G.**
Vacuum ejector fitted.
Str. 11/2—14/3/40.**G.**
Str. 23/1—3/3/44.**G.**
Str. 8/7—2/10/46.**G.**
Str. 2/2—21/3/49.**G.**
Str. 11/2—8/3/52.**G.**
Str. 15/10—17/11/56.**G.**
Str. 15/4—15/5/57.**N/C.**

BOILERS:
3027.
3014 *(exJ69 7370)* 2/11/28.
2986 *(exJ69 7086)* 22/12/31.
2964 *(ex7027)* 3/9/36.
3064 *(exJ69 7353)* 14/3/40.
3094 *(ex7039)* 3/3/44.
3037 *(exJ69 7195)* 2/10/46.
3167 *(exJ69 8577)* 21/3/49.
23737 *(ex?)* 8/3/52.
23743 *(exJ69 68596)* 17/11/56.

SHEDS:
Stratford.
Peterborough East 2/1/26.
Sheffield 26/3/26.
Stratford 17/8/27.
Parkeston 8/3/47.

In April 1923 No.46 had a vacuum ejector added, followed in May by No.43, and five more got them in 1924: Nos.7041, 7042, 7044, 7045 and 7048. No.7050 got it in November 1928, No.7047 in March 1929 and No.7049 completed this fitting when ex works 10th May 1929.

Carriage heating apparatus, with connection at both ends, began to be fitted from February 1924 on No.7041 but this was not completed until 16th January 1931 when No.7046 was ex works.

The twenty shunters, Nos.21 to 40, had only steam brake fitted until the LNER decided they would make very suitable passenger station pilots.

In July 1923 No.25 had vacuum ejector added to its steam brake, was changed from loose to screw couplings, and got a set of ten-spoke passenger wheels. No.23 also had vacuum ejector added in February 1924. No more had vacuum added until March 1935 (No.7028) when fifteen of the remaining eighteen were fitted, the last being No.7024 in May 1940. Only Nos.7029, 7032 and 7033 did not get vacuum because they worked from 1929/31 to 26th July 1953 as the shunters on the docks at Boston.

Nos.7029, 7032, and 7033 duly became 68655, 68658 and 68659 and although on 26th July 1953 all three went to Stratford shed, they were the only J68 with just steam brake to withdrawal.

Originally the ten passenger engines, Nos.41 to 50, had Royal Blue paint and the ten shunters, Nos.21 to 30, had black, all with a fine vermilion lining.

During the 1914-18 war, all changed into dark shop grey without lining which was their livery when taken over by the LNER.

7034 cont./
Stratford 10/4/49.

RENUMBERED:
7034 27/8/25.
8660 27/9/46.
68660 19/3/49.

CONDEMNED: 4/12/60.
Cut up at Stratford.

_____

7035

Stratford.

To traffic 27/10/1923.

REPAIRS:
Str. 25/2—30/4/26.**G.**
Str. 31/8—2/11/28.**G.**
Additional rails on bunker.
Str. 10/10—27/11/31.**G.**
Str. 3/5—4/6/36.**G.**
Vacuum ejector fitted.
Str. 1/10—18/11/39.**G.**
Str. 12/4—5/6/43.**G.**
Str. 11/8—9/9/46.**G.**
Str. 6/11—17/12/49.**G.**
Str. 11/2—1/3/52.**C/L.**
Str. 13/4—9/5/53.**G.**
Str. 11/12/56—12/1/57.**G.**

BOILERS:
3028.
2966 *(exJ69 7335)* 30/4/26.
3008 *(ex7030)* 27/11/31.
37 *(exJ69 7163)* 4/6/36.
2975 *(exJ69 7088)* 18/11/39.
3083 *(ex7024)* 5/6/43.
3176 *(new)* 9/9/46.
3176 reno.23740 1/3/52.
23769 *(ex?)* 9/5/53.
23757 *(exJ69 68501)* 12/1/57.

SHEDS:
Stratford.
Parkeston 24/6/51.
Stratford 15/3/53.
Hitchin 12/2/56.

RENUMBERED:
7035 30/4/26.
8661 3/9/46.
68661 17/12/49.

CONDEMNED: 18/12/59.
Cut up at Stratford.

_____

7036

Stratford.

To traffic 1/11/1923.

REPAIRS:
Str. 25/2—5/5/27.**G.**
Additional rails on bunker.
Str. 27/3—16/5/30.**G.**
Str. 10/5—21/6/35.**G.**
Str. 6/1—14/2/40.**G.**
Str. 15—18/5/40.**L.**
Vacuum ejector fitted.
Str. 28/7—14/8/42.**L.**
Str. 28/5—28/6/44.**G.**
Str. 24/2—13/4/48.**G.**
Str. 12/8—1/9/51.**G.**
Str. 8/11—11/12/54.**G.**
Str. 24/6—24/7/57.**C/L.**

BOILERS:
31.
34 *(exJ69 7328)* 21/6/35.
3065 *(ex7039)* 14/2/40.
2980 *(exJ69 7198)* 28/6/44.
3088 *(exJ69 8619)* 13/4/48.
23808 *(new)* 1/9/51.
23717 *(exJ69 68603)* 11/12/54.

SHEDS:
Stratford.
York 8/8/27.
Ardsley 15/3/28.
Stratford 10/5/35.
Colchester 12/2/56.
Stratford 11/5/58.

RENUMBERED:
7036 5/5/27.
8662 5/1/47.
68662 10/4/48.

CONDEMNED: 18/8/58.
Cut up at Stratford.

_____

7037

Stratford.

To traffic 6/11/1923.

REPAIRS:
Str. 1/3—2/6/26.**G.**
Str. 14/12/28—28/2/29.**G.**
Additional rails on bunker.
Str. 15/5—16/6/32.**G.**
Str. 10/1—19/2/37.**G.**
Vacuum ejector fitted.
Str. 15/2—15/3/41.**G.**
Str. 3—23/9/44.**G.**
Str. 5/12/48—16/1/49.**G.**
Str. 17/12/51—12/1/52.**G.**
Str. 20/3—21/4/56.**G.**

BOILERS:
32.
3040 *(exJ69 7328)* 16/6/32.
3093 *(new)* 19/2/37.
3026 *(exJ69 7087)* 15/3/41.
3156 *(new)* 23/9/44.
23729 *(ex?)* 12/1/52.
23711 *(exJ69 68575)* 21/4/56.

SHED:
Stratford.

RENUMBERED:
7037 2/6/26.
8663 13/1/47.
68663 15/1/49.

CONDEMNED: 11/10/60.
Cut up at Stratford.

_____

7038

Stratford.

To traffic 10/11/1923.

REPAIRS:
Str. 5/10—20/11/25.**G.**
Str. 30/11/27—16/2/28.**G.**
Additional rails on bunker.
Str. 28/1—5/4/30.**G.**
Str. 20/8—23/10/31.**G.**
Str. 14/8—22/9/33.**H.**
Str. 27/3—9/5/35.**G.**
Vacuum ejector fitted.
Str. 14/12/37—5/1/38.**G.**
Str. 22/9—11/11/39.**G.**
Str. 14/1—22/2/44.**G.**
Str. 26/1—17/3/47.**G.**
Str. 17/3—15/4/52.**G.**
Str. 14/2—12/3/55.**G.**

BOILERS:
33.
37 *(exJ69 7387)* 5/4/30.
3058 *(new)* 23/10/31.
2955 *(exJ69 7355)* 9/5/35.
3102 *(new)* 5/1/38.
3045 *(ex7027)* 11/11/39.
3085 *(ex7028)* 22/2/44.
3078 *(exJ69 8556)* 17/3/47.
23742 *(ex?)* 15/4/52.
23807 *(exJ69 68491)* 12/3/55.

SHEDS:
Cambridge.
March 17/5/24.
Norwich 26/7/53.
Lowestoft 13/11/55.

RENUMBERED:
7038 20/11/25.
8664 5/1/47.
68664 15/4/52.

CONDEMNED: 2/9/58.
Cut up at Stratford.

_____

7039

Stratford.

To traffic 17/11/1923.

REPAIRS:
Str. 23/6—21/10/26.**G.**
Additional rails on bunker.
Str. 7/1—7/3/29.**G.**
Str. 24/10—12/12/31.**G.**
Str. 26/7—27/8/36.**G.**
Vacuum ejector fitted.
Str. 4/11—8/12/39.**G.**
Str. 2/1—2/2/44.**G.**
Str. 8/9—20/10/47.**G.**
Str. 11/2—10/3/51.**G.**
Str. 13/11—5/12/53.**G.**
Str. 26/9—27/10/56.**G.**

BOILERS:
34.
3006 *(exJ69 7053)* 12/12/31.
3065 *(exJ69 7345)* 27/8/36.
3094 *(exJ69 7051)* 8/12/39.
3049 *(ex7042)* 2/2/44.
3050 *(exJ69 8636)* 20/10/47.
23801 *(new)* 10/3/51.
23786 *(ex?)* 5/12/53.
23718 *(ex68647)* 27/10/56.

SHED:
Stratford.

RENUMBERED:
7039 21/10/26.
8665 9/1/47.
68665 10/3/51.

CONDEMNED: 7/12/59.
Cut up at Stratford.

_____

By Grouping, the GER initials were already being blocked out and 19in. yellow painted and unshaded numbers were being put on grey paint. This style was continued and ex Stratford 27th February 1924, this is how No.23 was turned out.

The ten built in October/November 1923 had standard black with fine red lining, and at least to 16th October 1923 on No.33E, L&NER was used.

All ten numbered 31 to 40 had the area suffix E added to their number from new. The last five, from No.36E, out 1ˢᵗ November 1923, are known to have been LNER without ampersand.

The other twenty continued in grey, most of them still having it after their LNER 1924 number was applied and No.7030 *see* page 76, top still had it ex works 9ᵗʰ February 1927 when the extra coal rails were fitted.

7040

Stratford.

To traffic 22/11/1923.

REPAIRS:
Str. 1/10—17/12/26.**G.**
Str. 23/11/29—11/1/30.**G.**
Additional rails on bunker.
Str. 11/7—2/8/33.**G.**
Str. 4/7—10/8/37.**G.**
Vacuum ejector fitted.
Str. 26/1—15/3/41.**G.**
Str. 22/3—13/4/43.**G.**
Str. 1—21/10/44.**G.**
Str. 24/2—12/4/48.**G.**
Str. 29/10—24/11/51.**G.**
Str. 28/3—23/4/55.**G.**

BOILERS:
   35.
   40 *(ex7030)* 11/1/30.
 3071 *(new)* 2/8/33.
 2997 *(ex7048)* 10/8/37.
 3097 *(exJ69 7052)* 15/3/41.
 3024 *(ex spare & 7027)*
13/4/43.
 3025 *(exJ69 7365)* 21/10/44.
 3087 *(exJ69 8495)* 12/4/48.
23723 *(ex?)* 24/11/51.
23877 *(ex Cow. & 68505)*
23/4/55.

SHEDS:
Stratford.
Colchester 29/1/56.
Stratford 11/5/58.

RENUMBERED:
7040 17/12/26.
8666 9/1/47.
68666 10/4/48.

CONDEMNED: 18/8/58.
Cut up at Stratford.

Early in 1925 Southern Area made moves to have the 1924 number put on if L&NER or LNER had already been applied. Few of the Eastern section were dealt with and with this one Stratford made a wrong interpretation. They changed 33ᴇ to 7033 correctly but should have left L&NER standing instead of blacking that out. Date of change was not recorded but the date of the photograph is 24th July 1926.

Apart from Nos.7031 to 7040, which had standard red lining, by no means all the other twenty received it before the June 1928 instruction to discard it was effective. Few rather than many got it and from 1928 only unlined black was used to withdrawal.

From June 1942 until into 1946 only NE was put on but Stratford still used 7½in. size for it, with 12in. numbers

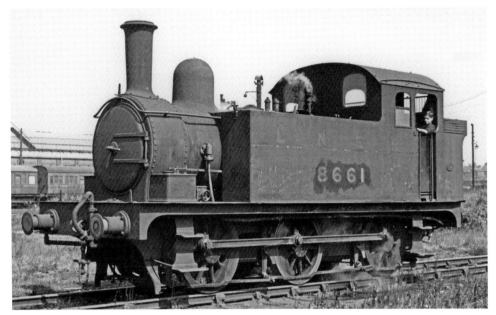

Restoration of LNER was overtaken by the renumbering which began in January 1946. Numbers 8637 to 8666 were allocated to J68 class and only 8637 was not taken up, No.7041 having gone to the War Department in October 1939. No.7035 became 8661 on 3rd September 1946 whilst in Stratford works for a General repair. As it had been decided that no further orders for shaded transfers were to be placed, Stratford had to use existing stock as best they could, hence the 9in. instead of 12in. figures.

When No.8665 was ex works 20th October 1947, transfers were then exhausted and it had painted and unshaded numbers in Gill sans style but with the LNER modification to the figure 6.

(below) In April 1948, Nos.68666 (12th) and 68662 (13th) were the first to show the new ownership, so no J68 carried a regional prefix E. Lettering was still 7½in. but 10in. numbers were used.

From July 1948 the number was moved to the bunker and at 10in., figures and letters were matched but the lettering ceased to be used from September 1949.

The 15½in. size BR emblem was used from 24th September 1949 when No.68639 was ex works and all except Nos.68646 and 68649 had this style when withdrawn.

Ex works 14th September 1957, No.68646 had the BR crest and with the lion facing the wrong way to conform to heraldry.

No.68649 was the only other to get the BR crest, ex works 9th May 1958, and also with the wrongly facing lion. Neither visited works again and so no correction was made. J68 class became extinct on 10th September 1961 when 68642, 68646 and 68649 were all withdrawn.

Forty more engines, Nos.367 to 396, and 265 to 274, were built at Stratford from April 1894 to June 1896. All were rebuilt as No.340 between February 1904 and June 1913. Condensing apparatus was fitted when new so the tank side plates were built up to cover the chamber. From June 1900 to August 1901, twenty further engines, Nos.305 (189 until 1909), 190 to 198, and 160 to 169 were built at Stratford. All except Nos.161, 164, and 169 got the 180lb. longer firebox boiler from August 1910 to January 1922.

The class was completed with Nos.51 to 60, and 81 to 90, built at Stratford from May to September 1904. These were built with the 180lb., longer firebox boilers, but they had wider cabs and bunkers giving sides flush with the wide tanks holding 1200 gallons of water. This also increased coal capacity by 5 cwts.

CLASS J 69

7328

Stratford.

To traffic 3/1890.
Class R24 - passenger.

REPAIRS:
Str. 25/2—11/9/08.**G.**
Rebuilt to Class R24 Rbt.
Str. ?/?—?/8/12.**G.**
Rebuilt to Class J67/2 (Diag.37 boiler de-rated). Westinghouse brake replaced by steam, condensing gear removed.
Str. ?/?—?/2/17.**G.**
Reverted to Class J69/1 (boiler up-rated).
Pbo. 12/8—13/9/22.**G.**
At 1/1/23: J69/1. Steam brake.
Str. 30/12/24—26/2/25.**G.**
Str. 6/5—15/9/27.**G.**
Additional rails on bunker.
Str. 5/1—24/4/28.**L.**
Str. 6/10—30/11/29.**G.**
Str. 12/1—19/2/32.**G.**
Str. 26/10—24/11/33.**H.**
Str. 16/3—1/5/35.**G.**
Vacuum ejector fitted.
Str. 23/10—10/11/37.**G.**
Str. 11/5—14/9/39.**G.**
Str. 19/1—15/3/42.**G.**
Str. 15/10—16/12/44.**G.**
Str. 14/2—19/4/48.**G.**
Str. 1/8—1/9/51.**G.**
Str. 7—29/1/55.**G.**
Str. 3/6/58. *Not repaired.*

BOILERS:
  328.
  328 *(new)* 11/9/08.
  3040 *(new)* 15/9/27.
   34 *(exJ68 7039)* 19/2/32.
  3064 *(ex7377)* 1/5/35.
   36 *(exJ68 7031)* 10/11/37.
  3034 *(ex7367)* 14/9/39.
  3069 *(ex7373)* 15/3/42.
  3162 *(new)* 16/12/44.
  23807 *(new)* 1/9/51.
  23736 *(ex68606)* 29/1/55.

SHEDS:
March.
Boston 27/12/35.
Peterborough East 20/10/37.
New England 30/4/39.
Leicester 3/7/43.
Stratford 27/11/49.
Cambridge 26/7/53.
New England 25/3/56.
Grantham 1/4/56.

New England 29/4/56.

RENUMBERED:
  7328 26/2/25.
  8491 1/9/46.
  68491 19/4/48.

CONDEMNED: 3/6/58.
Cut up at Stratford.

7335

Stratford.

To traffic 4/1890.
Class R24 - passenger.

REPAIRS:
Str. 17/9/03—16/1/04.**G.**
Rebuilt to Class R24 Rbt.
Str. ?/?—?/10/12.**G.**
Rebuilt to Class J67/2 (Diag.37 boiler de-rated). Westinghouse brake replaced by steam, condensing gear removed.
Str. 3/10/16—12/2/17.**G.**
Rebuilt to J69/1.
At 1/1/23: J69/1. Steam brake.
Str. 3/5—13/7/23.**G.**
Str. 7/11/25—23/1/26.**G.**
Str. 15/10/28—30/1/29.**G.**
Additional rails on bunker.
Str. 22/9—25/10/32.**G.**
Str. 10/10—1/11/35.**G.**
Vacuum ejector fitted.
Str. 11—12/2/38.**H.** (2 days)
Str. 20/5—26/6/40.**G.**
Str. 11—29/9/44.**G.**
Str. 9/8—20/9/47.**G.**
Str. 3/11—9/12/50.**G.**
Str. 19/12/53—16/1/54.**G.**
Str. 27/7—29/8/57.**G.**
Don. 31/8/60. *Not repaired.*

BOILERS:
  335.
  335 *(new)* 16/1/04.
  2966 *(new)* 12/2/17.
   36 *(ex7274)* 23/1/26.
  3052 *(new)* 30/1/29.
  3047 *(ex7082)* 25/10/32.
  3013 *(ex7272)* 1/11/35.
  3081 *(ex7053)* 12/2/38.
  3040 *(exJ68 7042)* 26/6/40.
  3014 *(exJ68 7032)* 29/9/44.
  3090 *(ex8601)* 20/9/47.
  23708 *(ex?)* 9/12/50.
  23801 *(exJ68 68665)* 16/1/54.
  23727 *(ex68565)* 29/8/57.

SHEDS:
Ipswich.
Stratford 24/3/27.
King's Lynn 7/1/34.
March 12/1/34.
Cambridge 27/1/43.
Bury St Edmunds 27/5/45.
Darnall 23/2/58.
Mexborough 16/3/58.
Grimesthorpe 6/3/60.

RENUMBERED:
  7335 23/1/26.
  8497 17/3/46.
  68497 9/12/50.

CONDEMNED: 19/9/60.
Cut up at Doncaster.

7337

Stratford.

To traffic 4/1890.
Class R24 - passenger.

REPAIRS:
Str. 16/5—18/8/04.**G.**
Rebuilt to Class R24 Rbt.
Wolwich Ar. 14/5—23/11/20.**G.**
At 1/1/23: J69/1. Westinghouse brake. Condensing apparatus.
Str. ?/?—?/12/27.**G.**
Vacuum ejector fitted. Condensing apparatus removed. Additional rails on bunker
Cow. 1/1—21/2/31.**G.**
Cow. ?/?—26/1/35.**G.**
Cow. ?/?—12/9/35.**H.**
Cow. ?/?—5/2/36.**L.**
Cow. ?/?—17/12/38.**H.**
Cow. ?/?—15/4/40.**L.**
Cow. ?/?—22/6/40.**L.**
Cow. ?/?—4/4/42.**G.**
Spark arrestor fitted.
Cow. ?/?—31/1/44.**L.**
Cow. ?/?—4/4/44.**L.**
Inv. ?/?—29/6/46.**H.**
Cow. ?/?—9/10/48.**L.**
Cow. 13/7—19/8/49.**H/I.**
Gor. 19/6—4/8/51.**G.**
Str. 17/2—26/3/57.**G.**

BOILERS:
  337.
  337 *(new)* 18/8/04.
  3002 *(new)* 23/11/20.
  C1700 *(ex7386)* 21/2/31.
  C1692 *(ex7356)* 26/1/35.
  C1700 *(ex7392)* 4/4/42.

23841 *(ex?)* 4/8/51.
23722 *(ex68546)* 26/3/57.

SHEDS:
Stratford.
Parkhead 7/2/28.
Stirling ?/3/40.
Carlisle Canal ?/2/42.
Brunswick 25/2/51.
Trafford Park 11/10/52.
Brunswick 8/11/52.
Lincoln 8/2/53.
Boston 26/7/53.
Stratford 17/4/55.
King's Lynn 25/9/55.
South Lynn 20/4/58.
King's Lynn 27/7/58.
March 20/11/60.
Stratford 11/6/61.

RENUMBERED:
  7337 *after* 17/1/25.
  8499 5/5/46.
  68499 9/10/48.

CONDEMNED: 16/9/62.
Cut up at Stratford.

7338

Stratford.

To traffic 5/1890.
Class R24 - passenger.

REPAIRS:
Str. ?/?—?/3/01.**G.**
Str. 10/9/09—14/1/10.**G.**
Rebuilt to Class R24 Rbt.
At 1/1/23: J69/1. Westinghouse brake. Condensing apparatus.
Str. 24/5—21/7/23.**G.**
Str. 14/9—8/12/25.**G.**
Str. 7/7—5/10/28.**G.**
Vacuum ejector fitted. condensing apparatus removed. Additional rails on bunker.
Cow. 9—17/11/28.**N/C.**
Footsteps and bunker handrails fitted.
Cow. 31/12/29—31/1/30.**G.**
Cow. 30/3—30/4/31.**H/I.**
Cow. 13/5—10/6/32.**G.**
Cow. 13—31/7/33.**H/I.**
Cow. 4—15/8/33.**N/C.**
Cow. 15—31/1/36.**C/H.**
Cow. 3/3—9/4/37.**G.**
Cow. 1—3/5/41.**G.**
Spark arrestor fitted for work at ROF Longtown.

Because this class was designed for passenger train working they had steel 10-spoke balanced wheels and the reversing gear was screw operated.

(above) The wider cabs on Nos.7051 to 7060 and 7081 to 7090 had their keyhole entrance made narrower to give better protection but no side window was ever put in.

When the condensing apparatus was removed - No.7347 lost it in August 1928 - the separate chamber on the tank top remained, as did the vertical air vent pipes.

In 1912 Nos.327 to 336 were all de-rated to shunters, losing Westinghouse brake, having reverse changed from screw to lever, and their wheels replaced by the cast iron 15-spoke unbalanced type. The working pressure was reduced to 160lb. Except for Nos.328 and 335, the other eight were put in LNER class J67.

By Grouping Nos.328 and 335 though still shunters had from February 1917 boilers again working at 180lb so the LNER included them in J69 class.

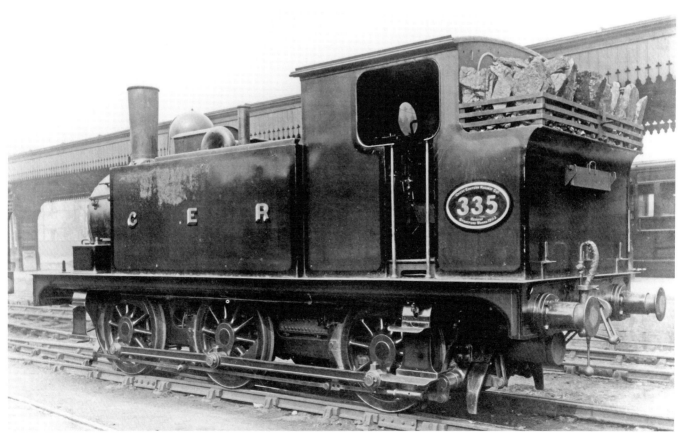

Cow. 17/6—14/7/43.**G.**
Str. 25/9—7/11/47.**G.**
Str. 4/2—10/3/51.**G.**
Str. 25/1—20/2/54.**G.**
Str. 9/9—4/10/57.**G.**

BOILERS:
  338.
  338 *(new)* ?/3/01.
  338 *(new)* 14/1/10.
  3051 *(new)* 5/10/28.
  3051 reno.C1686 31/1/30.
  C1693 *(ex7357)* 10/6/32.
  C1696 *(ex7374)* 9/4/37.
  C1686 *(ex7368)* 14/7/43.
  3155 *(ex8566)* 7/11/47.
  23800 *(new)* 10/3/51.
  23806 *(ex68498)* 20/2/54.
  23801 *(ex68497)* 4/10/57.

SHEDS·
Stratford.
Eastfield 5/11/28.
Thornton Jct. 26/3/29.
Carlisle Canal 5/5/41.
Stratford 7/7/44.
Parkeston 16/5/48.
Stratford 23/7/50.
Parkeston 8/4/51.
Stratford 6/2/55.
Parkeston 13/11/60.
Stratford 1/1/61.

RENUMBERED:
  7338 8/12/25.
  8500 20/10/46.
  68500 10/3/51.

CONDEMNED: 13/1/61.
Cut up at Stratford.

_____

7339

Stratford.

To traffic 5/1890.
Class R24 - passenger.

REPAIRS:
Str. 26/8—24/10/04.**G.**
Rebuilt to Class R24 Rbt.
Str. 3/10/16—11/1/17.**G.**
Str. 1/11/19—20/3/20.**G.**
Str. 9/5—15/8/22.**G.**
At 1/1/23: J69/1. Westinghouse
brake. Condensing apparatus.
Str. 13/5—17/8/24.**G.**
Vacuum ejector fitted.
Str. 11/6—16/10/26.**G.**
*Westinghouse replaced by steam
and vacuum ejector. Condensing
apparatus removed. Additional
rails on bunker.*
Str. 1/4—17/7/29.**G.**

Str. 1/6—20/7/31.**G.**
Str. 30/7—3/9/32.**H.**
Str. 27/7—6/9/35.**G.**
Str. 24/3—5/8/39.**G.**
Rebuilt to J67/2.
Str. 10/7—7/8/40.**L.**
Damage by enemy action.
Str. 18/4—22/5/42.**G.**
Str. 11/6—22/7/44.**G.**
Str. 26/5—30/6/46.**G.**
Rebuilt to J69/1.
Str. 25/11—20/12/48.**L.**
Str. 27/11/49—7/1/50.**G.**
Str. 18/11—18/12/52.**G.**
Str. 3/10—10/11/56.**G.**

BOILERS:
  339.
  339 *(new)* 24/10/04.
  392 *(ex7392)* 11/1/17.
  47 *(exJ68 7047)* 20/3/20.
  2976 *(ex7394)* 16/10/26.
  30 *(ex7194)* 17/7/29.
  26 *(ex7354)* 20/7/31.
  3059 *(ex7053)* 6/9/35.
  2814 *(exJ67 7207)* 5/8/39.
  2857 *(exJ66 7288)* 22/5/42.
  3170 *(new)* 30/6/46.
  23757 *(ex?)* 18/12/52.
  23815 *(ex68507)* 10/11/56.

SHEDS:
Stratford.
Lincoln 12/11/26.
Immingham 19/11/26.
Retford 5/5/27.
Stratford 2/8/33.
Ipswich 11/2/36.
Norwich 13/3/40.
Melton Constable 17/9/45.
Norwich 19/5/46.
Ipswich 14/7/46.
Norwich 10/9/46.
Boston 26/7/53.
Lincoln 9/6/57.

RENUMBERED:
  7339 17/8/24.
  8501 1/12/46.
  68501 18/12/48.

CONDEMNED: 17/4/61.
Into Doncaster for c/u: 16/8/60.

_____

7340

Stratford.

To traffic 5/1890.
Class R24 - passenger.

REPAIRS:
Str. ?/?—?/12/03.**G.**
Rebuilt to Class R24 Rbt.

Str. 9/10/13—26/2/14.**G.**
Str. 15/3—13/9/18.**G.**
Str. 28/3—12/9/22.**G.**
At 1/1/23: J69/1. Westinghouse
brake. Condensing apparatus.
Str. 11/8—22/11/24.**G.**
Str. 23/9—24/12/26.**G.**
Additional rails on bunker.
Str. 19/10/28—11/1/29.**G.**
Str. 13/9—3/10/29.**G.**
*Westinghouse brake replaced
by steam and vacuum ejector.
Condensing apparatus and
steam heating removed.*
Str. 19/1—21/3/31.**G.**
Str. 3/11—10/12/34.**G.**
Str. 3/3—11/4/38.**G.**
Str. 10/8—10/9/41.**G.**
Str. 28/5—29/7/44.**G.**
Str. 1/3—21/4/47.**G.**
Str. 7—27/5/50.**G.**
Str. 10/2—7/3/53.**G.**
Str. 17/11—22/12/56.**G.**

BOILERS:
  340.
  340 *(new)* ?/12/03.
  394 *(ex7394)* 13/9/18.
  2980 *(ex7363)* 22/11/24.
  3012 *(ex7351)* 11/1/29.
  2972 *(exJ68 7046)* 21/3/31.
  2951 *(ex7269)* 10/12/34.
  2996 *(exJ68 7032)* 11/4/38.
  3073 *(ex7055)* 10/9/41.
  3079 *(ex7194)* 29/7/44.
  3178 *(new)* 21/4/47.
  3206 *(new)* 27/5/50.
  23763 *(ex?)* 7/3/53.
  23817 *(ex68573)* 22/12/56.

SHEDS:
Stratford.
Immingham 23/10/29.
Ipswich 11/2/36.
Bury St Edmunds 5/6/38.
King's Lynn 10/2/46.
Retford 1/6/58.
Doncaster 9/11/58.
Retford 5/7/59.

RENUMBERED:
  7340 22/11/24.
  8502 7/10/46.
  68502 27/5/50.

CONDEMNED: 6/2/61.
Into Doncaster for c/u: 6/2/61.

_____

7341

Stratford.

To traffic 5/1890.
Class R24 - passenger.

REPAIRS:
Str. 6/6—13/10/02.**G.**
Rebuilt to Class R24 Rbt.
Str. 3/8—28/12/17.**G.**
At 1/1/23: J69/1. Westinghouse
brake. Condensing apparatus.
Str. 29/10/23—29/2/24.**G.**
Vacuum ejector fitted.
Str. ?/?—?/11/28.**G.**
*Additional rails on bunker.
Condensing apparatus removed.*
Cow. ?/?—30/3/29.**L.**
Cow. ?/?—10/9/32.**G.**
Cow. ?/?—15/1/33.**H.**
Cow. ?/?—23/8/37.**G.**
Cow. ?/?—26/4/41.**H.**
Cow. ?/?—5/7/43.**L.**
Cow. ?/?—25/9/43.**H.**
Cow. ?/?—2/11/44.**L.**
Cow. 15/5—6/6/47.**G.**
Cow. 13—18/12/48.**L.**
Cow. 14/11—10/12/49.**H/I.**
Cow. 3—28/9/52.**G.**
Cow. 2—13/2/53.**N/C.**
Cow. 23/10—13/11/54.**C/L.**

BOILERS:
  341.
  341 *(new)* 13/10/02.
  50 *(exJ68 7050)* 28/12/17.
  39 *(new)* 29/2/24.
  39 reno.C1687 30/3/29.
  C1686 *(ex7338)* 10/9/32.
  C1831 *(new)* 23/8/37.
  C1701 *(ex8505)* 6/6/47.
  23867 *(ex68551)* 28/9/52.

SHEDS:
Stratford.
Eastfield 19/11/28.
Stirling *by* 1/4/29.
Parkhead 11/9/32.
Eastfield ?/?.
Parkhead ?/3/33.

RENUMBERED:
  341E 29/2/24.
  7341 ?/11/28. ???
  8503 10/11/46.
  68503 10/12/49.

CONDEMNED: 3/1/57.
Cut up at Cowlairs ?

_____

7342

Stratford.

To traffic 5/1890.
Class R24 - passenger.

REPAIRS:
Str. 4/3—30/9/02.**G.**
Rebuilt to Class R24 Rbt.

Ex works 7th June 1946, No.8587, a J67 with 1000 gallons tanks, was fitted with a Diagram 37 boiler working at 180lb and with safety valves ahead of the firebox. In the 1946 stock alterations it was simply changed to J69.

Following No.8587, another eleven small tank J67 were similarly re-boilered but not until 14th March 1950 was Part 2 of J69 introduced to identify them. These eleven were 8585 (1st September 1947), 68591 (9th November 1948), 68520 (4th February 1950), 68510 (10th March 1950), 68522 (22nd March 1950), 68519 (22nd April 1950), 68517 (10th February 1951), 68498 (18th August 1951), 68512 (24th February 1951), 68513 (12th June 1952) and finally 68588 (27th June 1953).

Ex works 19th September 1953, No.68517 had a Diagram 39 boiler and so reverted to J67 but it was the only one to do so. These changes caused difficulties in recording and despite the J67 proof by the safety valve position, J69/2 was still shown on the buffer beam.

The remaining eleven then stayed as J69 Part 2 through to withdrawal.

No.7336 as No.68498, ex works 18th August 1951, had then been given a new Diagram 37 boiler and so became a J69 Part 2. It was the last J69 with the original 1000 gallons tank capacity and this was retained to its 16th September 1962 condemnation as Departmental No.44 which it had become from 21st of August 1959.

Unlike the shunters, J69 engines had the boiler handrails continued along the smokebox and above the door. Only two exceptions were noted, Nos.7056 in 1938 (see page 154, top) and 68520 in 1956 (see page 165, centre).

7342 cont./
Str. 5/1—24/4/18.**G**.
Str. 18/12/22—16/6/23.**G**.
At 1/1/23: *J69/1. Westinghouse brake. condensing apparatus.*
Str. 6/5—23/8/27.**G**.
Westinghouse brake replaced by steam. Additional rails on bunker. Condensing apparatus removed.
Cow. 19/10/27—?/?.**?**.
Cow. ?/?—6/9/30.**G**.
Cow. ?/?—25/5/33.**H**.
Cow. ?/?—26/10/35.**L**.
Cow. ?/?—7/10/36.**G**.
Cow. ?/?—10/8/40.**G**.
Cow. ?/?—6/6/42.**G**.
Cow. 24/5—21/6/47.**G**.
Cow. 7/4—16/5/52.**G**.
Cow. 23—24/10/52.**N/C**.
Cow. 18—19/11/53.**N/C**.

BOILERS:
   342.
   342 *(new)* 30/9/02.
   2969 *(new)* 24/4/18.
   2950 *(ex7193)* 16/6/23.
   2982 *(exStr & 7270)* 6/9/30.
   C1687 *(ex7057)* 10/8/40.
   C1829 *(ex7391)* 6/6/42.
   C1831 *(ex8503)* 21/6/47.
   23865 *(ex68567)* 16/5/52.

SHEDS:
Stratford.
Thornton Jct. 13/10/27.
Dunfermline ?/?2/42.
Thornton Jct. 12/1/46.

RENUMBERED:
   7342 *after* 16/6/23.
   8504 3/11/46.
68504 16/5/52.

CONDEMNED: 23/1/56.
Cut up at Cowlairs.

_____

7343

Stratford.

To traffic 5/1890.
Class R24 - passenger.

REPAIRS:
Str. 22/1—1/9/03.**G**.
Rebuilt to Class R24 Rbt.
Str. 21/5—7/10/20.**G**.
At 1/1/23: *J69/1. Westinghouse brake. Condensing apparatus.*
Str. ?/?—?/7/23.**G**.
Str. 27/1—28/4/28.**G**.
Westinghouse brake replaced by steam.

Additional rails on bunker.
Condensing apparatus removed.
Cow. ?/?—3/11/31.**G**.
Cow. ?/?—24/2/34.**G**.
Cow. ?/?—6/12/35.**H**.
Cow. ?/?—18/2/38.**H**.
Cow. ?/?—24/11/38.**L**.
Cow. 14/12/40—11/1/41.**G**.
Cow. ?/?—20/11/43.**H**.
Inv.   ?/?—2/12/44.**H**.
Cow. 24/3—12/4/47.**G**.
Cow. 31/1—26/2/51.**H/I**.

BOILERS:
   343.
   343 *(new)* 1/9/03.
   3000 *(new)* 7/10/20.
   3044 *(new)* 28/4/28.
   3044 reno.C1689 3/11/31.
   C1690 *(ex7347)* 24/2/34.
   C1701 *(ex7374)* 11/1/41.
   3161 *(new)* 12/4/47.
   3161 reno.23877 26/2/51.

SHEDS:
Stratford.
St Margarets 12/5/28.
Dumfries 9/7/52.

RENUMBERED:
   7343 *after* 31/1/25..
   8505 3/11/46.
68505 24/2/51.

CONDEMNED: 11/11/53.
Cut up at Cowlairs.

_____

7344

Stratford.

To traffic 5/1890.
Class R24 - passenger.

REPAIRS:
Str. ?/?—?/4/1900.**G**.
Str. 15/5—14/11/13.**G**.
Rebuilt to Class R24 Rbt.
Str. 3/6—14/10/22.**G**.
At 1/1/23: *J69/1. Westinghouse brake. Condensing apparatus.*
Str. 12/11/24—30/1/25.**G**.
Str. 17/11/27—31/3/28.**G**.
Additional rails on bunker.
Condensing apparatus removed.
Str. 26/5—25/7/30.**G**.
Str. 5/3—16/4/35.**G**.
Vacuum ejector fitted.
Str. 21/3—23/4/38.**G**.
Longmoor. 28/10/39.**L**.
Vacuum ejector removed.

BOILERS:
   344.

344 *(new)* ?/4/1900.
344 *(new)* 14/11/13.
3017 *(ex7381)* 30/1/25.
2998 *(ex7196)* 25/7/30.
3092 *(new)* 16/4/35.
2970 *(ex7269)* 23/4/38.

SHEDS:
Stratford.
Norwich 2/10/26.
Yarmouth 19/5/29.
Stratford 21/8/29.
Norwich 9/9/35.
Yarmouth 17/5/36.
Norwich 3/6/37.
Yarmouth 23/3/39.
Stratford 9/10/39.
WD Longmoor 14/10/39 *(o/l)*.

RENUMBERED:
7344 30/1/25.

SOLD TO W.D.: 19/10/40.
Sold to Steelbreaking & Dismantling Co., Chesterfield 3/1947 as WD 70088. C/u 1949.

_____

7345

Stratford.

To traffic 5/1890.
Class R24 - passenger.

REPAIRS:
Str. 15/1—14/8/03.**G**.
Rebuilt to Class R24 Rbt.
Str. 18/7—15/12/16.**G**.
Str. 14/12/22—6/3/23.**G**.
At 1/1/23: *J69/1. Westinghouse brake. Condensing apparatus.*
Str. 29/10—13/12/24.**G**.
Str. 7/7—30/9/27.**G**.
Additional rails on bunker.
Str. 20/12/29—8/2/30.**G**.
Westinghouse replaced by steam and vacuum ejector. Condensing apparatus removed.
Str. 1/12/31—10/1/32.**G**.
Str. 1—20/7/36.**G**.
Str. 15/8—2/10/40.**G**.
Str. 13/10—1/11/40.**L**.
Str. 6—15/5/42.**H**.
Str. 6/8—30/9/44.**G**.
Str. 5/11—17/12/48.**G**.
Str. 23/4—16/5/52.**G**.
Str. 26/8—12/10/56.**G**.
Str. 2/6/60. *Not repaired.*

BOILERS:
   345.
   345 *(new)* 14/8/03.
   2963 *(new)* 15/12/16.
   3020 *(new)* 6/3/23.

2961 *(ex7090)* 8/2/30.
3065 *(new)* 10/1/32.
3012 *(ex7354)* 20/7/36.
2964 *(exJ68 7034)* 2/10/40.
3021 *(exJ68 7026)* 15/5/42.
3099 *(exJ68 8643)* 17/12/48.
23815 *(new)* 16/5/52.
23805 *(exJ68 68648)* 12/10/56.

SHEDS:
Stratford.
Parkeston 25/9/39.
Stratford 8/9/40.
Parkeston 8/6/46.
Stratford 7/12/46.
New England 9/10/55.
Doncaster 4/12/55.

RENUMBERED:
   7345 13/12/24.
   8507 16/11/46.
68507 11/12/48.

CONDEMNED: 6/6/60.
Cut up at Stratford.

_____

7346

Stratford.

To traffic 5/1890.
Class R24 - passenger.

REPAIRS:
Str. 12/10/03—13/2/04.**G**.
Rebuilt to Class R24 Rbt.
Str. 10/3—10/7/20.**G**.
Str. 3/10—9/12/22.**G**.
Str. 20/9/24—17/1/25.**G**.
Str. 2/12/26—12/2/27.**G**.
Str. 20/12/29—15/2/30.**G**.
Westinghouse brake replaced by steam and vacuum ejector. Additional rails on bunker. Condensing apparatus removed.
Str. 15/2—9/3/34.**G**.
Str. 30/3—10/8/39.**G**.
Str. 25/7—28/8/43.**G**.
Str. 31/10—17/11/45.**L**.
Str. 13/10—13/11/46.**G**.
Str. 23/11/49—28/1/50.**G**.
Str. 8/6—8/8/53.**G**.
Str. 22/2—29/3/57.**G**.

BOILERS:
   346.
   346 *(new)* 13/2/04.
   2991 *(new)* 10/7/20.
   3028 *(exJ68 7035)* 12/2/27.
   35 *(exJ68 7040)* 15/2/30.
   2974 *(exJ68 7047)* 9/3/34.
   3082 *(ex7167)* 10/8/39.
   2976 *(ex7060)* 28/8/43.
   3054 *(exJ68 8651)* 13/11/46.

(top) **Until 1925 the Macallan variable blast pipe was standard on the passenger engines. The forward rod controlled that and the other was for the condensing apparatus.**

(above) **From 1925 the variable blast pipes were taken off and replaced by the plain type.**

(left) **Steam heating apparatus for carriage warming was put on from 1924 and there was a connecting hose at both ends.**

Until 1926 the bunker top had three open coal rails of flat bar iron.

Between 17th April 1926 and 20th June 1930, all had the coal rail spaces closed by the fitting of three more rails into the spaces.

7346 cont./
23775 *(ex?)* 8/8/53.
23787 *(ex68498)* 29/3/57.

SHEDS:
Stratford.
Doncaster 20/5/31.
Stratford 15/6/37.
Parkeston 6/7/37.
Stratford 25/9/39.
Hitchin 10/11/39.
Stratford 11/5/40.
Parkeston 25/11/44.
Stratford 8/6/46.
Colchester 1/11/53.
Stratford 29/1/56.
Retford 14/10/56.
Doncaster 5/10/58.

RENUMBERED:
7346 17/1/25.
8508 7/11/46.
68508 28/1/50.

CONDEMNED: 2/2/61.
Into Doncaster for c/u: 2/2/61.

7347

Stratford.

To traffic 2/1892.
Class R24 - passenger.

REPAIRS:
Str. ?/?—?/2/1899.**G**.
Str. 25/8/04—6/2/05.**G**.
Rebuilt to Class R24 Rbt.
Woolwich Ar. 9/1—6/10/20.**G**.
At 1/1/23: *J69/1. Westinghouse brake. Condensing apparatus.*
Str. 31/5—?/7/24.**L**.
Vacuum ejector fitted.
Str. 2/11/25—5/2/26.**G**.
Str. ?/?—?/8/28.**G**.
Additional rails on bunker.
Condensing apparaus removed.
Cow. ?/?—28/9/28.**L**.
Cow. ?/?—9/9/33.**G**.
Cow. ?/?—24/5/34.**H**.
Cow. ?/?—20/4/35.**H**.
Cow. ?/?—7/5/37.**H**.
Cow. ?/?—26/11/38.**G**.
Cow. ?/?—5/9/42.**H**.
Cow. ?/?—28/8/43.**L**.
Cow. 13/9—11/10/45.**G**.
Cow. 28/9—12/10/46.**L**.
Cow. 6—24/9/48.**G**.
Cow. 30/4—31/5/52.**G**.
Cow. 24/10—19/11/55.**H/I**.

BOILERS:
347.
347 *(new)* ?/2/1899.

347 *(new)* 6/2/05.
267 *(ex7267)* 6/10/20.
42 *(exJ68 7049)* 5/2/26.
42 reno.C1690 circa 1930.
C1684 *(ex7089)* 9/9/33.
3029 *(exStr & 7382)* 26/11/38.
3153 *(new exStr)* 11/10/45.
23881 *(new)* 31/5/52.

SHEDS:
Stratford.
Parkeston ?/?.
Polmont 13/9/25.

RENUMBERED:
7347 ?/7/24.
8524 10/10/46.
68524 24/9/48.

CONDEMNED: 16/6/59.
Cut up at Cowlairs 27/11/59.

7348

Stratford.

To traffic 2/1892.
Class R24 - passenger.

REPAIRS:
Str. 17/9/03—16/1/04.**G**.
Rebuilt to Class R24 Rbt.
Str. 5/3—6/7/16.**G**.
Str. 11/4—31/8/21.**G**.
At 1/1/23: *J69/1. Westinghouse brake. Condensing apparatus.*
Str. 8/3—5/5/23.**G**.
Str. 19/3—1/7/25.**G**.
Str. 22/9—22/12/27.**G**.
Vacuum ejector fitted. Additional rails on bunker. Condensing apparatus removed.
Cow. 10—18/2/28.**N/C**.
Footsteps and bunker handrails fitted.
Cow. 25/12/29—23/1/30.**G**.
Cow. 12/1—13/2/32.**G**.
Cow. 19/7—2/9/33.**G**.
Cow. 23/8—4/10/39.**G**.
Cow. 11/11—5/12/42.**H/I**.
Cow. 13/5—7/6/47.**G**.
Str. 4/12/53. *Not repaired.*

BOILERS:
348.
348 *(new)* 16/1/04.
2960 *(new)* 6/7/16.
2952 *(ex7058)* 31/8/21.
2998 *(ex7375)* 1/7/25.
2992 *(ex7086)* 22/12/27.
2992 reno.C1691 23/1/30.
3011 *(ex7379)* 4/10/39.
3166 *(new)* 7/6/47.

SHEDS:
Stratford.
Scottish Area 7/2/28.
St Margarets 19/2/28.
Aberdeen Ferryhill ?/6/34.
Thornton Jct. 14/11/34.
Carlisle Canal 28/2/40.
St Margarets 16/12/46.
Kittybrewster 18/3/51.
Lincoln 6/1/52.

RENUMBERED:
7348 1/7/25.
8525 12/1/47.

CONDEMNED: 14/12/53.
Cut up at Stratford.

7349

Stratford.

To traffic 3/1892.
Class R24 - passenger.

REPAIRS:
Str. ?/?—?/6/04.**G**.
Rebuilt to Class R24 Rbt.
Str. 24/3—6/7/16.**G**.
At 1/1/23: *J69/1. Westinghouse brake. Condensing apparatus.*
Str. 20/1—17/3/23.**G**.
Str. 19/11/24—14/3/25.**G**.
Str. 25/3—18/6/27.**G**.
Additional rails on bunker.
Str. 25/10—30/11/29.**G**.
Westinghouse brake replaced by steam and vacuum ejector. Condensing apparatus removed.
Str. 22/8—23/9/32.**G**.
Str. 5/9—2/10/36.**G**.
Str. ?/4—25/5/40.**G**.
Str. 4—24/10/42.**G**.
Str. 14/7—30/8/44.**G**.
Str. 29/8—9/10/48.**G**.
Str. 24/3—10/4/52.**G**.
Str. 26/3—12/5/56.**G**.

BOILERS:
349.
349 *(new)* ?/6/04.
2959 *(new)* 6/7/16.
190 *(ex7392)* 18/6/27.
3018 *(ex7053)* 30/11/29.
32 *(exJ68 7037)* 23/9/32.
38 *(ex7090)* 2/10/36.
34 *(exJ68 7036)* 25/5/40.
3191 *(new)* 9/10/48.
23812 *(new)* 10/4/52.
23729 *(exJ68 68663)* 12/5/56.

SHEDS:
Stratford.
Boston 17/12/29.

Grantham 14/12/32.
Stratford 27/4/40.
Parkeston 10/2/45.
Stratford 8/3/47.
Parkeston 1/11/59.
Stratford 24/1/60.

RENUMBERED:
7349 14/3/25.
8526 24/11/46.
68526 9/10/48.

CONDEMNED: 3/10/60.
Cut up at Stratford.

7350

Stratford.

To traffic 3/1892.
Class R24 - passenger.

REPAIRS:
Str. 1/10/09—4/1/10.**G**.
Rebuilt to Class R24 Rbt.
Str. 26/7—20/12/18.**G**.
Str. 1/9—17/11/21.**G**.
At 1/1/23: *J69/1. Westinghouse brake. Condensing apparaus.*
Str. 11/6—14/10/24.**G**.
Str. 4/11/26—5/2/27.**G**.
Str. 10/2—17/3/28. **H**.
Str. 21/12/28—15/3/29.**G**.
Westinghouse brake replaced by steam and vacuum ejector. Additional rails on bunker. Condensing apparatus removed.
Str. 13/2—29/3/32.**G**.
Str. 14/10—8/11/35.**G**.
Str. 23—28/2/38.**L**.
Spark arrestor fitted.
Str. 5/1—24/7/39.**G**.
Str. 17/12/42—20/2/43.**G**.
Str. 12/8—21/11/46.**G**.
Str. 15/12/49—4/2/50.**G**.
Str. 21/9—17/10/53.**G**.

BOILERS:
350.
350 *(new)* 4/1/10.
2976 *(new)* 20/12/18.
2974 *(ex7394)* 14/10/24.
3038 *(new)* 5/2/27.
2999 *(ex7058)* 29/3/32.
31 *(exJ68 7036)* 8/11/35.
3023 *(ex7196)* 24/7/39.
2964 *(ex7345)* 20/2/43.
3093 *(ex7395)* 21/11/46.
23784 *(ex?)* 17/10/53.

SHEDS:
Stratford.
Trafford Park 8/4/29.
Grantham 26/7/32.

Until after Grouping all the boilers had 4-column Ramsbottom safety valves mounted on the rear ring of the barrel ahead of the firebox.

The LNER standardized on Ross 'pop' safety valves and put some of these on in place of Ramsbottom. Ex works 16th June 1925, No.7356 had the boiler built in 1914 for J68 No.28 which had been so changed.

All boilers built by the LNER from 1926 had the Ross 'pop' valves mounted directly on the boiler, and on Stratford maintained engines, usually without a casing at their base.

Unlike the shunters, J69 class did not have the whistle at the side of the safety valves but on a standpipe just in front of the cab.

In BR days the Stratford habit of enclosing safety valves spread to the 'pop' type, and a number had these covers put on.

The building by the LNER of many N7 class displaced J69 off the London suburban services and between 22nd July 1926 (No.7385) and 28th April 1933 (No.7055), fifty-nine class J69 became shunters, condensing apparatus was taken off. Lever reverse replaced screw, a steam brake was fitted and the Westinghouse pump and piping removed. Most of them had the destination board bracket removed from smokebox door and the back of the bunker.

7350 cont./
Boston 30/1/36.
Ardsley 7/8/40.
New England 26/9/44.
Boston 18/2/46.
Colwick 15/4/47.
Stratford 27/11/49.
Parkeston 17/9/50.
Stratford 18/2/51.
New England 9/10/55.
Retford 4/12/55.

RENUMBERED:
7350 14/10/24.
8527 22/12/46.
68527 4/2/50.

CONDEMNED: 20/6/58.
Cut up at Stratford.

7351

Stratford.

To traffic 3/1892.
Class R24 - passenger.

REPAIRS:
Str. ?/?—?/12/03.**G.**
Rebuilt to Class R24 Rbt.
Str. 11/4—25/8/21.**G.**
At 1/1/23: *J69/1. Westinghouse
brake. Condensing apparatus.*
Str. 6/7—8/9/23.**G.**
Str. 12/6—19/8/25.**G.**
Str. 17/8—19/12/28.**G.**
*Westinghouse brake replaced
by steam. Additional rails on
bunker. Condensing apparatus
removed.*
Str. 4/3—12/4/33.**G.**
Str. 17/12/36—29/1/37.**G.**
Gor. 7/10—22/11/41.**G.**
Str. 20/11—22/12/44.**G.**
Str. 25/1—5/3/48.**G.**
Str. 6/9—6/10/51.**G.**
Str. 29/9—29/10/54.**G.**
Str. 15/11—7/12/57.**G.**

BOILERS:
　351.
　351 (new) ?/12/03.
3012 (new) 25/8/21.
3032 (ex7085) 19/12/28.
3048 (ex7054) 12/4/33.
　32 (ex7349) 29/1/37.
2966 (ex7383 & sp) 22/11/41.
3057 (ex7369) 22/12/44.
3053 (ex8574) 5/3/48.
23719 (ex?) 6/10/51.
23803 (ex68534) 29/10/54.
23746 (ex68513) 7/12/57.

SHEDS:
Stratford.
Gorton 12/1/29.
Brunswick 15/1/29.
Trafford Park 21/4/33.
Brunswick 14/9/34.
Trafford Park 29/1/37.
Brunswick 11/5/37.
Gorton 11/10/41.
Walton-on-the-Hill 22/11/41.
Boston 31/3/43.
Lincoln 7/10/51.

RENUMBERED:
7351 19/8/25.
8528 31/8/46.
ᴇ**8528** 5/3/48.
68528 6/10/51.

CONDEMNED: 28/10/59.
Cut up at Stratford.

7352

Stratford.

To traffic 3/1892.
Class R24 - passenger.

REPAIRS:
Str. ?/?—?/2/1900.**G.**
Str. 28/2—29/8/06.**G.**
Rebuilt to Class R24 Rbt.
Str. 10/10/22—3/3/23.**G.**
At 1/1/23: *J69/1. Westinghouse
brake. Condensing apparatus.*
Str. 8/11/24—24/1/25.**G.**
Str. 18/2—19/5/27.**G.**
Str. 18/5—22/7/29.**G.**
*Westinghouse brake replaced
by steam. Additional rails on
bunker. Condensing apparatus
removed.*
Str. 19/12/32—3/2/33.**G.**
Str. 31/8—7/10/38.**G.**
Rebuilt to J67/2.
Gor. 23/3—9/5/42.**G.**
Str. 23/7—20/10/45.**G.**
Str. 1/2—23/3/48.**G.**
Str. 17/9—13/10/51.**G.**
Str. 26/4—22/5/54.**G.**
Rebuilt to J69/1.
Str. 7/2—15/3/57.**C/H.**
Str. 14—28/5/57.**C/L.**

BOILERS:
　352.
　352 (new) ?/2/1900.
　352 (new) 29/8/06.
　192 (ex7192) 3/3/23.
2997 (ex7376) 19/5/27.
2994 (ex7056) 22/7/29.
3068 (new) 3/2/33.
2909 (exJ66 7326) 7/10/38.

2911 (exJ67 7019) 20/10/45.
2855 (exJ67 8509) 23/3/48.
23911 (ex?) 13/10/51.
23702 (ex68566) 22/5/54.

SHEDS:
Stratford.
Lincoln 12/8/29.
Immingham 21/7/30.
Louth 19/9/31.
Immingham 26/7/35.
Lincoln 15/6/37.
Ardsley 24/3/39.
Gorton 28/9/40.
Bidston 2/10/40.
Trafford Park 6/12/40.
Ardsley 3/12/42.
New England 6/8/43.
Frodingham 31/1/45.
New England 25/5/45.
Boston 3/7/45.
Lincoln 25/11/45.
Frodingham 7/4/46.
Lincoln 19/5/46.
Hitchin 26/7/53.
Stratford 30/5/54.
King's Lynn 25/9/55.
Cambridge 6/11/55.
Stratford 19/2/56.

RENUMBERED:
7352 24/1/25.
8529 1/9/46.
68529 23/3/48.

CONDEMNED: 18/8/58.
Cut up at Stratford.

7353

Stratford.

To traffic 3/1892.
Class R24 - passenger.

REPAIRS:
Str. ?/?—?/12/04.**G.**
Rebuilt to Class R24 Rbt.
Str. 24/12/14—27/4/15.**G.**
Str. 16/10—29/12/22.**G.**
At 1/1/23: *J69/1. Westinghouse
brake. Condensing apparatus.*
Str. 25/6—25/10/24.**G.**
Str. 26/8—9/12/26.**G.**
Additional rails on bunker.
Str. 27/7—16/11/28.**G.**
*Westinghouse brake replaced by
steam. Condensing apparatus
removed.*
Str. 22/5—9/7/32.**G.**
Str. 5/7—20/8/35.**G.**
Vacuum ejector fitted.
Str. 23/2—18/3/38.**G.**
Str. 26/11/39—16/1/40.**G.**

Str. 28/6—1/8/44.**G.**
Str. 24/11/46—10/1/47.**G.**
Str. 31/1—2/4/47.**L.**
Str. 10/12/49—7/1/50.**C/L.**
Str. 10/9—10/10/50.**G.**
Str. 30/9—31/10/53.**G.**
Str. 27/11/56—19/1/57.**G.**

BOILERS:
　353.
　353 (new) ?/12/04.
2954 (new) 27/4/15.
3009 (ex7371) 9/12/26.
　338 (ex7338) 16/11/28.
3014 (exJ68 7034) 9/7/32.
3039 (exJ68 7026) 20/8/35.
3064 (ex7328) 18/3/38.
　37 (exJ68 7035) 16/1/40.
2984 (exJ68 7022) 1/8/44.
3048 (exJ68 7048) 10/1/47.
23701 (ex?) 10/10/50.
23703 (exJ68 68659) 31/10/53.
23763 (ex68502) 19/1/57.

SHEDS:
Stratford.
Gorton 22/12/28.
Brunswick 1/1/29.
Gorton 18/12/31.
Trafford Park 21/12/31.
March 6/9/35.
Cambridge 10/2/43.
South Lynn 8/12/48.
Cambridge 21/12/48.
Darnall 23/2/58.
Barrow Hill 20/4/58.
Retford 25/5/58.
Doncaster 5/10/58.
Retford 5/7/59.

RENUMBERED:
7353 25/10/24.
8530 14/12/46.
68530 7/1/50.

CONDEMNED: 14/2/61.
Into Doncaster for c/u: 14/2/61.

7354

Stratford.

To traffic 3/1892.
Class R24 - passenger.

REPAIRS:
Str. 22/1—27/10/03.**G.**
Rebuilt to Class R24 Rbt.
Str. 9/7/20—19/3/21.**G.**
Str. 22/11/22—10/2/23.**G.**
At 1/1/23: *J69/1. Westinghouse
brake. Condensing apparatus.*
Str. 30/3—25/6/25.**G.**

Not all lost these brackets when changed to shunter as shown by No.7369, and on bunker of No.7379 *see* page 153, centre.

No.7367 became a shunter with steam brake only from 17th August 1929 and was renumbered No.8543 on 19th May 1946. Despite this inability to work passenger trains it kept its destination board brackets until it was taken out of running stock on 2nd November 1959.

In 1930/31, ten engines, Nos.7083, 7084, 7085, 7168, 7266, 7267, 7269, 7270, 7361 and 7373 were fitted with trip cock gear for working the East London line and they retained condensing apparatus so that they could work under the Thames to the Southern Railway. From 1927 most of the others had their condensing apparatus removed.

Until June 1930 all had a typical Great Eastern stovepipe chimney with a half round beaded edge at its top.

Str. 13/1—31/3/28.**G.**
7354 cont./
Additional rails on bunker.
Str. 23/8—10/9/29.**G.**
*Westinghouse brake replaced
by steam and vacuum ejector.
Condensing apparatus removed.*
Str. 22/3—6/6/31.**G.**
Str. 20/11/34—14/1/35.**G.**
Str. 1/3—2/4/38.**G.**
Gor. 15—23/9/39.**L.**
Chimney shortened.
Gor. 17/11/40—22/2/41.**G.**
Gor. 2—23/10/43.**G.**
Rebuilt to J67/2.
Gor. 1/12/46—8/1/47.**L.**
Gor. 30/11/47—22/1/48.**G.**
Gor. 13—27/5/50.**G.**
Gor. 9/12/50.**C/L.**
Firehole ring welded.
Gor. 12/9—17/10/53.**G.**

BOILERS:
354.
354 *(new)* 27/10/03.
3003 *(new)* 19/3/21.
26 *(exJ68 7026)* 31/3/28.
3012 *(ex7340)* 6/6/31.
3080 *(new)* 14/1/35.
3077 *(ex7052)* 2/4/38.
2898 *(ex7366)* 23/10/43.
2900 *(ex8540)* 22/1/48.
2868 *(ex8547)* 27/5/50.
2868 reno. 23951 9/12/50.
23955 *(ex?)* 17/10/53.

SHEDS:
Stratford.
Doncaster 18/9/29.
Trafford Park 13/1/32.
Walton-on-the-Hill 2/2/33.
Gorton 2/2/35.
Wrexham 25/9/39.
Trafford Park 3/5/40.
Wrexham 22/2/41.
Walton-on-the-Hill 1/2/42.
Gorton 28/11/43.
Walton-on-the-Hill 19/11/44.
Gorton 25/2/45.
Walton-on-the-Hill 16/2/47.
Wrexham 4/9/47.

RENUMBERED:
7354 25/6/25.
8531 6/10/46.
ᴇ8531 22/1/48.
68531 25/6/49.

CONDEMNED: 3/10/55.*Into
Gorton for c/u:* 8/10/55,
c/u 12/11/55.

7355

Stratford.

To traffic 3/1892.
Class R24 - passenger.

REPAIRS:
Str. 18/2—10/6/04.**G.**
Rebuilt to Class R24 Rbt.
Str. 5/10/17—22/2/18.**G.**
Str. 23/11/21—24/2/22.**G.**
At 1/1/23: J69/1. Westinghouse
brake. Condensing apparatus.
Str. 21/4—12/7/24.**G.**
Vacuum ejector fitted.
Str. 24/2—23/4/26.**G.**
Additional rails on bunker.
Str. 2/5—1/8/28.**G.**
Str. ?/?—?/3/30.**?.**
Condensing apparatus removed.
Str. 31/5—18/7/30.**G.**
Condensing apparatus refitted.
Str. 7/11—12/12/32.**G.**
Str. 7/2—21/3/35.**G.**
Str. 25/8—21/9/37.**G.**
Str. 2/5—3/6/40.**G.**
Trip cocks fitted.
Str. 11/1—5/2/43.**L.**
Str. 17/3—28/4/44.**G.**
Str. 28/1—29/3/47.**G.**
Str. 22/10—25/11/50.**G.**
Str. 7—12/5/51.**C/L.**
Str. 3/10—12/11/55.**G.**

BOILERS:
355.
355 *(new)* 10/6/04.
341 *(ex7341)* 22/2/18.
3033 *(new)* 12/7/24.
3001 *(ex7357)* 1/8/28.
2955 *(ex7373)* 12/12/32.
2987 *(ex7389)* 21/3/35.
3078 *(ex7393)* 21/9/37.
3020 *(ex7274)* 3/6/40.
3081 *(exJ68 7049)* 28/4/44.
3085 *(exJ68 8664)* 29/3/47.
23704 *(ex?)* 25/11/50.
23793 *(ex?)* 12/11/55.

SHEDS:
Stratford.
Parkeston 10/12/26.
Stratford 21/3/35.
Stratford Works 16/12/58.

RENUMBERED:
7355 12/7/24.
8532 23/11/46.
68532 25/11/50.
DEPT'L 43 9/1/59.

WITHDRAWN: 16/12/58.
CONDEMNED: 21/8/59.
Cut up at Stratford.

7356

Stratford.

To traffic 3/1892.
Class R24 - passenger.

REPAIRS:
Str. ?/?—?/12/1899.**G.**
Str. 17/8—20/11/11.**G.**
Rebuilt to Class R24 Rbt.
Str. 17/9—18/12/19.**G.**
At 1/1/23: J69/1. Westinghouse
brake. Condensing apparatus.
Str. 13/2—16/6/25.**G.**
Str. ?/?—?/2/28.**G.**
*Vacuum ejector fitted. Additional
rails on bunker. Condensing
apparatus removed.*
Cow. ?/?—?/4/28.**N/C.**
*Footsteps and bunker handrails
fitted.*
Cow. ?/?—10/5/32.**G.**
Cow. ?/?—28/9/34.**G.**
Cow. ?/?—23/10/37.**L.**
Cow. 15/2—18/3/40.**G.**
Cow. 27/4—19/5/43.**L.**
Cow. 10/7—9/8/44.**G.**
Cow. 30/12/46—22/1/47.**G.**
Cow. 15/4—24/5/47.**L.**
Cow. 13/4—13/5/49.**H/I.**

BOILERS:
356.
356 *(new)* ?/12/1899.
356 *(new)* 20/11/11.
270 *(ex7270)* 18/12/19.
28 *(exJ68 7028)* 16/6/25.
28 reno. C1692 circa 1930.
C1830 *(new)* 28/9/34.
C1691 *(ex7348)* 18/3/40.
C1696 *(ex7338)* 9/8/44.
3019 *(exStr. & 7379)* 22/1/47.

SHEDS:
Stratford.
Norwich 2/10/26.
Stratford 15/1/27.
St Margarets 23/3/28.
Dunfermline ?/11/40.
Thornton Jct. ?/2/42.
Eastfield 4/4/43.
Polmont 8/9/43.
Dumfries 13/5/52.
St Margarets 9/7/52.
Bathgate 8/10/52 *(as S.B.)*.
St Margarets 14/7/53.

RENUMBERED:
7356 16/6/25.
8533 1/12/46.
68533 13/5/49.

CONDEMNED: 14/7/53.
Cut up at Cowlairs.

7357

Stratford.

To traffic 4/1892.
Class R24 - passenger.

REPAIRS:
Str. ?/?—?/12/04.**G.**
Rebuilt to Class R24 Rbt.
Str. 7/5—22/10/20.**G.**
At 1/1/23: J69/1. Westinghouse
brake. Condensing apparatus.
Str. 25/7—23/3/23.**G.**
Str. 26/1—12/5/25.**G.**
Str. 20/1—11/4/28.**G.**
*Westinghouse brake replaced
by steam. Additional rails on
bunker. Condensing apparatus
removed.*
Cow. 11—17/5/28.**N/C.**
*Footsteps and bunker handrails
fitted.*
Cow. 13/2—20/7/31.**G.**
Cow. 5/7—25/8/34.**G.**
Cow. 16/3—16/4/38.**G.**
Cow. 10/6—7/7/43.**G.**
Str. 18—30/8/44.**L.**
After collision.
Str. 1/5—30/6/47.**G.**
Str. 11/3—7/4/51.**G.**

BOILERS:
357.
357 *(new)* ?/12/04.
3001 *(new)* 22/10/20.
2956 *(ex7196)* 11/4/28.
C1698 *(ex7376)* 20/7/31.
3018 *(ex7358)* 16/4/38.
C1692 *(ex7337)* 7/7/43.
3183 *(new)* 30/6/47.
23803 *(new)* 7/4/51.

SHEDS:
Stratford.
Scottish Area 7/5/28.
Thornton Jct. 18/5/28.
Stratford 7/6/44.

RENUMBERED:
7357 12/5/25.
8534 26/9/46.
68534 7/4/51.

CONDEMNED: 30/8/54.
Cut up at Stratford.

7358

Stratford.

To traffic 4/1892.
Class R24 - passenger.

Beginning with No.7361, ex works 20th June 1930, a cast iron North Eastern pattern 2½ inches shorter chimney was fitted on engines which Stratford maintained, but the twenty transferred to the Scottish Area in 1928/9 all retained the stovepipe.

Until 1933 the wooden roof on the cab had only a shallow arch and the rain strips at each edge were straight.

Starting in 1933 the Stratford maintained engines had the wood cab roof replaced by a steel one of higher arched profile, and on which the rain strips were curved to divert the water to run off only at each corner.

Twenty engines were sent to Scotland during 1927-28, ten (Nos.7057, 7342, 7343, 7357, 7358, 7368, 7374, 7379, 7386, 7392) had been altered to steam brake only whilst the other ten (Nos.7089, 7337, 7338, 7341, 7347, 7348, 7356, 7375, 7376, 7391) had Westinghouse brake with vacuum ejector for alternative train braking. No.68551 (ex7375) was one of the latter. Note that its front sandbox carried the number plate and had an inspection door on the side, both peculiar to Cowlairs after Nationalisation.

(left) The engines in Scotland kept their wooden cab roofs, and with two exceptions did so on those returned to being maintained by Stratford. No.7392 went to Scottish area 14th October 1927 and on 25th August 1946 was re-numbered 8568. On 27th January 1952 it returned to work on the Eastern Region and despite a general repair at Stratford, 7th April 1956, kept a wood roof to its 8th May 1958 withdrawal, though it did get a cast iron chimney.

(below) The twenty sent to Scottish Area during 1927-28 all made an early visit to Cowlairs to be fitted with the shunters steps and handrails on the lower part of the bunker. No.7348 went north on 7th February 1928 and was in Cowlairs 10th to18th February for steps and rails to be added before allocation on 19th February to St. Margarets shed.

114

7358 cont.
REPAIRS:
Str.   ?/?—?/1/1900.**G.**
Str.   ?/?—?/12/04.**G.**
Rebuilt to Class R24 Rbt.
Str.   12/5—13/9/17.**G.**
At 1/1/23: *J69/1. Westinghouse*
brake. Condensing apparatus.
Str.   17/3—18/9/23.**G.**
Str.   ?/?—?/3/28.**G.**
Westinghouse brake replaced
by steam. Additional rails on
bunker. Condensing apparatus
removed.
Cow.   ?/?—31/12/32.**G.**
Cow.   ?/?—17/5/35.**G.**
Cow.   19/6—13/7/37.**G.**
Cow.   ?/?—10/8/40.**H.**
Cow.   ?/?—31/8/40.**L.**
Inv.   6/1—24/2/45.**H.**
Cow.   5—30/10/48.**G.**
Cow.   17/3—25/4/54.**G.**
Not in use for 156 days in 1944.

BOILERS:
   358.
   358 *(new)* ?/1/1900.
   358 *(new)* ?/12/04.
   339 *(ex7339)* 13/9/17.
   3022 *(new)* 18/9/23.
   3022 reno. C1694 circa 1930.
   3018 *(exStr.7349)* 31/12/32.
   3096 *(new exStr.)* 13/7/37.
   3070 *(ex8623)* 30/10/48.
   23876 *(ex68544)* 25/4/54.

SHEDS:
Stratford.
Kipps 31/3/28.
Burntisland *before* 14/6/30.
Thornton Jct. 22/7/33.
Dundee 12/7/54.

RENUMBERED:
   7358 *before* ?/3/28.
   8535 25/8/46.
68535 30/10/48.

CONDEMNED: 20/8/59.
Cut up at Cowlairs 25/12/59.

_____

7359

Stratford.

To traffic 4/1892.
Class R24 - passenger.

REPAIRS:
Str. ?/?—?/6/04.**G.**
Rebuilt to Class R24 Rbt.
At 1/1/23: *J69/1. Westinghouse*
brake. Condensing apparatus.
Str. 2/1—28/4/23.**G.**

Str. 14/10—29/11/24.**G.**
Str. 6/1—12/3/27.**G.**
Additional rails on bunker.
Str. 25/10—7/12/29.**G.**
Westinghouse brake replaced
by steam and vacuum ejector.
Condensing apparatus removed.
Str. 25/5—11/7/34.**G.**
Str. 7/5—8/9/39.**G.**
Rebuilt to J67/2.
Str. 8/12/43—5/1/44.**G.**
Str. 25/8—29/9/46.**G.**
Str. 13/5—24/6/49.**G.**
Str. 5/9—4/10/52.**G.**
Str. 14/12/55—17/2/56.**G.**

BOILERS:
   359.
   359 *(new)* ?/6/04.
   3021 *(new)* 28/4/23.
   2983 *(ex7056)* 12/3/27.
   2976 *(ex7339)* 7/12/29.
   2985 *(ex7360)* 11/7/34.
   2854 *(exJ67 7403)* 8/9/39.
   2906 *(ex7190)* 5/1/44.
   2863 *(exJ66 7323)* 29/9/46.
   2907 *(exJ67 8515)* 24/6/49.
   23926 *(ex?)* 4/10/52.
   23914 *(exJ66 68383)* 17/2/56.

SHEDS:
Stratford.
Lincoln 4/1/30.
Louth 31/1/30.
Doncaster 4/11/30.
March 27/3/36.
King's Lynn 4/4/36.
Cambridge 4/5/39.
Melton Constable 14/3/48.
Norwich 28/4/48.
Melton Constable 14/8/49.

RENUMBERED:
   7359 29/11/24.
   8536 7/4/46.
68536 24/6/49.

CONDEMNED: 21/2/58.
Cut up at Stratford.

_____

7360

Stratford.

To traffic 4/1892.
Class R24 - passenger.

REPAIRS:
Str. 23/4—17/11/03.**G.**
Rebuilt to Class R24 Rbt.
Str. 9/4—26/6/20.**G.**
Str. 8/8—21/10/22.**G.**
At 1/1/23: *J69/1. Westinghouse*
brake. Condensing apparatus.

Str. 15/12/24—14/2/25.**G.**
Str. 18/7—7/10/27.**G.**
Additional rails on bunker.
Str. 22/10—5/12/28.**G.**
Str. 18/12/28—25/1/29.**L.**
Westinghouse brake replaced by
steam. Condensing apparatus
removed.
Str. 19/2—24/4/31.**G.**
Str. 23/4—1/6/34.**G.**
Str. 6/8—10/9/37.**G.**
Str. 9—14/4/38.**L.**
Str. 2/6—27/7/40.**G.**
Rebuilt to J67/2.
Str. 5/4—20/7/43.**G.**
Str. 5—27/10/45.**G.**
Rebuilt to J69/1.
Str. 29/2—22/4/48.**G.**
Str. 24/8—15/9/51.**G.**
Str. 18/10—19/11/54.**G.**

BOILERS:
   360.
   360 *(new)* 17/11/03.
   2990 *(new)* 26/6/20.
   3010 *(ex7058)* 7/10/27.
   2985 *(ex7331)* 24/4/31.
   3079 *(new)* 1/6/34.
   3007 *(ex7055)* 10/9/37.
   2905 *(exJ67 7016)* 27/7/40.
   2879 *(exJ67 7262)* 20/7/43.
   3092 *(ex7387)* 27/10/45.
   3057 *(ex8528)* 22/4/48.
   23809 *(new)* 15/9/51.
   23719 *(ex68528)* 19/11/54.

SHEDS:
Stratford.
Lincoln 4/2/29.

RENUMBERED:
   7360 14/2/25.
   8537 31/3/46.
68537 22/4/48.

CONDEMNED: 20/6/58.
Cut up at Stratford.

_____

7361

Stratford.

To traffic 4/1892.
Class R24 - passenger.

REPAIRS:
Str. ?/?—?/9/1899.**G.**
Str. 29/3—6/10/06.**G.**
Rebuilt to Class R24 Rbt.
Str. 5/11/20—24/3/21.**G.**
Str. 9/10—14/12/22.**G.**
At 1/1/23: *J69/1. Westinghouse*
brake. Condensing apparatus.
Str. 3/6—26/7/24.**G.**

Str. 15/12/26—9/4/27.**G.**
Vacuum ejector fitted.
Str. 7/4—20/6/30.**G.**
Additional rails on bunker.
Str. ?/?—13/5/31.**L.**
Trip cocks fitted.
Str. 20/2—27/3/35.**G.**
Str. 3/8—15/9/39.**G.**
Str. 12—28/3/42.**L.**
Str. 8/12/42—15/1/43.**G.**
Str. 13/8—12/9/46.**G.**
Str. 31/3—1/4/47.**N/C.**
Trip cocks refitted.
Str. 14/9—13/10/49.**G.**
Str. 26/4—13/5/50.**C/L.**
Str. 20/4—29/5/53.**G.**
Str. 5/2—9/3/57.**G.**

BOILERS:
   361.
   361 *(new)* ?/9/1899.
   361 *(new)* 6/10/06.
   3004 *(new)* 24/3/21.
   2974 *(ex7350)* 9/4/27.
   195 *(ex7195)* 20/6/30.
   3088 *(new)* 27/3/35.
   3101 *(ex7269)* 15/9/39.
   3017 *(exJ68 7043)* 15/1/43.
   3175 *(new)* 12/9/46.
   3041 *(exJ68 8639)* 13/10/49.
   23709 *(ex68495)* 29/5/53.
   23737 *(exJ68 68660)* 9/3/57.

SHEDS:
Stratford.
Doncaster 28/4/27.
Mexborough 25/2/28.
Doncaster 12/5/28.
Stratford 21/4/31.

RENUMBERED:
   7361 26/7/24.
   8538 1/6/46.
68538 13/10/49.

CONDEMNED: 10/9/61.
Cut up at Stratford.

_____

7362

Stratford.

To traffic 4/1892.
Class R24 - passenger.

REPAIRS:
Str. ?/?—?/12/01.**G.**
Str. 7/9/16—29/3/17.**G.**
Rebuilt to Class R24 Rbt.
Str. 5/9—20/12/21.**G.**
At 1/1/23: *J69/1. Westinghouse*
brake. Condensing apparatus.
Str. 14/10/24—22/1/25.**G.**
Str. 2/6—27/8/27.**G.**

These shunters aids were fitted on both sides of the engine, note that No.7057 was one which kept the brackets for the destination boards despite their then being quite useless.

(centre) Nos.7338 and 7357 were returned to the GE Section in 1944 in exchange for Class J67 Nos.7329 and 7399, which were required at Galashiels to work the lightly laid Lauder branch. Despite for subsequent General repairs at Stratford works, No.7338 (later 68500) kept its low cab roof to withdrawal on 13th January 1961 but did get a cast iron chimney and had the NBR type shunters footsteps removed. No.7357 (68534) was treated in like fashion except that the steps were retained. It was withdrawn 30th August 1954.

(below) Nine more returned south during 1951-52 (Nos.68499, 8525, 68550, 68552, 68555, 68567, 68568, 68623, 68635) leaving a further nine (Nos.68503, 68504, 68505, 68524, 68533, 68535, 68544, 68551, 68562) which remained in Scotland until withdrawn, the last one being No.68535 from Dundee shed on 20th August 1959. No.68552 (ex7376) returned south on 17th February 1952 and when shopped at Stratford 3rd March 1956, came out with a steel cab roof and cast iron chimney. Its NBR style cab footsteps were removed (the only one of the nine so altered) and the only evidence of Cowlairs attention was the horizontal handrail left on the bunker and the backing plates behind the coal rails. No.68555 (7379) was the only other ex Scottish J69 that received a new steel roof at Stratford, but it kept its stovepipe chimney. No.68520 is a J69 Part 2, i.e. with small tanks.

By the end of the LNER the GER stovepipes had seen twenty years use in the Scottish Area and were in increasing need of replacement.

When this 13th April 1952 photograph was taken, No.8504 was about to go to Cowlairs because its GE stovepipe had a hole in the side under the rim.

7362 cont./
Additional rails on bunker.
Str. 21/3—2/5/30.**G.**
Str. 20/2—2/4/35.**G.**
Vacuum ejector fitted.
Str. 30/1—2/3/38.**G.**
Longmoor. 28/10/39.**L.**
Vacuum ejector removed.

BOILERS:
362.
362 *(new)* ?/12/01.
2965 *(new)* 29/3/17.
24 *(exJ68 7024)* 22/1/25.
3019 *(ex7389)* 2/5/30.
3089 *(new)* 2/4/35.
3105 *(new)* 2/3/38.

SHEDS:
Cambridge.
Stratford 20/1/25.
Peterborough East 1/10/27.
Boston 8/7/29.
Peterborough East 20/9/29.
Stratford 16/12/29.
Colchester 26/3/39.
W.D. Longmoor 14/10/39 *(o/l)*.
Stratford 3/12/39 *paper transfer.*

RENUMBERED:
7362 22/1/25.

SOLD: To W.D. 19/10/40.
*Last seen as WD 70089 at
Cairnryan in July 1947, ultimate
fate unknown.*

_____

7363

Stratford.

To traffic 5/1892.
Class R24 - passenger.

REPAIRS:
Str. ?/?—?/12/04.**G.**
Rebuilt to Class R24 Rbt.
Str. 25/10/18—17/4/19.**G.**
Str. 16/8—28/10/22.**G.**
At 1/1/23: *J69/1. Westinghouse
brake. Condensing apparatus.*
Str. 17/6—3/10/24.**G.**
Str. 23/2—17/4/26.**G.**
Additional rails on bunker.
Str. 30/12/27—8/3/28.**G.**
Str. 23/8—13/9/29.**G.**
*Westinghouse brake replaced
by steam and vacuum ejector.
Condensing apparatus and
steam heat removed.*
Str. 9/7—12/9/31.**G.**
Gor. 10/4—13/7/32.**H.**
Str. 16/5—21/6/35.**G.**
Str. 28/11/38—19/1/39.**G.**

Rebuilt to J67/2.
Gor. 22/5—27/6/42.**G.**
Gor. 19/11—30/12/44.**G.**
Str. 29/8—21/11/47.**G.**
Gor. 6/2—11/3/48.**L.**
Gor. 20/12/49—25/1/50.**C/L.**
Gor. 10/10—11/11/50.**H/I.**
Gor. 14/10—8/11/52.**G.**
Str. 29/12/55. *Not repaired.*

BOILERS:
363.
363 *(new)* ?/12/04.
2980 *(new)* 17/4/19.
3034 *(new)* 3/10/24.
30 *(ex7339)* 12/9/31.
3016 *(exJ68 7028)* 21/6/35.
2900 *(exJ67 7202)* 19/1/39.
2913 *(exJ66 8375)* 21/11/47.
2913 reno. 23950 11/11/50.
23953 *(exJ67 68584)* 8/11/52.

SHEDS:
Stratford.
Gorton 4/10/29.
Trafford Park 8/10/29.
Brunswick 3/3/33.
Trafford Park 20/5/35.
Brunswick 17/12/36.
Trafford Park 11/5/37.
Lincoln 8/2/53.
Hitchin 26/7/53.

RENUMBERED:
7363 3/10/24.
8540 19/5/46.
E8540 11/3/48.
68540 5/2/49.

CONDEMNED: 16/1/56.
Cut up at Stratford.

_____

7364

Stratford.

To traffic 5/1892.
Class R24 - passenger.

REPAIRS:
Str. ?/?—?/11/1900.**G.**
Str. 24/8/18—14/5/19.**G.**
Rebuilt to Class R24 Rbt.
At 1/1/23: *J69/1. Westinghouse
brake. Condensing apparatus.*
Str. 16/2—28/5/24.**G.**
Str. ?/?—?/2/27.**G.**
Str. ?/?—?/7/29.**G.**
Additional rails on bunker.

BOILERS:
364.
364 *(new)* ?/11/1900.
2981 *(new)* 14/5/19.

2951 *(ex7054)* 28/5/24.
2984 *(exJ67 7332)* ?/7/29.

SHEDS:
Colchester.
Stratford 12/8/29..

RENUMBERED:
7364 28/5/24.

CONDEMNED: 21/1/31 *after
collision at Northumberland
Park.*
Cut up at Stratford.

_____

7365

Stratford.

To traffic 5/1892.
Class R24 - passenger.

REPAIRS:
Str. 27/8—7/12/04.**G.**
Rebuilt to Class R24 Rbt.
At 1/1/23: *J69/1. Westinghouse
brake. Condensing apparatus.*
Str. 14/11/23—26/2/24.**G.**
Str. 11/6—30/9/26.**G.**
*Westinghouse brake replaced
by steam and vacuum ejector.
Additional rails on bunker.
Condensing apparatus removed.*
Str. 25/1—26/4/29.**G.**
Str. 9/1—20/3/31.**G.**
Str. 27/8—8/10/34.**G.**
Str. 9/5—3/6/38.**G.**
Str. 26/8—27/9/41.**G.**
Str. 8/9—5/10/44.**G.**
Str. 24/10—6/12/48.**G.**
Str. 3—22/3/52.**G.**
Str. 26/4—11/6/55.**G.**

BOILERS:
365.
365 *(new)* 7/12/04.
191 *(ex7191)* 26/2/24.
3015 *(ex7373)* 20/3/31.
2976 *(ex7359)* 8/10/34.
3090 *(exJ68 7030)* 3/6/38.
3025 *(ex7393)* 27/9/41.
3031 *(ex7390)* 5/10/44.
3086 *(ex8545)* 6/12/48.
23810 *(new)* 22/3/52.

SHEDS:
Stratford.
Immingham 10/11/26.
Lincoln ?/?.
King's Cross 8/10/34.
Hitchin 16/8/36.
Lincoln 26/7/53.

RENUMBERED:
7365 26/2/24.
8541 7/9/46.
68541 6/12/48.

CONDEMNED: 12/8/58.
Cut up at Stratford.

_____

7366

Stratford.

To traffic 5/1892.
Class R24 - passenger.

REPAIRS:
Str. 21/6—21/9/05.**G.**
Rebuilt to Class R24 Rbt.
Str. 3/8—30/12/16.**G.**
Str. 9/10/22—10/3/23.**G.**
At 1/1/23: *J69/1. Westinghouse
brake. Condensing apparatus.*
Str. 21/1—13/3/25.**G.**
Str. 13/8—11/11/26.**G.**
Heating apparatus fitted.
Str. 18/9—13/12/28.**G.**
*Westinghouse brake replaced
by steam. Additional rails on
bunker. Condensing apparatus
and steam heating removed.*
Str. 26/5—15/7/31.**G.**
Str. 23/9—30/10/34.**G.**
Gor. 21/3—24/6/39.**G.**
Rebuilt to Class J67/2.
Gor. 20/11—13/12/41.**L.**
Gor. 23/5—9/7/43.**G.**
Rebuilt to J69/1.
Str. 21/1—17/2/45.**G.**
Str. 11/8—9/9/46.**L.**
Str. 10/10—16/11/48.**G.**
Str. 24/2—15/3/52.**G.**
Str. 15/6—30/7/55.**C/L.**
Str. 4/12/56—5/1/57.**G.**

BOILERS:
366.
366 *(new)* 21/9/05.
2964 *(new)* 30/12/16.
3010 *(ex7360)* 15/7/31.
2959 *(ex7052)* 30/10/34.
2898 *(exJ65 7151)* 24/6/39.
32 *(ex spare & 7351)* 9/7/43.
3163 *(new)* 17/2/45.
3196 *(new)* 16/11/48.
23741 *(ex?)* 15/3/52.
23883 *(ex68570)* 5/1/57.

SHEDS:
Stratford.
Gorton 12/1/29.
Bidston 16/1/29.
Trafford Park 20/6/29.
Brunswick 17/4/31.
Trafford Park 26/5/31.

7366 cont./
Walton-on-the-Hill 2/11/31.
Trafford Park 31/7/41.
Gorton 30/11/41.
Trafford Park 22/12/41.
New England 9/7/43.
South Lynn 6/4/44.
Cambridge 16/11/47.
King's Lynn 3/12/47.
South Lynn 2/5/48.
King's Lynn 27/7/58.
Stratford 24/7/60.

RENUMBERED:
7366 13/3/25.
8542 26/9/46.
68542 13/11/48.

CONDEMNED: 16/9/62.
Cut up at Stratford.

7367

Stratford.

To traffic 4/1894.
Class R24 - passenger.

REPAIRS:
Str. 27/5—25/8/04.**G.**
Rebuilt to Class R24 Rbt.
Str. 28/5—18/11/20.**G.**
Str. 23/10—22/12/22.**G.**
At 1/1/23: J69/1. Westinghouse
brake. Condensing apparatus.
Str. 24/6—18/10/24.**G.**
Str. 28/1—28/4/27.**G.**
Str. 26/6—17/7/28.**G.**
Additional rails on bunker.
Str. 11/7—17/8/29.**G.**
Westinghouse brake replaced by
steam. Condensing apparatus
and steam heating removed.
Str. 26/7—3/10/30.**G.**
Str. 18/1—23/2/35.**G.**
Str. 29/8—11/10/38.**G.**
Spark arrestor fitted.
Str. 5/1—20/2/42.**G.**
Str. 11/9—11/10/44.**G.**
Str. 10/12/45—17/1/46.**G.**
Str. 13/5—11/6/49.**G.**
Str. 19/7—22/8/52.**G.**
Str. 22/7—25/8/56.**G.**
Str. 2/11—16/12/59.**G.**

BOILERS:
367.
367 *(new)* 25/8/04.
2999 *(new)* 19/11/20.
38 *(exJ68 7045)* 28/4/27.
3020 *(ex7345)* 3/10/30.
3034 *(exJ68 7045)* 23/2/35.
3087 *(exJ68 7033)* 11/10/38.
3086 *(exJ68 7023)* 20/2/42.

3047 *(ex7087)* 11/10/44.
3066 *(exJ68 8656)* 11/6/49.
23816 *(new)* 22/8/52.
23823 *(new)* 25/8/56.
23823 reno. SB3387 16/12/59.

SHEDS:
Stratford.
Hitchin 6/12/30.
Doncaster 26/5/31.
Ardsley 16/7/36.
Doncaster 18/3/37.
Boston 9/6/37.
Stratford 26/5/57.
Lincoln 1/6/58.
Stratford works 16/12/59.

RENUMBERED:
7367 18/10/24.
8543 19/5/46.
68543 11/6/49.
DEPT'L 45 2/11/59.

WITHDRAWN: 2/11/59, and
after undergoing a 'shopping' at
Stratford, it was put to work as
a replacement for Dept'l No.31
(J66 68382).

CONDEMNED: 16/9/62.
Cut up at Stratford.

7368

Stratford.

To traffic 4/1894.
Class R24 - passenger.

REPAIRS:
Str. 16/6—6/11/06.**G.**
Rebuilt to Class R24 Rbt.
Str. 19/9/20—9/4/21.**G.**
At 1/1/23: J69/1. Westinghouse
brake. Condensing apparatus.
Str. 9/3—15/6/28.**G.**
Westinghouse brake replaced
by steam. Add. rails on bunker.
Condensing apparatus removed.
Cow. ?/?—25/2/33.**G.**
Cow. ?/?—12/3/35.**H.**
Cow. ?/?—15/6/36.**L.**
Cow. ?/?—1/2/38.**G.**
Cow. ?/?—22/4/39.**L.**
Cow. ?/?—13/7/40.**H.**
Cow. ?/?—31/8/40.**L.**
Cow. ?/?—12/3/41.**L.**
Cow. ?/?—19/7/41.**L.**
Cow. ?/?—19/4/42.**L.**
Cow. ?/?—3/4/43.**G.**
Inv. ?/?—24/2/45.**H.**
Cow. 19/2—7/3/47.**G.**
Cow. 9—26/8/49.**G.**
Cow. 30/6—15/8/52.**G.**

BOILERS:
368.
368 *(new)* 6/11/06.
3006 *(new)* 9/4/21.
3000 *(ex7343)* 15/6/28.
3000 reno.C1695 circa 1930.
C1694 *(ex7358)* 25/2/33.
C1686 *(ex7341)* 1/2/38.
C1687 *(ex7342)* 3/4/43.
3160 *(new)* 7/3/47.
23872 *(ex8504)* 15/8/52.

SHEDS:
Stratford.
Polmont 19/7/28.

RENUMBERED:
7368 ?/?/??.
8544 6/10/46.
68544 26/8/49.

CONDEMNED: 31/1/55.
Cut up at Cowlairs.

7369

Stratford.

To traffic 4/1894.
Class R24 - passenger.

REPAIRS:
Str. ?/?—?/12/04.**G.**
Rebuilt to Class R24 Rbt.
Str. 27/10/14—5/3/15.**G.**
At 1/1/23: J69/1. Westinghouse
brake. Condensing apparatus.
Str. 8/9—22/11/23.**G.**
Str. 5/3—2/6/26.**G.**
Str. ?/?—4/2/27. **L.**
Steam heating fitted.
Str. 26/5—15/9/28.**G.**
Additional rails on bunker.
Str. 15/7—15/8/29.**G.**
Westinghouse brake replaced by
steam. Condensing apparatus
and steam heating removed.
Str. 29/5—4/7/32.**G.**
Str. 7/5—11/6/37.**G.**
Vacuum ejector fitted.
Str. 5/3—8/4/41.**G.**
Str. 28/10—18/11/44.**G.**
Str. 3/10—13/11/48.**G.**
Str. 5—19/1/52.**G.**
Str. 19/9—15/10/54.**G.**
Str. 23/6—9/8/57.**G.**

BOILERS:
369.
369 *(new)* ?/12/04.
2953 *(new)* 5/3/15.
3050 *(new)* 15/9/28.
2973 *(ex7167)* 4/7/32.
35 *(ex7389)* 11/6/37.

3057 *(ex7268)* 8/4/41.
3086 *(ex7367)* 18/11/44.
3172 *(ex8565)* 13/11/48.
23732 *(ex?)* 19/1/52.
23802 *(ex68494)* 15/10/54.
23709 *(ex68538)* 9/8/57.

SHEDS:
Stratford.
King's Lynn 4/1/49.
South Lynn 11/5/58.
King's Lynn 1/6/58.
Lincoln 27/7/58.
Colwick 25/1/59.

RENUMBERED:
369E 22/11/23.
7369 *by* 29/9/24.
8545 5/10/46.
68545 13/11/48.

CONDEMNED: 3/2/61.
Into Doncaster for c/u: 3/2/61.

7370

Stratford.

To traffic 5/1894.
Class R24 - passenger.

REPAIRS:
Str. 5/10/4—11/1/05.**G.**
Rebuilt to Class R24 Rbt.
Str. 24/3—14/7/21.**G.**
At 1/1/23: J69/1. Westinghouse
brake. Condensing aparatus.
Str. 9/1—7/7/23.**G.**
Str. 27/6—15/10/25.**G.**
Str. 23/6—2/10/28.**G.**
Westinghouse brake replaced
by steam. Add. rails on bunker.
Condensing apparatus removed.
Str. 24/9—6/11/31.**G.**
Str. 3/8—19/9/34.**G.**
Str. 6/10—2/12/39.**G.**
Str. 11/4—28/5/40.**G.**
Str. 17/4—13/5/44.**G.**
Str. 11/5—10/6/47.**G.**
Str. 2—31/10/51.**G.**
Str. 24/12/56—26/1/57.**G.**

BOILERS:
370.
370 *(new)* 11/1/05.
3011 *(new)* 14/7/21.
3014 *(ex7052)* 15/10/25.
2996 *(ex7374)* 2/10/28.
3062 *(ex7090)* 19/9/34.
3102 *(exJ68 7038)* 2/12/39.
2985 *(ex7395)* 13/5/44.
3181 *(new)* 10/6/47.
23722 *(ex?)* 31/10/51.
23703 *(ex68530)* 26/1/57.

Ex Cowlairs 16th May 1952 after a 'General' 68504 had a Cowlairs version of a stovepipe put on. This seems to have been riveted to the existing base, and it had a flat beading around the top. Note the plates now fixed on the sandbox.

No.68562 got a similar change when ex Cowlairs 20th April 1954 from a Heavy Intermediate repair, as had been given to 68551 at a General repair, ex works 19th May 1952, *see* page 114, top.

Stratford had needed to deal with some cast chimneys during and soon after the War. Ex works 14th April 1945, No.7165 had a stovepipe put outside the existing cast base and riveted to it. At the top they still used half-round beading.

No.7365 had been given the same treatment when ex Stratford 5th October 1944 and appears to have a shorter chimney. Its number was changed to 8541 on 7th September 1946.

7370 cont./
SHEDS:
Stratford.
Gorton 6/11/28.
Trafford Park 14/11/28.
Brunswick 11/2/31.
Gorton 21/4/31.
Brunswick 18/12/31.
King's Cross 19/9/34.
Stratford 19/10/34.
Ardsley 27/5/35.
Hatfield 7/9/44.
King's Cross 1/10/44.
New England 31/1/45.
Boston 30/9/45.
New England 18/2/46.
Stratford 1/9/49.

RENUMBERED:
7370 15/10/25.
8546 29/9/46.
68546 31/10/51.

CONDEMNED: 5/5/58.
Cut up at Stratford.

_____

7371

Stratford.

To traffic 5/1894.
Class R24 - passenger.

REPAIRS:
Str. 8/11/06—5/3/07.**G.**
Rebuilt to Class R24 Rbt.
Str. 11/2—5/5/21.**G.**
Str. 16/8—2/11/22.**G.**
At 1/1/23: J69/1. Westinghouse
brake. Condensing apparatus.
Str. 6/3—14/6/24.**G.**
Vacuum ejector fitted.
Str. 6/8—24/12/26.**G.**
*Westinghouse brake replaced
by steam. Add. rails on bunker.
Condensing apparatus and
steam heating removed.*
Str. 18/8—17/10/29.**G.**
Str. 8/12/30—13/2/31.**G.**
Str. 6/3—7/4/33.**G.**
Str. 12/7—26/8/36.**G.**
Gor. 1/3—27/5/39.**G.**
Gor. 20/2—7/4/44.**G.**
Rebuilt to J67/2.
Gor. 14/12/47—16/2/48.**G.**
Gor. 23/12/50—13/1/51.**G.**

BOILERS:
371.
371 *(new)* 5/3/07.
3009 *(new)* 5/5/21.
47 *(ex7339)* 24/12/26.
36 *(ex7335)* 17/10/29.
3045 *(exJ68 7049)* 13/2/31.

2991 *(ex7271)* 7/4/33.
3056 *(exJ68 7049)* 26/8/36.
2868 *(ex7086)* 7/4/44.
2898 *(ex8531)* 16/2/48.
23952 *(ex?)* 13/1/51.

SHEDS:
Stratford.
Walton-on-the-Hill 17/1/27.
Retford 28/2/28.
Stratford 13/3/33.
Wigan 22/6/33.
Trafford Park 14/4/34.
Walton-on-the-Hill 27/5/39.
Brunswick 23/8/40.
Gorton 16/4/44.
Brunswick 10/9/44.
Widnes 22/5/50.
Brunswick ?/5/51.
Wrexham 5/9/53.
Brunswick 7/11/53.

RENUMBERED:
7371 14/6/24.
8547 22/9/46.
E8547 16/2/48.
68547 2/4/49.

CONDEMNED: 16/4/56.
Into Gorton for c/u: 21/4/56. C/u
2/6/56.

_____

7372

Stratford.

To traffic 5/1894.
Class R24 - passenger.

REPAIRS:
Str. 5/10/04—17/1/05.**G.**
Rebuilt to Class R24 Rbt.
Str. 11/1—25/7/18.**G.**
Str. 12/12/21—11/3/22.**G.**
At 1/1/23: J69/1. Westinghouse
brake. Condensing apparatus.
Str. 31/1—6/5/24.**G.**
Vacuum ejector fitted.
Str. 25/1—26/3/26.**G.**
Str. 16/6—5/10/28.**G.**
Additional rails on bunker.
Str. 30/3—30/5/31.**G.**
Str. 30/11—20/12/33.**G.**
Str. 6/11—6/12/35.**G.**
Str. 3—28/7/38.**G.**
Str. 1—4/8/39.**L.**
Trip cocks fitted, ex 7083.
Str. 4/4—12/5/42.**G.**
Str. 28/2—8/4/46.**G.**
Str. 20—21/3/47.**N/C.**
Trip cocks re-fitted.
Str. 4/1—9/2/48.**H.**
Str. 25/10—10/12/49.**G.**
Str. 21/10/53. *Not repaired.*

BOILERS:
372.
372 *(new)* 17/1/05.
380 *(new7380)* 25/7/18.
2970 *(ex7388)* 6/5/24.
3056 *(ex7165)* 30/5/31.
391 *(exJ68 7042)* 20/12/33.
2990 *(exJ68 7050)* 6/12/35.
3089 *(ex7362)* 28/7/38.
3104 *(ex7265)* 12/5/42.
3168 *(new)* 8/4/46.

SHEDS:
Stratford.
Cambridge 15/1/29.
Stratford 6/12/35.
Colchester 16/5/48.
Stratford 8/8/48.

RENUMBERED:
7372 6/5/24.
8548 6/4/46.
E8548 9/2/48.
68548 10/12/49.

CONDEMNED: 9/11/53.
Cut up at Stratford.

_____

7373

Stratford.

To traffic 5/1894.
Class R24 - passenger.

REPAIRS:
Str. 2/8—23/11/06.**G.**
Rebuilt to Class R24 Rbt.
Str. 4/4—12/8/22.**G.**
At 1/1/23: J69/1. Westinghouse
brake. Condensing apparatus.
Str. 30/6—30/8/24.**G.**
Vacuum ejector fitted.
Str. 27/6—19/8/25.**L.**
Str. 11/8—24/12/26.**G.**
Additional rails on bunker.
Str. 29/4—10/5/30.**N/C.**
Trip cocks fitted.
Str. 4/11—19/12/30.**G.**
Str. 10/10—14/11/32.**G.**
Str. 10/2—19/3/37.**G.**
Str. 6/7—14/8/41.**G.**
Str. 24/12/44—19/1/45.**G.**
Str. 22—25/3/47.**N/C.**
Trip cocks re-fitted.
Str. 11/2—19/3/48.**H.**
Str. 4/1—9/2/49.**G.**
Str. 28/1—28/2/52.**G.**
Str. 2/12/54—8/2/55.**C/L.**
Str. 12/11—8/12/56.**G.**

BOILERS:
373.
373 *(new)* 23/11/06.

3015 *(new)* 12/8/22.
2955 *(ex7060)* 19/12/30.
3052 *(ex7335)* 14/11/32.
3069 *(ex7051)* 19/3/37.
3071 *(exJ68 7031)* 14/8/41.
3038 *(ex7378)* 19/1/45.
3073 *(exJ68 8658)* 19/3/48.
23738 *(ex?)* 28/2/52.
23739 *(ex68569)* 8/12/56.

SHED:
Stratford.

RENUMBERED:
7373 30/8/24.
8549 25/5/46.
E8549 19/3/48.
68549 9/2/49.

CONDEMNED: 11/2/62.
Cut up at Stratford.

_____

7374

Stratford.

To traffic 6/1894.
Class R24 - passenger.

REPAIRS:
Str. 5/10/04—13/1/05.**G.**
Rebuilt to Class R24 Rbt.
Str. 26/4—28/7/20.**G.**
Str. 4/4—2/6/22.**G.**
At 1/1/23: J69/1. Westinghouse
brake. Condensing apparatus.
Str. 16/3—27/6/25.**G.**
Str. 12/4—23/7/28.**G.**
*Westinghouse brake replaced
by steam. Add. rails on bunker.
Condensing apparatus removed.*
Cow. 21—24/8/28.**N/C.**
*Footsteps and bunker handrails
fitted.*
Cow. 15/4—15/5/31.**G.**
Cow. 2/3—6/4/32.**H.**
Cow. 25/8—5/9/32.**L.**
Cow. 14/12/34—4/2/35.**G.**
Cow. 3—23/10/40.**G.**
Cow. 2—8/11/40.**L.**
Inv. 5/4—25/5/45.**G.**
Cow. 3/4—5/5/50.**G.**
Str. 7/3—28/4/56.**G.**
Str. 17/2—8/3/58.**C/H.**
Don. 25/7/61. *Not repaired.*

BOILERS:
374.
374 *(new)* 13/1/05.
2996 *(new)* 28/7/20.
2969 *(ex7190)* 23/7/28.
2969 *reno.C1696* 15/5/31.
C1701 *(ex7391)* 4/2/35.
2982 *(ex7342)* 23/10/40.

7374 cont./
3096 *(ex8535)* 5/5/50.
23752 *(ex68553)* 28/4/56.
23803 *(ex68528)* 8/3/58.

SHEDS:
Stratford.
Cambridge 17/11/26.
Scottish Area 15/8/28.
Thornton Jct. 21/8/28.
Stratford 10/2/52.
Colwick 11/12/55.
Boston 21/2/60.

RENUMBERED:
7374 27/6/25.
8550 13/10/46.
68550 5/5/50.

CONDEMNED: 27/7/61.
Cut up at Doncaster.

_____

7375

Stratford.

To traffic 6/1894.
Class R24 - passenger.

REPAIRS:
Str.   ?/?—?/12/04.**G**.
Rebuilt to Class R24 Rbt.
Str.   28/5—6/10/20.**G**.
At 1/1/23: J69/1. *Westinghouse*
brake. Condensing apparatus.
Str.   6/3—28/5/25.**G**.
Str.   21/10/27—28/1/28.**G**.
Vacuum ejector fitted. Additional
rails on bunker. Condensing
apparatus removed.
Cow. ?/?—20/?/31.**H**.
Cow. ?/?—11/8/34.**G**.
Cow. ?/?—26/9/35.**L**.
Cow. ?/?—1/2/37.**H**.
Cow. ?/?—28/12/40.**G**.
Cow. ?/?—15/1/44.**H**.
Cow. 3—25/10/46.**G**.
Cow. 7/6—2/7/49.**H/I**.
Cow. 17/4—19/5/52.**G**.

BOILERS:
375.
375 *(new)* ?/12/04.
2998 *(new)* 6/10/20.
270 *(ex7356)* 28/5/25.
270 reno.C1697 1930.
C1689 *(ex7343)* 11/8/34.
C1695 *(ex7089)* 28/12/40.
3029 *(ex7347)* 25/10/46.
23871 *(ex8562)* 19/5/52.

SHEDS:
Stratford.
Eastfield 27/2/28.

(1/4/29 working at Alloa, o/l,
whilst No.7341 of Stirling was in
shops).
Yoker 1/4/51.
Dawsholm 4/11/51.
Dundee 11/4/54.

RENUMBERED:
7375 28/5/25.
8551 14/9/46.
68551 2/7/49.

CONDEMNED: 21/6/57.
Cut up at Kilmarnock 7/57.

_____

7376

Stratford.

To traffic 6/1894.
Class R24 - passenger.

REPAIRS:
Str.   ?/?—?/7/06.**G**.
Rebuilt to Class R24 Rbt.
Str.   26/4—7/8/20.**G**.
At 1/1/23: J69/1. *Westinghouse*
brake. Condensing apparatus.
Str.   19/12/23—27/3/24.**G**.
Vacuum ejector fitted.
Str.   1/1—14/4/27.**G**.
Additional rails not fitted on
bunker. Condensing apparatus
removed.
Cow. 8—20/2/28.**N/C**.
Steam heating, footsteps and
bunker handrails fitted.
Cow. 7/3—10/4/29.**L**.
Cow. 31/12/30—16/4/31.**G**.
Cow. 3—4/8/31.**N/C**.
Cow. 24/9—25/10/35.**G**.
Cow. 6/9—11/10/38.**G**.
Drop grate fitted.
Cow. 11/11—3/12/42.**G**.
Cow. 3—19/2/44.**L**.
Cow. 21/5—20/6/44.**H**.
Cow. 28/10—7/11/46.**L**.
Cow. 21/5—11/6/48.**G**.
Str.   12/1—3/3/56.**G**.
Str.   13—16/3/56.**N/C**.
Str.   26/3—12/4/56.**N/C**.
Str.   2—13/1/61.**N/C**.

BOILERS:
376.
376 *(new)* ?/7/06.
2997 *(new)* 7/8/20.
3004 *(ex7361)* 14/4/27.
3004 reno.C1698 10/4/29.
C1685 *(ex7337)* 16/4/31.
C1698 *(ex7357)* 11/10/38.
3018 *(ex7357)* 20/6/44.
C1689 *(ex8568)* 11/6/48.
23811 *(exJ68 68656)* 3/3/56.

SHEDS:
Stratford.
Cambridge 31/1/25.
Scottish Area 1/11/27.
Eastfield 16/11/27.
Parkhead 26/10/32.
Aberdeen Ferryhill 4/8/33.
Eastfield 13/11/33.
Kittybrewster 5/4/51.
St Margarets 14/6/51.
Stratford 17/2/52.
Colwick 11/12/55.
Colchester 18/3/56.
Parkeston 1/11/59.
Stratford 28/2/60.

RENUMBERED:
7376 27/3/24.
8552 27/10/46.
68552 11/6/48.

CONDEMNED: 10/9/61.
Cut up at Stratford.

_____

7377

Stratford.

To traffic 10/1895.
Class R24 - passenger.

REPAIRS:
Str. ?/?—?/7/06.**G**.
Rebuilt to Class R24 Rbt.
At 1/1/23: J69/1. *Westinghouse*
brake. Condensing apparatus.
Str. 10/1—15/4/24.**G**.
Vacuum ejector fitted.
Str. 14—29/10/25.**L**.
Str. 12/3—8/8/26.**G**.
Westinghouse brake replaced
by steam. Additional rails on
bunker. Condensing apparatus
and steam heating removed.
Str. 16/3—22/6/29.**G**.
Str. 7/11/31—15/1/32.**G**.
Str. 22/12/34—1/2/35.**G**.
Str. 3/9—7/10/38.**G**.
Rebuilt to J67/2.
Str. 6/4—6/5/41.**G**.
Str. 16/1—28/2/44.**G**.
Str. 23/6—17/8/46.**G**.
Rebuilt to J69/1.
Str. 7/9—8/10/49.**G**.
Str. 4—24/12/52.**G**.
Str. 1—24/3/56.**G**.
Str. 29/3—12/4/56.**N/C**.

BOILERS:
377.
377 *(new)* ?/7/06.
2962 *(ex7196)* 15/4/24.
3064 *(new)* 15/1/32.
3084 *(new)* 1/2/35.

2896 *(exJ66 7294)* 7/10/38.
2910 *(exJ67 7257)* 6/5/41.
2854 *(ex7359)* 28/2/44.
3173 *(new)* 17/8/46.
23752 *(ex?)* 24/12/52.
23740 *(ex68588)* 24/3/56.

SHEDS:
Stratford.
Neasden 27/9/26.
Lincoln 2/11/26.
Staveley 29/11/53.
Lincoln 13/12/53.
Wrexham 21/4/57.
Bidston 1/11/58.

RENUMBERED:
7377 15/4/24.
8553 17/8/46.
68553 8/10/49.

CONDEMNED: 18/12/58.
Into Gorton for c/u: 20/12/58.
C/u 17/1/59.

_____

7378

Stratford.

To traffic 10/1895.
Class R24 - passenger.

REPAIRS:
Str. 8/6—30/8/04.**G**.
Rebuilt to Class R24 Rbt.
Str. 21/5—19/4/21.**G**.
At 1/1/23: J69/1. *Westinghouse*
brake. Condensing apparatus.
Str. 18/9—24/11/23.**G**.
Str. 28/1—29/4/26.**G**.
Additional rails on bunker.
Steam heating fitted 2/2/27.
Str. 18/12/28—25/3/29.**G**.
Westinghouse brake replaced
by steam. condensing apparatus
and steam heating removed.
Str. 2/11—24/12/31.**G**.
Str. 8—27/10/36.**G**.
Vacuum ejector fitted.
Str. 25/11/40—10/1/41.**G**.
Str. 8/10—4/11/44.**G**.
Str. 4/2—18/4/47.**G**.
Str. 31/7—26/8/50.**G**.
Str. 19/10—21/11/53.**G**.
Str. 15/3—26/4/57.**G**.

BOILERS:
378.
378 *(new)* 30/8/04.
3007 *(new)* 19/4/21.
3024 *(exJ68 7031)* 25/3/29.
3005 *(ex7382)* 24/12/31.
2995 *(ex7381)* 2710/36.
3038 *(exJ67 7332)* 10/1/41.

No.7305 (8596 from 1st September 1946) was ex Stratford 11th August 1945 with this parallel-sided stovepipe fixed to the base of a cast chimney.

No.8603 had a first-aid repair done to its cast chimney either to cover a hole or to close a crack. It was ex Stratford from a General repair 21st July 1945 and became 8603 from 8th September 1946.

Although the change from stovepipe to cast chimney cut the height by 2½ inches, Stratford fitted some even shorter ones, probably spare from withdrawn 2-4-2 tanks. No.8629 was so fitted ex works 26th June 1946 and re-numbered from 7083 and with LNER restored.

No. 68626 carried a shorter cast chimney from its October 1957 repair to withdrawal on 3rd May 1962.

7378 cont./
3080 *(exJ68 7024)* 4/11/44.
3178 *(ex8502)* 26/8/50.
23701 *(ex?)* 21/11/53.
23771 *(exJ68 68642)* 26/4/57.

SHEDS:
Stratford.
Gorton 17/4/29.
Walton-on-the-Hill 21/6/30.
Trafford Park 2/11/31.
Stratford 24/12/31.
Parkeston 18/1/48.
Stratford 8/1/50.
Parkeston 6/2/55.
Cambridge 14/10/56.
Colwick 23/2/58.
Lincoln 11/10/59.
Boston 29/4/61.
Lincoln 11/6/61.

RENUMBERED:
378ᴇ 24/11/23.
7378 29/4/26.
8554 10/11/46.
68554 26/8/50.

CONDEMNED: 25/7/61.
Into Doncaster for c/u: 25/7/61.

7379

Stratford.

To traffic 10/1895.
Class R24 - passenger.

REPAIRS:
Str.   20/10/03—12/2/04.**G**.
Rebuilt to Class R24 Rbt.
Str.   17/11/19—19/2/20.**G**.
At 1/1/23: J69/1. Westinghouse
brake. Condensing apparatus.
Str.   6/6—4/10/23.**G**.
Str.   13/7—15/10/25.**G**.
Str.   12/5—1/8/28.**G**.
*Westinghouse brake replaced
by steam. Add. rails on bunker.
Condensing apparatus removed.*
Cow. 21—28/9/28.**N/C**.
*Footsteps and bunker handrails
fitted.*
Cow. 19/2—3/3/29.**L**.
Cow. 18/9—23/11/29.**L**.
Cow. 28/2—10/5/30.**H**.
Cow. 11/8—4/9/31.**L**.
Cow. 23/11/32—24/2/33.**G**.
Cow. 29/10—6/12/34.**L**.
Cow. 5/11—15/12/36.**G**.
Cow. 5/7—16/8/39.**G**.
Cow. 5/2—15/4/42.**G**.
Cow. 20/8—6/9/46.**G**.
Cow. 6/10—4/11/50.**G**.
Str.   3/8—12/9/53.**C/H**.

Str.   3—30/4/55.**H/I**.

BOILERS:
379.
379 *(new)* 12/2/04.
356 *(ex7356)* 19/2/20.
2952 *(ex7348)* 15/10/25.
2952 reno.C1699 3/3/29.
3011 *(exStr & 7084)* 24/2/33.
3019 *(exStr, J68 7050)* 16/8/39.
C1690 *(ex7391)* 6/9/46.
2982 *(ex8550)* 4/11/50.
23782 *(ex?)* 12/9/53.

SHEDS:
Stratford.
Scottish Area 12/9/28.
Burntisland 28/9/28.
Thornton Jct. 22/7/33.
Ipswich 17/2/52.
Cambridge 26/7/53.
Bury St Edmunds 27/9/53.
Cambridge 31/1/54.
South Lynn 26/9/54.
Cambridge 20/3/55.
Norwich 4/3/56.
Ipswich 16/2/58.

RENUMBERED:
379ᴇ 4/10/23.
7379 15/10/25.
8555 22/9/46.
68555 4/11/50.

CONDEMNED: 5/5/58.
Cut up at Stratford.

7380

Stratford.

To traffic 10/1895.
Class R24 - passenger.

REPAIRS:
Str. 17/5—20/8/04.**G**.
Rebuilt to Class R24 Rbt.
Str. 26/10/17—8/4/18.**G**.
At 1/1/23: J69/1. Westinghouse
brake. Condensing apparatus.
Str. 23/8—3/11/23.**G**.
Str. 5/1—30/4/27.**G**.
Steam heating fitted.
Str. 28/10/29—4/1/30.**G**.
*Westinghouse brake replaced
by steam and vacuum ejector.
Add. rails on bunker.Condensing
apparatus removed.*
Str. 30/5—23/6/33.**G**.
Str. 2/12/36—14/1/37.**G**.
Str. 8/4—15/5/40.**G**.
Str. 7—16/5/42.**L**.
Str. 3/2—25/3/44.**G**.
Str. 7/8—12/9/46.**G**.

Str. 18/9—22/10/49.**G**.
Str. 30/6—15/8/52.**G**.
Str. 7—17/10/52.**N/C**.
Str. 28/7—18/9/53.**N/C**.
Str. 4/3—12/4/57.**G**.

BOILERS:
380.
380 *(new)* 20/8/04.
388 *(ex7388)* 8/4/18.
48 *(exJ68 7048)* 30/4/27.
2981 *(ex7394)* 4/1/30.
22 *(exJ68 7021)* 23/6/33.
3061 *(ex7058)* 14/1/37.
3032 *(ex7163)* 15/5/40.
3078 *(ex7053)* 25/3/44.
3177 *(new)* 12/9/46.
3175 *(ex8538)* 22/10/49.
23819 *(new)* 15/8/52.
23724 *(ex68621)* 12/4/57.

SHEDS:
Stratford.
Parkeston 13/4/41.
Stratford 23/5/42.
Parkeston 13/11/49.
Stratford 8/4/51.
King's Lynn 25/9/55.
South Lynn 20/4/58.
New England 1/6/58.
Doncaster 15/6/58.
Langwith Jct. 27/3/60.
Retford 22/1/61.
Stratford 18/6/61.

RENUMBERED:
380ᴇ 3/11/23.
7380 *by* 30/4/27.
8556 9/3/46.
68556 22/10/49.

CONDEMNED: 16/9/62.
Cut up at Stratford.

7381

Stratford.

To traffic 10/1895.
Class R24 - passenger.

REPAIRS:
Str. 29/8—18/12/07.**G**.
Rebuilt to Class R24 Rbt.
Str. 21/6—5/10/22.**G**.
At 1/1/23: J69/1. Westinghouse
brake. Condensing apparatus.
Str. 28/10/24—7/2/25.**G**.
Str. 10/2—8/4/27.**G**.
Additional rails on bunker.
Str. 10/1—22/2/30.**G**.
*Westinghouse brake replaced
by steam and vacuum ejector.
Condensing apparatus removed.*

Str. 4/11—8/12/32.**G**.
Str. 9/8—4/9/36.**G**.
Str. 5/12/39—19/1/40.**G**.
Str. 7/5—10/6/44.**G**.
Str. 18/10—6/12/48.**G**.
Str. 11/12/51—5/1/52.**G**.
Str. 22/4—19/7/55.**G**.

BOILERS:
381.
381 *(new)* 18/12/07.
3017 *(new)* 5/10/22.
46 *(ex7305)* 7/2/25.
2993 *(ex7165)* 22/2/30.
2995 *(ex7059)* 8/12/32.
3055 *(ex7194)* 4/9/36.
3063 *(ex7197)* 19/1/40.
3102 *(ex7370)* 10/6/44.
3163 *(ex8542)* 6/12/48.
23728 *(ex?)* 5/1/52.
23723 *(exJ68 68666)* 19/7/55.

SHEDS:
Stratford.
Gorton 1/5/31.
Wigan 22/5/31.
Stratford 4/11/32.
Parkeston 10/4/49.
Stratford 17/9/50.
Norwich 16/11/52.
Ipswich 18/1/53.
Boston 26/7/53.

RENUMBERED:
7381 7/2/25.
8557 9/10/46.
68557 4/12/48.

CONDEMNED: 20/10/59.
Cut up at Stratford.

7382

Stratford.

To traffic 10/1895.
Class R24 - passenger.

REPAIRS:
Str. 14/10/04—24/2/05.**G**.
Rebuilt to Class R24 Rbt.
Str. 14/11/19—28/2/20.**G**.
At 1/1/23: J69/1. Westinghouse
brake. Condensing apparatus.
Str. 12/12/23—8/4/24.**G**.
Vacuum ejector fitted.
Str. 4/6—25/9/26.**G**.
*Westinghouse brake changed
to steam (with vacuum ejector).
Additional rails on bunker.
Condensing apparatus removed.*
Str. 21/12/28—3/4/29.**G**.
Str. 29/8—16/11/31.**G**.
Str. 8/2—2/3/36.**H**.

7382 cont./
Str. 1/6—2/7/38.**G.**
Rebuilt to J67/2.
Str. 10/2—20/3/41.**G.**
Str. 1/12/43—25/1/44.**G.**
Str. 10/7—10/8/46.**G.**
Rebuilt to J69/1.
Str. 12/3—14/4/49.**G.**
Str. 2—31/10/52.**G.**
Str. 22/4—1/6/56.**G.**

BOILERS:
382.
382 *(new)* 24/2/05.
2986 *(new)* 28/2/20.
168 *(ex7168)* 25/9/26.
3005 *(ex7059)* 3//29.
27 *(exJ68 7027)* 16/11/31.
3029 *(ex7060)* 2/3/36.
2918 *(new)* 2/7/38.
2851 *(exJ66 7298)* 20/3/41.
2831 *(exJ67 7329)* 25/1/44.
3174 *(new)* 10/8/46.
23882 *(new)* 31/10/52.
23812 *(ex68526)* 1/6/56.

SHEDS:
Stratford.
Lincoln 8/11/26.
Immingham 18/11/26.
New Holland ?/?.
Immingham 27/10/28.
New Holland 31/7/29.
Louth 4/11/30.
Immingham 19/9/31.
Lincoln 29/7/35.
Staveley 6/5/53.
Lincoln 26/7/53.
Doncaster 24/3/57.
Colwick 12/6/60.

RENUMBERED:
7382 8/4/24.
8558 10/8/46.
68558 14/4/49.

CONDEMNED: 13/1/61.
Into Doncaster for c/u: 13/1/61.

7383

Stratford.

To traffic 11/1895.
Class R24 - passenger.

REPAIRS:
Str. 19/5—25/8/04.**G.**
Rebuilt to Class R24 Rbt.
Str. 27/4—26/7/18.**G.**
At 1/1/23: *J69/1. Westinghouse brake. Condensing apparatus.*
Str. 20/1—24/3/23.**G.**
Str. 24/12/24—1/4/25.**G.**

Str. ?/?—15/1/27.**N/C.**
Steam heating fitted.
Str. 9/9—25/11/27.**G.**
Additional rails on bunker.
Str. 6/12/29—23/1/30.**G.**
Westinghouse brake replaced by steam plus vacuum ejector. Condensing apparatus removed.
Str. 8/4—12/5/33.**G.**
Str. 28/4—17/6/36.**G.**
Gor. 17/12/39—3/2/40.**G.**
Gor. 19/9—7/11/42.**H/I.**
Gor. 18/7—3/10/47.**G.**
Gor. 3—24/6/50.**G.**

BOILERS:
383.
383 *(new)* 25/8/04.
2972 *(new)* 26/7/18.
2965 *(ex7362)* 1/4/25.
3025 *(exJ68 7032)* 23/1/30.
3045 *(ex7371)* 12/5/33.
2966 *(ex7384)* 17/6/36.
3035 *(ex7191)* 3/2/40.
3056 *(ex7371)* 3/10/47.
3095 *(ex68598)* 24/6/50.

SHEDS:
Stratford.
Gorton 1/5/31.
Trafford Park 22/5/31.
Walton-on-the-Hill 24/7/41.
Gorton 7/11/42.
Trafford Park 13/12/42.
Walton-on-the-Hill 25/7/43.
Brunswick 26/3/44.
Shown allocated to Wrexham by 1/51 but trans Brunswick 3/52.
Trafford Park 13/6/53.
Brunswick 19/9/53.
Wrexham 1/1/55.
Brunswick 15/1/55.
Birkenhead 7/5/55.
Wrexham 14/1/56.

RENUMBERED:
7383 by 25/10/24.
8559 11/8/46.
68559 5/3/49.

CONDEMNED: 30/4/56.
Into Gorton for c/u 5/5/56. Sent to Darlington 16/5/56 for c/u.

7384

Stratford.

To traffic 11/1895.
Class R24 - passenger.

REPAIRS:
Str. 31/12/07—4/4/08.**G.**
Rebuilt to Class R24 Rbt.

At 1/1/23: *J69/1. Westinghouse brake. Condensing apparatus.*
Str. 15/11/23—29/1/24.**G.**
Str. 22/11/26—11/2/27.**G.**
Additional rails on bunker.
Str. 25/10—14/12/29.**G.**
Westinghouse brake replaced by steam plus vacuum ejector. Condensing apparatus removed.
Str. 31/12/31—12/2/32.**G.**
Str. 9/12/35—3/1/36.**G.**
Str. 9/10/38—1/7/39.**G.**
Rebuilt to J67/2.
Str. 19/4—2/7/43.**G.**
Str. 25/9—3/11/45.**G.**
Rebuilt to J69/1.
Str. 12/6—13/8/49.**H/I.**
Str. 3/10—1/11/52.**G.**
Str. 28/10—1/12/56.**G.**

BOILERS:
384.
384 *(new)* 4/4/08.
2987 *(ex7197)* 11/2/27.
2966 *(exJ68 7035)* 12/2/32.
168 *(ex7168)* 3/1/36.
2897 *(exJ67 7199)* 1/7/39.
2890 *(exJ67 7331)* 2/7/43.
3084 *(ex7269)* 3/11/45.
23754 *(ex?)* 1/11/52.
23826 *(new)* 1/12/56.

SHEDS:
Ipswich.
Stratford 21/3/25.
Gorton 2/1/30.
Trafford Park 10/1/30.
Grantham 25/7/32.
New England 1/9/36.
Ardsley 20/9/39.
Boston 30/4/40.
Lincoln 1/3/59.

RENUMBERED:
7384 29/1/24.
8560 29/9/46.
68560 13/8/49.

CONDEMNED: 10/1/61.
Into Doncaster for c/u: 10/1/61.

7385

Stratford.

To traffic 11/1895.
Class R24 - passenger.

REPAIRS:
Str. 13/7—13/11/07.**G.**
Rebuilt to Class R24 Rbt.
Str. 3/12/20—20/4/21.**G.**
At 1/1/23: *J69/1. Westinghouse brake. Condensing apparatus.*

Str. 14/11/23—26/1/24.**G.**
Vacuum ejector fitted.
Str. 11/3—22/7/26.**G.**
Westinghouse brake replaced by steam plus vacuum ejector. Additional rails on bunker. Condensing apparatus removed.
Str. 30/12/28—26/4/29.**G.**
Str. 15/12/32—19/1/33.**G.**
Str. 16/8—16/9/36.**G.**
Str. 9—14/3/38.**L.**
Spark arrestor fitted.
Str. 5/2—26/3/40.**G.**
Str. 28/5—24/6/44.**G.**
Str. 8/4—21/5/47.**G.**
Str. 19/2—1/4/50.**G.**
Str. 18/5—20/6/53.**G.**

BOILERS:
385.
385 *(new)* 13/1/07.
3008 *(new)* 20/4/21.
3007 *(ex7378)* 26/4/29.
3046 *(exJ68 7041)* 19/1/33.
2991 *(ex7371)* 16/9/36.
3062 *(ex7370)* 26/3/40.
3063 *(ex7381)* 24/6/44.
3079 *(ex8502)* 21/5/47.
3203 *(new)* 1/4/50.
23773 *(ex?)* 20/6/53.

SHEDS:
Stratford.
King's Cross 10/9/24.
Stratford 27/10/24.
Neasden 27/9/26.
Annesley 12/12/27.
Leicester 21/1/28.
Woodford 21/2/28.
Boston 3/3/32.
Grantham 19/1/33.
Boston 4/1/36.
Stratford 12/4/40.
Parkeston 23/7/50.
Stratford 8/3/53.
Colchester 6/2/55.
Retford 16/9/56.

RENUMBERED:
7385 26/1/24. ??
8561 3/11/46.
68561 1/4/50.

CONDEMNED: 14/7/58.
Cut up at Stratford.

7386

Stratford.

To traffic 12/1895.
Class R24 - passenger.

7386 cont./
REPAIRS:
Str.   27/10/03—19/3/04.**G.**
Rebuilt to Class R24 Rbt.
Woolwich Ar. 16/1—20/8/20.**G.**
At 1/1/23: J69/1. Westinghouse
brake. Condensing apparatus.
Str. ?/?—?/5/23.**G.**
Str.   12/8—10/11/27.**G.**
Westinghouse brake replaced
by steam. Add. rails on bunker.
Condensing apparatus removed.
Cow. ?/?—?/?/28.**N/C.**
Footsteps and bunker handrails
fitted.
Cow. ?/?—27/12/30.**G.**
Cow. ?/?—3/9/32.**H.**
Cow. ?/?—7/6/35.**H.**
Cow. ?/?—24/9/37.**H.**
Cow. ?/?—12/5/38.**G.**
Cow. ?/?—6/8/40.**G.**
Cow. ?/?—25/7/42.**H.**
Cow. 12/8—6/9/45.**G.**
Cow. 8/9—15/10/51.**G.**
Cow. 17/3—20/4/54.**H/I.**
Cow. 24/12/54—29/1/55.**C/L.**

BOILERS:
  386.
  386 *(new)* 19/3/04.
  2995 *(new)* 20/8/20.
   395 *(ex7395)* 10/11/27.
   395 reno.C1700 circa 1928.
  C1688 *(ex7342)* 27/12/30.
  C1694 *(ex7368)* 12/5/38.
  C1830 *(ex7089)* 6/9/45.
  23880 *(new)* 15/10/51.

SHEDS:
Stratford.
Parkhead 2/12/27.
St Margarets *by* 28/10/32.
Haymarket 5/3/45.
St Margarets 20/8/45.
Dumfries 11/1/51.
Polmont 3/3/55.

RENUMBERED:
  7386 *before* 12/8/27.
  8562 12/5/46.
  68562 15/10/51.

CONDEMNED: 15/8/56.
Cut up at Cowlairs.

7387

Stratford.

To traffic 12/1895.
Class R24 - passenger.

REPAIRS:
Str. ?/?—?/2/06.**G.**

Rebuilt to Class R24 Rbt.
Str. 24/1—28/8/19.**G.**
At 1/1/23: J69/1. Westinghouse
brake. Condensing apparatus.
Str. 12/9—7/12/23.**G.**
Str. 10/2—22/4/27.**G.**
Steam heating fitted.
Str. 6/12/29—1/2/30.**G.**
Westinghouse brake replaced
by steam plus vacuum ejector.
Additional rails on bunker.
Condensing apparatus removed.
Str. 15/11—5/12/34.**G.**
Str. 28/10—6/11/36.**L.**
Str. 8/5—1/6/38.**G.**
Str. 16—28/6/38.**L.**
Str. 22/9—21/11/39.**G.**
Str. 25/4—23/5/42.**G.**
Str. 8/7—4/8/45.**G.**
Str. 13/1—23/2/49.**G.**
Str. 30/6—20/8/52.**G.**
Str. 1—27/10/56.**G.**

BOILERS:
  387.
  387 *(new)* ?/2/06.
  391 *(ex7391)* 28/8/19.
   37 *(new)* 7/12/23.
  2983 *(ex7359)* 1/2/30.
  3015 *(ex7365)* 5/12/34.
  2998 *(ex7059)* 1/6/38.
  3092 *(ex7196)* 23/5/42.
  2986 *(ex7165)* 4/8/45.
  3021 *(ex8507)* 23/2/49.
  23749 *(ex?)* 20/8/52.
  23825 *(new)* 27/10/56.

SHEDS:
Stratford.
Cambridge 1/11/38.
Stratford 30/12/38.
Parkeston 8/1/39.
Stratford 25/9/39.
Parkeston 8/6/46.
Stratford 6/9/47.
Parkeston 1/11/59.
Stratford 28/2/60.

RENUMBERED:
  387ᴇ 7/12/23.
  7387 *by* 10/2/27.
  8563 26/5/46.
  68563 19/2/49.

CONDEMNED: 3/10/60.
Cut up at Stratford.

7388

Stratford.

To traffic 12/1895.
Class R24 - passenger.

REPAIRS:
Str. ?/?—?/1204.**G.**
Rebuilt to Class R24 Rbt.
Str. 5/10/17—15/3/18.**G.**
At 1/1/23: J69/1. Westinghouse
brake. Condensing apparatus.
Str. 12/12/23—2/4/24.**G.**
Vacuum ejector fitted.
Str. 29/1—10/2/25.**L.**
Str. 1/10—15/12/26.**G.**
Steam heating fitted.
Str. 11/2—27/4/29.**G.**
Additional rails on bunker.
Str. 9/5—10/7/31.**G.**
Str. ?/?—?/4/32.**L.**
Condensing apparatus removed.
Str. 27/2—6/4/34.**G.**
Str. 5/11—11/12/36.**G.**
Str. 10/8—22/9/39.**G.**
Vacuum ejector removed.

BOILERS:
  388.
  388 *(new)* ?/12/04.
  2970 *(new)* 15/3/18.
   50 *(ex7341)* 2/4/24.
  2984 *(ex7364)* 10/7/31.
  3072 *(new)* 6/4/34.
  3005 *(ex7378)* 11/12/36.
   31 *(ex7350)* 22/9/39.

SHEDS:
Stratford.
March 10/10/27.
Cambridge 14/5/28.
Stratford 6/4/34.
WD Longmoor 4/10/39.

RENUMBERED:
7388 2/4/24.

SOLD TO W.D.: 19/10/40.
O/l to WD Longmoor 4/10/39.
Became WD 84, then 70084.
Disposed May 1948 to John
Lysaght Ltd., Scunthorpe and
renumbered 27. Scrapped 1/58.

7389

Stratford.

To traffic 12/1895.
Class R24 - passenger.

REPAIRS:
Str. ?/?—?/9/04.**G.**
Rebuilt to Class R24 Rbt.
Str. 28/11/22—10/2/23.**G.**
At 1/1/23: J69/1. Westinghouse
brake. Condensing apparatus.
Str. 8/1—11/4/25.**G.**
Str. 2/6—6/9/27.**G.**
Steam heating fitted.

Additional rails on bunker.
Str. 3/2—15/3/30.**G.**
Westinghouse brake replaced
by steam plus vacuum ejector.
Condensing apparatus removed.
Str. 16/4—13/5/32.**G.**
Str. 22/8—17/9/34.**G.**
Str. 21/12/36—21/1/37.**G.**
Str. 1/4—25/8/39.**G.**
Str. 21/1—21/2/42.**G.**
Str. 6—26/5/44.**G.**
Str. 10/6—27/7/46.**G.**
Str. 22/9—4/11/48.**G.**
Str. 19/11—29/12/51.**G.**
Str. 28/1—9/2/52.**C/L.**
Str. 3/3—5/4/57.**G.**

BOILERS:
  389.
  389 *(new)* ?/9/04.
  3019 *(new)* 10/2/23.
   47 *(ex7371)* 15/3/30.
  2987 *(ex7384)* 13/5/32.
   35 *(ex7346)* 17/9/34.
  3072 *(ex7388)* 21/1/37.
  3084 *(ex7377)* 25/8/39.
  3090 *(ex7365)* 21/2/42.
  3061 *(ex7271)* 26/5/44.
  3172 *(new)* 27/7/46.
  3194 *(new)* 4/11/48.
  23727 *(ex?)* 29/12/51.
  23750 *(ex68577)* 5/4/57.

SHEDS:
Stratford.
Hatfield 12/11/30.
Stratford 24/6/51.
Yarmouth 27/11/55.
Lowestoft 4/3/56.
Stratford 1/11/59.

RENUMBERED:
  7389 11/4/25.
  8565 27/7/46.
  68565 4/11/48.

CONDEMNED: 6/8/62.
Cut up at Stratford ???

7390

Stratford.

To traffic 12/1895.
Class R24 - passenger.

REPAIRS:
Str. 18/7—3/10/05.**G.**
Rebuilt to Class R24 Rbt.
Str. 27/9/18—30/5/19.**G.**
At 1/1/23: J69/1. Westinghouse
brake. Condensing apparatus.
Str. 20/7—15/12/23.**G.**
Str. 30/10—24/12/25.**G.**

(above) **Carlisle based 68499 had a Cowlairs stovepipe at a light repair 9th October 1948 and was so fitted when transferred to Liverpool on 25th February 1951.**

(left) **Back at English sheds, No.68499 had a General repair on 4th August 1951 at Gorton (as shown here) when its chimney was unaltered. However, Stratford gave it a final General on 26th March 1957 and fitted it with a cast iron chimney (*see* page 164, centre).**

(below) **Shortage of foundry capacity caused more stovepipes to be fitted at Stratford during and just after the war. Ex works 11th March 1949, No.68577 had one of the shorter stovepipes and with a flat beading at its top.**

(above) **No.7089** went to Scottish Area 13th May 1928 from a General repair at Stratford, ex works 25th April 1928 at which it got the extra coal rails, the only GER feature to be changed. It called at Cowlairs 24th to 31st May 1928 to be fitted with shunters steps and a bunker handrail. Because it had Westinghouse and vacuum brakes it then worked as passenger pilot at Perth until January 1942 when it moved to Stirling and in August 1942 to Dunfermline, where it stayed until June 1951.

(centre) Ex Cowlairs 25th April 1945, the LNER was cut to NE and on Sunday 1st September 1946, Dunfermline shed renumbered it to 8635 in normal 12in. shaded transfers. Despite boiler changes in 1933, 1940 and 1945, Ramsbottom safety valves remained but their shapely brass enclosure was lost to a sharply angled steel one. Note the LNER number plate still on the bunker whilst the 0-6-0T was waiting to enter Cowlairs 18th January 1947.

Out of Cowlairs 8th February 1947, it then had a newly built boiler with Ross 'pops' to which a square enclosure was added. From a light repair 16th July 1948, it came out as 68635. Although not repainted, Cowlairs did not simply add a 6 but put on a complete new set of transfers as shown by the spacing relative to NE. The number plate was moved from the bunker to the sandbox. A smokebox number plate was put on at Cowlairs 3rd June 1950. On 24th June 1951 No.68635 returned to the Eastern Region.

7390 cont./
Str. 29/9—5/11/27.**G.**
Str. 27/1—9/2/28.**L.**
Additional rails on bunker.
Str. 21/7—31/10/28.**H.**
Steam heating fitted.
Str. 12/12/28—25/1/29.**G.**
Westinghouse brake replaced
by steam plus vacuum ejector.
Condensing apparatus removed.
Str. 10/1—27/2/31.**G.**
Str. 9/2—23/3/34.**G.**
Str. 16—28/8/34.**L.**
Str. 16/5—26/6/37.**G.**
Str. 9/7—9/8/41.**G.**
Str. 21/8—20/9/44.**G.**
Str. 13/9—20/10/47.**G.**
Str. 11/9—7/10/50.**G.**
Str. 21/2—20/3/54.**G.**
Str. 28/11—21/12/57.**G.**

BOILERS:
390.
390 *(new)* 3/10/05.
88 *(ex7088)* 30/5/19.
3030 *(new)* 15/12/23.
36 *(ex7371)* 27/2/31.
3030 *(exJ68 7029)* 23/3/34.
2979 *(exJ68 7029)* 26/6/37.
3031 *(exJ68 7046)* 9/8/41.
3155 *(new)* 20/9/44.
3186 *(new)* 20/10/47.
23702 *(ex?)* 7/10/50.
23789 *(ex?)* 20/3/54.
23806 *(ex68500)* 21/12/57.

SHEDS:
Stratford.
Lincoln 4/2/29.
Cambridge 8/9/34.
South Lynn 16/11/47.
Cambridge 1/3/59.
King's Lynn 14/6/59.
Stratford 24/7/60.

RENUMBERED:
390E 15/12/23.
7390 24/12/25.
8566 6/10/46.
68566 7/10/50.

CONDEMNED: 5/9/62.
Cut up at Stratford ?

7391

Stratford.

To traffic 1/1896.
Class R24 - passenger.

REPAIRS:
Str. 7/2—25/6/13.**G.**
Rebuilt to Class R24 Rbt.

Str. 5/7—6/12/18.**G.**
At 1/1/23: J69/1. Westinghouse
brake. Condensing apparatus.
Str. 6/11/23—19/1/24.**G.**
Vacuum ejector fitted.
Str. 8/1—10/5/27.**G.**
Condensing apparatus removed.
Additional rails on bunker.
Cow. 6—12/1/28.**N/C.**
Footsteps and bunker handrails
fitted.
Cow. 24/12/29—18/1/30.**G.**
Cow. 11/9—8/10/30.**L.**
Cow. 13—17/7/31.**L.**
Fitted with large ejector.
Cow. 27/10—2/12/31.**G.**
Cow. 7/8—14/9/34.**G.**
Cow. 15/12/37—3/2/38.**G.**
Cow. 8/4—20/5/41.**G.**
Cow. 15—25/6/43.**L.**
Cow. 10/1—11/2/44.**H.**
Cow. 31/5—9/6/44.**L.**
Cow. 12—14/8/44.**L.**
Cow. 8/2—5/3/46.**G.**
Cow. 1—26/6/48.**G.**
Cow. 15/11—16/12/50.**G.**
Cow. 4—11/1/51.**N/C.**
Cow. 29/8—28/9/51.**C/H.**
Str. 7/10—1/11/52.**C/L.**
Str. 5/4—1/5/54.**G.**

BOILERS:
391.
391 *(new)* 25/6/13.
271 *(ex7271)* 6/12/18.
388 *(ex7380)* 10/5/27.
388 reno. C1701 18/1/30.
C1829 *(new)* 14/9/34.
C1690 *(ex7343)* 20/5/41.
C1694 *(ex7386)* 5/3/46.
C1690 *(ex8555)* 16/12/50.
C1690 reno.23862 28/9/51.
23800 *(ex68500)* 1/5/54.

SHEDS:
Stratford.
Ipswich ?/?.
Scottish Area 1/11/27.
Parkhead 12/11/27.
Ipswich 10/2/52.
Norwich 24/2/52.
Cambridge 26/7/53.
South Lynn 27/9/53.
Cambridge 7/2/54.
South Lynn 18/9/55.
Cambridge 29/1/56.

RENUMBERED:
7391 19/1/24 ???.
8567 3/11/46.
68567 26/6/48.

CONDEMNED: 19/8/57.
Cut up at Stratford.

7392

Stratford.

To traffic 1/1896.
Class R24 - passenger.

REPAIRS:
Str. 8/6—14/10/04.**G.**
Rebuilt to Class R24 Rbt.
Str. 30/9/15—25/2/16.**G.**
Str. 28/12/22—18/8/23.**G.**
At 1/1/23: J69/1. Westinghouse
brake. Condensing apparatus.
Str. 20/2—31/3/25.**G.**
Str. 12/3—11/6/27.**G.**
Additional rails on bunker.
Str. 23/8—13/9/27.**H.**
Westinghouse brake replaced by
steam. Condensing apparatus
removed.
Cow. 15/12/27—24/2/28.**N/C.**
Footsteps and bunker handrails
fitted.
Cow. 25/9—18/10/29.**L.**
Cow. 6/8—7/11/30.**G.**
Cow. 19/9—19/12/32.**G.**
Cow. 14/12/34—1/2/35.**G.**
Cow. 1/4—21/5/37.**G.**
Cow. 5—17/1/38.**L.**
Cow. 13/9—12/10/40.**G.**
Cow. 4—6/11/40.**L.**
Cow. 4—24/2/41.**H.**
Cow. 1—29/4/41.**L.**
Spark arrestor fitted for R.O.F.
Longtown.
Cow. 16/7—15/8/44.**G.**
Inv. 27/3—12/4/45.**H.**
Inv. 31/5—13/6/45.**L.**
Cow. 9/2—6/3/48.**G.**
Str. 27/2—7/4/56.**G.**

BOILERS:
392.
392 *(new)* 14/10/04.
2958 *(new)* 25/2/16.
190 *(ex7190)* 18/8/23.
165 *(ex7165)* 11/6/27.
165 reno.C1702 18/10/29.
C1700 *(ex7337)* 21/5/37.
C1689 *(ex7375)* 24/2/41.
C1829 *(ex8504)* 6/3/48.
23822 *(new)* 7/4/56.

SHEDS:
Stratford.
Scottish Area 14/10/27.
Eastfield 19/10/27.
St Margarets 5/11/27.
Carlisle Canal 5/5/41.
St Margarets 16/12/46.
Aberdeen Ferryhill 9/4/50.
Kittybrewster 18/3/51.
Lincoln 27/1/52.
Norwich 11/5/52.

Plaistow 25/5/52.
Stratford 21/6/53.

RENUMBERED:
7392 31/3/25.
8568 25/8/46.
68568 7/4/56.

CONDEMNED: 8/5/58.
Cut up at Stratford.

7393

Stratford.

To traffic 1/1896.
Class R24 - passenger.

REPAIRS:
Str. 28/3—6/9/06.**G.**
Rebuilt to Class R24 Rbt.
Str. 26/7—20/12/18.**G.**
At 1/1/23: J69/1. Westinghouse
brake. Condensing apparatus.
Str. 5/3—5/5/23.**G.**
Str. 28/10/26—22/1/27.**G.**
Additional rails on bunker.
Str. 25/10—7/12/29.**G.**
Westinghouse brake replaced
by steam plus vacuum ejector.
Condensing apparatus removed.
Str. 1/4—11/5/34.**G.**
Str. 19/7—20/8/37.**G.**
Str. 24/5—11/7/41.**G.**
Str. 29/12/43—25/1/44.**G.**
Str. 27/1—17/2/45.**G.**
Str. 1/12/48—15/1/49.**G.**
Str. 18/2—15/3/52.**G.**
Str. 13/8—29/9/56.**G.**

BOILERS:
393.
393 *(new)* 6/9/06.
2977 *(new)* 20/12/18.
3037 *(new)* 22/1/27.
3078 *(new)* 11/5/34.
3025 *(exJ68 7025)* 20/8/37.
3099 *(exJ68 7045)* 11/7/41.
3164 *(new)* 17/2/45.
23739 *(ex?)* 15/3/52.
23824 *(new)* 29/9/56.

SHEDS:
Stratford.
Parkeston 23/5/42.
Stratford 10/2/45.
Colchester 8/6/46.
Stratford 7/12/46.
Lincoln 3/1/54.
Boston 11/11/56.
Lincoln 9/12/56.
Doncaster 9/6/57.
Langwith Jct. 15/11/59.
Grimesthorpe 6/3/60.

During the 1950s the GER stovepipe chimney had to have a new middle portion put in. This was riveted inside the existing base and a top, still with half-round beading strapped to it. During its last eleven years at English sheds, it still kept the shunters step and handrail.

Before withdrawal on 16th September 1962, Stratford tidied up the chimney, still keeping to half-round beading and the wood cab roof survived to the end. But by July 1962 the number plate had gone. Of the nine engines transferred south from Scotland during 1951-52, only Nos.68525, 68555 and 68623 also ran to withdrawal still carrying stovepipe chimneys.

When No.68513 was ex works 12th June 1952 as a Part 2, it had a short stovepipe riveted chimney outside the existing base and, unusually for Stratford, had flat beading at the top.

Ex works 9th June 1933 No.7160 had been fitted for grease lubrication of coupling pins and big ends of the connecting rods. It was still so equipped at least to 20th September 1938. Note toolbox has been removed.

When No.7376 went to Scottish Area 1st November 1927, it still had the three open coal rails behind which Cowlairs put plating. Ex works 11th October 1938, it had been fitted with drop grate for the wet ash pit at Eastfield shed.

(below) For a reason not discovered, in 1927/28 Nos.7192 and 7082, working on the Chingford line, were fitted with a forward extension to their front footsteps. No.7355 also got them (*see* page 150, top).

7393 cont./
Langwith Jct. 13/3/60.

RENUMBERED:
7393 by 28/10/26.
8569 24/11/46.
68569 15/1/49.

CONDEMNED: 2/6/60.
Cut up at Stratford.

_____

7394

Stratford.

To traffic 1/1896.
Class R24 - passenger.

REPAIRS:
Str. 14/6—10/9/08.**G.**
Rebuilt to Class R24 Rbt.
Str. 1/2—21/8/18.**G.**
Str. 24/2—1/7/22.**G.**
At 1/1/23: *J69/1. Westinghouse brake. Condensing apparatus.*
Str. 3/6—4/10/24.**G.**
Str. 3/6—7/10/26.**G.**
Westinghouse brake replaced by steam plus vacuum ejector. Additional rails on bunker. Condensing apparatus removed.
Str. 22/7—28/9/29.**G.**
Str. 13/7—23/8/33.**G.**
Str. 14/2—22/3/37.**G.**
Str. 2/2—25/2/41.**G.**
Str. 21/11—11/12/43.**G.**
Str. 21/12/44—21/1/45.**L.**
Str. 30/12/45—24/1/46.**G.**
Str. 15/1—18/2/50.**G.**
Str. 15—30/3/53.**G.**
Str. 10/11—15/12/56.**G.**

BOILERS:
394.
394 *(new)* 10/9/08.
2974 *(new)* 21/8/18.
2976 *(ex7350)* 4/10/24.
2981 *(ex7054)* 7/10/26.
2997 *(ex7352)* 28/9/29.
3043 *(exJ68 7025)* 23/8/33.
3048 *(ex7351)* 22/3/37.
2995 *(ex7378)* 25/2/41.
2975 *(exJ68 7035)* 11/12/43.
3068 *(exJ68 7027)* 24/1/46.
3200 *(new)* 18/2/50.
23883 *(new)* 30/3/53.
23827 *(new)* 15/12/56.

SHEDS:
Stratford.
Walton-on-the-Hill 28/10/26.
Gorton 29/2/28.
Wigan 9/11/28.
Trafford Park 21/11/28.

Brunswick 26/6/31.
Wigan 7/11/32.
Gorton 31/5/33.
Stratford 13/7/33.
Norwich 30/5/41.
Lowestoft 10/10/43.
Norwich 14/11/43.
Melton Constable 23/5/46.
Norwich 21/4/48.
Melton Constable 28/11/48.
Norwich 15/12/48.
Boston 26/7/53.
Colwick 21/2/60.
Stratford 11/6/61.

RENUMBERED:
7394 4/10/24.
8570 15/9/46.
68570 18/2/50.

CONDEMNED: 10/9/61.
Cut up at Stratford.

_____

7395

Stratford.

To traffic 2/1896.
Class R24 - passenger.

REPAIRS:
Str. 4/10—15/12/10.**G.**
Rebuilt to Class R24 Rbt.
At 1/1/23: *J69/1. Westinghouse brake. Condensing apparatus.*
Str. 16/5—14/7/23.**G.**
Str. 29/12/24—26/2/25.**G.**
Str. 15/5—3/9/27.**G.**
Steam heating fitted. Additional rails on bunker.
Str. 20/12/29—5/2/30.**G.**
Westinghouse brake replaced by steam plus vacuum ejector. Condensing apparatus removed.
Str. 12/6—19/7/33.**G.**
Str. 31/5—15/7/36.**G.**
Str. 19/9—7/11/39.**G.**
Str. 13/2—27/3/44.**G.**
Str. 8/6—24/7/46.**G.**
Str. 6/11—10/12/49.**G.**
Str. 31/12/52—31/1/53.**G.**
Str. 24/11—23/12/55.**C/L.**
Str. 6/7 8/8/56.**C/L.**
Str. 6/5—7/6/57.**G.**

BOILERS:
395.
395 *(new)* 15/12/10.
2978 *(ex7083)* 3/9/27.
2981 *(ex7380)* 19/7/33.
3008 *(exJ68 7035)* 15/7/36.
2985 *(ex7359)* 7/11/39.
3093 *(exJ68 7046)* 27/3/44.
3171 *(new)* 24/7/46.

23759 *(ex?)* 31/1/53.
23775 *(ex68508)* 7/6/57.

SHEDS:
Stratford.
Hitchin 15/5/31.
Stratford 8/11/39.
Parkeston 6/9/47.
Stratford 1/2/48.
Parkeston 10/4/49.
Stratford 13/11/49.

RENUMBERED:
7395 26/2/25.
8571 19/7/46.
68571 10/12/49.

CONDEMNED: 4/12/60.
Cut up at Stratford.

_____

7396

Stratford.

To traffic 3/1896.
Class R24 - passenger.

REPAIRS:
Str. 8/7—4/11/09.**G.**
Rebuilt to Class R24 Rbt.
Str. 1/3—4/9/18.**G.**
Str. 26/4—28/7/22.**G.**
At 1/1/23: *J69/1. Westinghouse brake. Condensing apparatus.*
Str. 21/5—28/8/24.**G.**
Vacuum ejector fitted.
Str. 11/6—27/11/26.**G.**
Westinghouse brake replaced by steam (plus vacuum ejector). Additional rails on bunker. Condensing apparatus removed.
Str. 11/3—1/6/29.**G.**
Str. 2/1—25/3/32.**G.**
Str. 26/7—14/8/35.**H.**
Str. 16/1—4/3/38.**G.**
Rebuilt to J67/2.
Str. 22/12/40—19/2/41.**G.**
Str. 2/4—1/7/43.**G.**
Str. 26/11—20/12/45.**G.**
Str. 12/10—28/11/48.**G.**
Str. 29/11—28/12/51.**G.**
Str. 8/11/54. *Not repaired.*

BOILERS:
396.
396 *(new)* 4/11/09.
2975 *(new)* 4/9/18.
2986 *(ex7382)* 27/11/26.
3054 *(new)* 1/6/29.
2961 *(ex7345)* 25/3/32.
3027 *(ex7167)* 14/8/35.
2915 *(new)* 4/3/38.
2845 *(exJ66 7319)* 19/2/41.
2912 *(exJ67 7204)* 1/7/43.

2916 *(exJ67 7401)* 20/12/45.
2871 *(exJ67 8594)* 28/11/48.
23915 *(ex?)* 28/12/51.

SHEDS:
Stratford.
Lincoln 20/12/26.
Immingham 20/8/28.
Lincoln 17/4/35.
Louth 8/10/35.
Lincoln 7/11/35.
Hatfield 15/5/41.
Ipswich 16/3/52.

RENUMBERED:
7396 28/8/24.
8572 15/9/46.
68572 28/11/48.

CONDEMNED: 29/11/54.
Cut up at Stratford.

_____

7265

Stratford.

To traffic 4/1896.
Class R24 - passenger.

REPAIRS:
Str. 15/10/08—15/1/09.**G.**
Rebuilt to Class R24 Rbt.
Str. 29/10/17—28/3/18.**G.**
At 1/1/23: *J69/1. Westinghouse brake. Condensing apparatus.*
Str. 21/2—3/5/23.**G.**
Str. 20/3—8/7/25.**G.**
Str. 1/8—20/10/27.**G.**
Steam heating fitted. Additional rails on bunker.
Str. 9/10—23/11/29.**G.**
Westinghouse brake replaced by steam plus vacuum ejector. Condensing apparatus removed.
Str. 16/3—20/4/33.**G.**
Str. 19/12/37—18/1/38.**G.**
Str. 1/1—4/2/42.**G.**
Str. 7/9—7/10/44.**G.**
Str. 31/3—13/4/45.**L.**
After collision.
Str. 18/12/45—23/1/46.**G.**
Str. 24/8—11/10/48.**L.**
Str. 16/10—19/11/49.**G.**
Str. 7—15/1/52.**C/L.**
Str. 20/7—19/8/52.**G.**
Str. 1/11—1/12/56.**G.**
Str. 27/7/60. *Not repaired.*

BOILERS:
265.
265 *(new)* 15/1/09.
2971 *(new)* 28/3/18.
2968 *(exJ68 7046)* 8/7/25.
2994 *(ex7352)* 20/4/33.

After its 28th July 1951 repair at Stratford, No.68632 was an oddity in having rounded front corners to its tanks.

Until into the 1930's it was usual to carry a toolbox on the top of the left hand tank, just ahead of the cab.

7265 cont./
  3104 *(new)* 18/1/38.
  3052 *(ex7270)* 4/2/42.
  3157 *(new)* 7/10/44.
  3157 reno.23733 15/1/52.
  23817 *(new)* 19/8/52.
  23786 *(exJ68 68665)* 1/12/56.

SHEDS:
Stratford.
Peterborough E. 13/12/29.
Boston 29/3/30.
Grantham 3/1/33.
King's Cross 3/12/34.
Hornsey 27/2/35.
Stratford 13/5/35.
Parkeston 13/4/41.
Stratford 15/2/42.
Colchester 11/5/58.
Parkeston 1/11/59.

RENUMBERED:
  7265 8/7/25.
  8573 20/5/46.
  68573 9/10/48.

CONDEMNED: 1/8/60.
Cut up at Stratford.

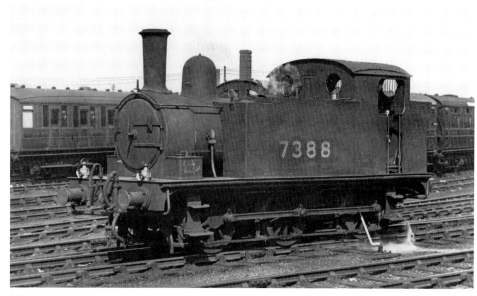

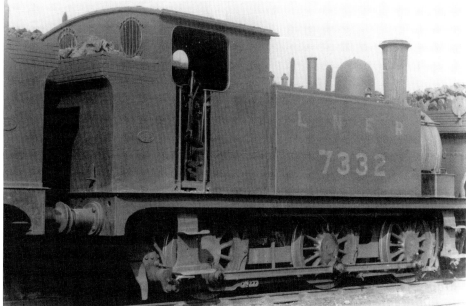

(top) **By 1934 the toolbox was being discarded because it blocked the forward view through the fireman's window.**
(centre) **When changed to shunters from 1927, the wheel operated reversing gear was changed to a lever.**
(bottom) **This 1931 photograph of No.7190 shows the cab side prepared for tablet exchanging apparatus to be fitted but there seems to be no record of this being done.**

7266

Stratford.

To traffic 4/1896.
Class R24 - passenger.

REPAIRS:
Str. 10/10/07—16/1/08.**G.**
Rebuilt to Class R24 Rbt.
Str. 27/3—29/6/20.**G.**
<u>At 1/1/23: *J69/1. Westinghouse</u>
<u>brake. Condensing apparatus.*</u>
Str. 9/5—26/8/23.**G.**
Str. 20/5—13/8/24.**G.**
Vacuum ejector fitted.
Str. 19/11/26—20/1/27.**G.**
Str. 2/10/28—10/1/29.**G.**
Additional rails on bunker.
Str. 3/10—28/11/30.**G.**
Str. ?/?—6/5/31.**N/C.**
Trip cocks fitted.
Str. 11/12/34—11/1/35.**G.**
Str. 7/9—6/10/39.**G.**
Str. 6/1—6/4/43.**G.**
Str. 24—26/3/47.**N/C.**
Trip cocks re-fitted.
Str. 24/7—3/9/47.**G.**
Str. 11/6—21/7/51.**G.**
Str. 13/9—8/10/54.**C/L.**
Str. 11/3—2/4/55.**G.**

BOILERS:
  266.
  266 *(new)* 16/1/08.
  2989 *(new)* 29/6/20.
  2957 *(ex7271)* 28/11/30.
  2972 *(ex7340)* 11/1/35.
  3066 *(exJ68 7043)* 6/10/39.
  3053 *(ex7305)* 6/4/43.
  3081 *(ex8532)* 3/9/47.
  23713 *(ex?)* 21/7/51.
  23742 *(exJ68 68664)* 2/4/55.

SHEDS:
Stratford.
Doncaster 29/4/27.
Stratford 22/4/31.
Colchester 22/12/40.
Stratford 20/7/41.

RENUMBERED:
  7266 13/8/24.
  8574 20/10/46.
  68574 21/7/51.

CONDEMNED: 19/1/59.
Cut up at Stratford.

7267

Stratford.

To traffic 4/1896.
Class R24 - passenger.

REPAIRS:
Str. 17/1—21/6/12.**G.**
Rebuilt to Class R24 Rbt.
Str. 17/4—24/7/20.**G.**
Str. 2/5—2/8/22.**G.**
<u>At 1/1/23: *J69/1. Westinghouse</u>
<u>brake. Condensing apparatus.*</u>
Str. 17/4—13/8/24.**G.**
Vacuum ejector fitted.
Str. 4/11/26—24/2/27.**G.**
Additional rails on bunker.
Steam heating fitted.
Str. 16/3—22/6/29.**G.**
Str. 31/5—25/6/30.**N/C.**
Trip cocks fitted.
Str. 1/3—8/4/32.**G.**
Str. 3—30/3/36.**G.**
Str. 5/10—15/11/40.**G.**
Str. 18/7—17/8/44.**G.**
Str. 22—26/3/47.**N/C.**
Trip cocks re-fitted.
Str. 9/4 28/5/47.**G.**
Str. 4/5—2/6/51.**G.**
Str. 5/2—9/3/56.**G.**
Str. 22/3—24/4/56.**N/C.**
Str. 30/12/56—22/1/57.**C/L.**

BOILERS:
  267.
  267 *(new)* 21/6/12.
  2993 *(new)* 24/7/20.
  387 *(exJ68 7047)* 24/2/27.
  2962 *(ex7377)* 8/4/32.
  3009 *(ex7081)* 30/3/36.
  3060 *(exJ68 7048)* 15/11/40.
  37 *(ex7353)* 17/8/44.
  3180 *(new)* 28/5/47.
  23711 *(ex?)* 2/6/51.
  23804 *(exJ68 68658)* 9/3/56.

SHEDS:
Stratford.
Colchester 20/7/41.
Parkeston 10/8/41.
Colchester 2/11/41.
Stratford 6/6/42.

RENUMBERED:
  7267 13/8/24.
  8575 20/7/46.
  68575 21/7/51.

CONDEMNED: 6/10/60.
Cut up at Stratford.

7268

Stratford.

To traffic 4/1896.
Class R24 - passenger.

REPAIRS:
Str. 25/10/10—20/1/11.**G.**
Rebuilt to Class R24 Rbt.
Str. 26/1—28/4/20.**G.**
Str. 18/12/22—13/1/23.**G.**
<u>At 1/1/23: *J69/1. Westinghouse</u>
<u>brake. Condensing apparatus.*</u>
Str. 1/9—3/12/24.**G.**
Str. 11/3—28/5/27.**G.**
Additional rails on bunker.
Str. 21/9/28—8/1/29.**G.**
Vacuum ejector fitted.
Str. 14/11—23/12/31.**G.**
Str. 4/2—3/3/36.**G.**
Str. 16/12/40—17/1/41.**G.**
Trip cocks fitted.
Str. 10—25/6/42.**L.**
Str. 13/8—23/9/44.**G.**
Str. 22—26/3/47.**N/C.**
Trip cocks re-fitted.
Str. 10/8—17/9/49.**G.**
Str. 26/9—3/10/49.**N/C.**
Str. 6/1—12/2/53.**G.**
Str. 20/12/54—24/2/55.**C/H.**
Str. 16/11/56—1/2/57.**C/L.**

BOILERS:
  268.
  268 *(new)* 20/1/11.
  265 *(ex7265 & sp)* 28/4/20.
  269 *(ex7269)* 28/5/27.
  3027 *(exJ68 7034)* 8/1/29.
  3063 *(new)* 23/12/31.
  3057 *(ex7191)* 3/3/36.
  3009 *(ex7267)* 17/1/41.
  3154 *(new)* 23/9/44.
  3071 *(ex8578)* 17/9/49.
  23760 *(ex?)* 12/2/53.
  23808 *(exJ68 68662)* 24/2/55.

SHEDS:
Stratford.
Yarmouth 13/8/29.
Stratford 26/11/31.
Colchester 10/10/32.
Stratford 26/3/39.
Colchester 8/9/40.
Stratford 22/12/40.
Colchester 2/11/41.
Stratford 17/5/42.

RENUMBERED:
  7268 3/12/24.
  8576 9/3/46.
  68576 19/9/49.

CONDEMNED: 12/3/58.
Cut up at Stratford.

7269

Stratford.

To traffic 5/1896.
Class R24 - passenger.

REPAIRS:
Str. 10/11/11—29/2/12.**G.**
Rebuilt to Class R24 Rbt.
Str. 14/7—9/12/22.**G.**
<u>At 1/1/23: *J69/1. Westinghouse</u>
<u>brake. Condensing apparatus.*</u>
Str. 19/7—26/9/24.**G.**
Str. 11/2—7/5/27.**G.**
Additional rails on bunker.
Str. 20—28/3/29.**N/C.**
Vacuum ejector fitted.
Str. 18/12/29—12/2/30.**G.**
Str. ?/?—28/4/31.**N/C.**
Trip cocks fitted.
Str. 9/8—5/9/34.**G.**
Str. 21/11—31/12/37.**G.**
Str. 21/6—27/7/39.**G.**
Str. 8/3—18/4/42.**G.**
Str. 15/4—18/5/45.**G.**
Str. 27/2—18/3/47.**N/C.**
Trip cocks re-fitted.
Str. 30/1—11/3/49.**G.**
Str. 11/8—10/9/52.**G.**
Str. 24/12/56—1/2/57.**G.**

BOILERS:
  269.
  269 *(new)* 29/2/12.
  3021 *(ex7359)* 7/5/27.
  2951 *(ex7364)* 12/2/30.
  2970 *(ex7088)* 5/9/34.
  3101 *(new)* 31/12/37.
  3036 *(ex7190)* 27/7/39.
  3084 *(ex7389)* 18/4/42.
  3167 *(new)* 18/5/45.
  3031 *(ex8541)* 11/3/49.
  23750 *(ex?)* 10/9/52.
  23749 *(ex68563)* 1/2/57.

SHEDS:
Stratford.
Parkeston 28/2/60.

RENUMBERED:
  7269 26/9/24.
  8577 21/1/46.
  68577 11/3/49.

CONDEMNED: 10/11/60.
Cut up at Stratford.

Those maintained at Cowlairs, when fitted with Ross 'Pops', were provided with a square casing around their base.

The usual type of buffer was the parallel shank with a hollow spindle, circular flange with wood packing behind it.

Some sent to Scotland had the GER stepped shank and to these Cowlairs fitted spindles with larger heads.

From 1927, when replacement buffers were needed, Group Standard type was fitted.

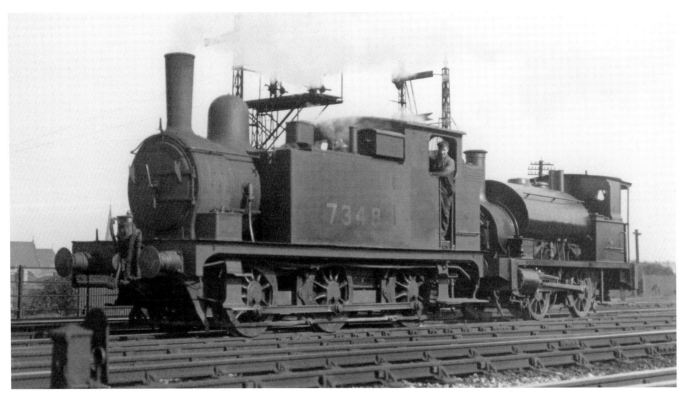

7270

Stratford.

To traffic 5/1896.
Class R24 - passenger.

REPAIRS:
Str. 3/1—27/5/10.**G.**
Rebuilt to Class R24 Rbt.
Str. 31/1—16/9/19.**G.**
Str. 2/11/21—17/1/22.**G.**
At 1/1/23: J69/1. Westinghouse
brake. Non-Condensing.
Str. 5/3—17/5/24.**G.**
Str. 23/12/26—9/4/27.**G.**
Additional rails on bunker.
Steam heating fitted.
Str. 30/3—23/7/29.**G.**
Vacuum ejector fitted.
Str. ?/?—28/4/31.**N/C.**
Trip cocks fitted.
Str. 4/12/32—4/1/33.**G.**
Str. 2/5—15/6/37.**G.**
Str. 3/8—4/9/41.**G.**
Str. 12/2—13/4/43.**L.**
Str. 18/3—12/4/45.**G.**
Str. 20—21/3/47.**N/C.**
Trip cocks re-fitted. Condensing
apparatus refitted by this time.
Str. 1/6—23/7/49.**G.**
Str. 31/7—2/8/49.**N/C.**
Str. 10/12/52—17/1/53.**G.**
Str. 28/10—23/11/57.**G.**

BOILERS:
270.
270 *(new)* 27/5/10.
2982 *(new)* 16/9/19.
2954 *(ex7197)* 23/7/29.
2993 *(ex7381)* 4/1/33.
3052 *(ex7373)* 15/6/37.
3046 *(ex7084)* 4/9/41.
3071 *(ex7373)* 12/4/45.
3159 *(ex8630)* 23/7/49.
23758 *(ex?)* 17/1/53.
23759 *(ex68571)* 23/11/57.

SHEDS:
Stratford.
Colchester 4/12/49.
Stratford 6/2/55.
Parkeston 20/11/60.
Stratford 1/1/61.

RENUMBERED:
7270 17/5/24.
8578 18/5/46.
68578 23/7/49.

CONDEMNED: 16/1/61.
Cut up at Stratford.

7271

Stratford.

To traffic 5/1896.
Class R24 - passenger.

REPAIRS:
Str. 11/9—16/12/08.**G.**
Rebuilt to Class R24 Rbt.
Str. 7/3—27/9/18.**G.**
At 1/1/23: J69/1. Westinghouse
brake. Condensing apparatus.
Str. 8/9/23—9/1/24.**G.**
Str. 18/8—8/10/25.**G.**
Str. 12/5—10/8/28.**G.**
Additional rails on bunker.
Steam heating fitted.
Str. 16/2—1/3/29.**N/C.**
Vacuum ejector fitted.
Str. 10/7—10/9/30.**G.**
Str. 10/11/32—7/2/33.**G.**
Str. 3—31/7/35.**G.**
Str. 19/1—25/2/38.**G.**
Str. 12—24/1/40.**L.**
Vacuum ejector removed.
Str. 30/5—22/6/40.**G.**
Vacuum ejector re-fitted.
Str. 10/4—11/5/44.**G.**
Condensing apparatus removed.
Str. 31/12/47—2/2/48.**G.**
Str. 26/12/51—26/1/52.**G.**
Str. 19/12/55—26/1/56.**G.**

BOILERS:
271.
271 *(new)* 16/12/08.
396 *(ex7396)* 27/9/18.
2957 *(ex7162)* 9/1/24.
2991 *(ex7083)* 10/9/30.
3070 *(new)* 7/2/33.
3058 *(exJ68 7038)* 31/7/35.
2994 *(ex7265)* 25/2/38.
3061 *(ex7380)* 22/6/40.
3043 *(ex7059)* 11/5/44.
C1686 *(ex8500)* 2/2/48.
23731 *(ex?)* 26/1/52.
23706 *(ex68601)* 26/1/56.

SHEDS:
Stratford.
Cambridge 22/8/28.
King's Lynn 11/5/36.
Cambridge 4/5/39.
Longmoor *(on loan)* 27/1/40.
Cambridge 30/5/40.
Bury St Edmunds 24/11/46.
Cambridge 15/2/48.
Stratford 14/9/52.
Colchester 11/5/58.
Stratford 1/11/59.

RENUMBERED:
271E 9/1/24.

7271 8/10/25.
8579 20/12/46.
E**8579** 2/2/48.
68579 26/1/52.

CONDEMNED: 18/1/60.
Cut up at Stratford.

_____

7272

Stratford.

To traffic 6/1896.
Class R24 - passenger.

REPAIRS:
Str. 28/11/07—19/3/08.**G.**
Rebuilt to Class R24 Rbt.
At 1/1/23: J69/1. Westinghouse
brake. Condensing apparatus.
Str. 24/7—6/11/23.**G.**
Str. ?/?—?/5/28.**G.**
Additional rails on bunker.
Str. 31/10—21//11/30.**G.**
Str. 16/9—2/10/35.**G.**
Str. ?/?—?/10/39.**L.**
Vacuum ejector fitted.
Str. ?/?—16/12/39.**G.**
Str. ?/?—10/4/40.**L.**
Vacuum brake removed.
Cow. ?/?—21/11/41.**G.***
Cow. ?/?—4/6/43.**G.***
Cow. ?/?—4/12/43.**L.***
* as WD 79 from Faslane.

BOILERS:
272.
272 *(new)* 19/3/08.
3031 *(new)* 6/11/23.
3013 *(exJ67 7333)* 21/11/30.
3067 *(ex7082)* 2/10/35.
3059 *(ex7339)* 16/12/39.

SHEDS:
Stratford.
Cambridge 9/5/28.
King's Lynn 6/8/28.
Cambridge 4/10/30.
Stratford 27/10/30.
WD Melbourne *(o/l)* 11/4/40.

RENUMBERED:
272E 6/11/23.
7272 *by* ?/5/28.

SOLD TO W.D.: 19/10/40.
Became WD 79 (later 70079).
Sold to Metal Industries Ltd.,
Faslane in 1946. By June 1950
it had been acquired by George
Wimpey for use in S.Wales.
Scrapped 1955.

_____

7273

Stratford.

To traffic 6/1896.
Class R24 - passenger.

REPAIRS:
Str. 21/9/07—31/1/08.**G.**
Rebuilt to Class R24 Rbt.
Str. 27/12/18—11/9/19.**G.**
At 1/1/23: J69/1. Westinghouse
brake. Non-Condensing.
Str. 27/11/23—30/1/24.**G.**
Str. 26/8—24/12/26.**G.**
Str. 23/8—10/1/29.**G.**
Additional rails on bunker.
Str. 13/9—2/10/29.**N/C.**
Westinghouse brake replaced by
steam plus vacuum ejector.
Str. 19/12/31—28/1/32.**G.**
Str. 8/4—1/6/35.**G.**
Gor. 23/4—12/6/37.**G.**
Gor. 9/3—13/4/40.**G.**
Gor. 8/4—2/6/45.**G.**
Str. 29/8—20/10/48.**G.**
Str. 20/1—9/2/52.**G.**
Str. 4/9—13/10/55.**G.**
Str. 23/9/59. *Not repaired.*

BOILERS:
273.
273 *(new)* 31/1/08.
350 *(ex7350)* 11/9/19.
3066 *(new)* 28/1/32.
2980 *(exJ68 7030)* 1/6/35.
2983 *(ex7086)* 13/4/40.
3077 *(ex7354)* 2/6/45.
3192 *(new)* 20/10/48.
23734 *(ex?)* 9/2/52.
23760 *(ex68576)* 13/10/55.

SHEDS:
Cambridge.
King's Lynn 17/5/28.
Cambridge 6/8/28.
Stratford 10/1/29.
Gorton 16/10/29.
Trafford Park 25/10/29.
Gorton 24/2/41.
Walton-on-the-Hill 23/11/41.
Trafford Park 15/1/42.
Northwich 5/8/42.
Trafford Park 10/6/43.
Walton-on-the-Hill 25/7/43.
Bidston 24/10/43.
Brunswick 20/2/44.
Gorton 1/10/44.
Trafford Park 19/11/44.
Gorton 14/1/45.
Walton-on-the-Hill 12/8/45.
New England 16/2/47.
Boston 20/4/47.
Lincoln 9/3/58.

7273 cont./
RENUMBERED:
273E 30/1/24.
7273 24/12/26.
8581 17/3/46.
68581 20/10/48.

CONDEMNED: 28/9/59.
Cut up at Stratford.

7274

Stratford.

To traffic 6/1896.
Class R24 - passenger.

REPAIRS:
Str. 12/12/07—20/3/08.**G.**
Rebuilt to Class R24 Rbt.
At 1/1/23: J69/1. Westinghouse
brake. Non-Condensing.
Str. ?/?—?/11/23.**G.**
Str. 3/10—31/12/25.**G.**
Str. ?/?—?/3/28.**G.**
Additional rails on bunker.
Str. 30/10—21/11/30.**G.**
Str. ?/?—?/9/35.**G.**
Str. ?/?—?/10/39.**N/C.**
Vacuum ejector fitted.
Str. ?/?—?/3/40.**G.**
Str. ?/?—?/5/40.**N/C.**
Vacuum ejector removed.
Cow. ?/?—22/11/41.**G.***
* as WD 78 from Faslane.

BOILERS:
274.
274 (new) 20/3/08.
36 (new) ?/11/23.
45 (exJ68 7050) 31/12/25.
21 (exJ68 7024) 21/11/30.
3020 (ex7367) ?/9/35.
3055 (ex7381) ?/3/40.

SHEDS:
Stratford.
Colchester ?/?.
Stratford 21/11/30.
Parkeston 24/12/39.
Stratford 17/3/40.
WD Melbourne (on loan)
10/5/40.

RENUMBERED:
274E ?/11/23.
7274 31/12/25.

SOLD TO W.D.: 19/10/40.
Became WD 78 (later 70078).
Sold to Metal Industries Ltd.,
Faslane in 1946. Became MIL 3.
Scrapped 1955.

7305

Numbered 189 to 1/1/09.

Stratford.

To traffic 6/1900.
Class R24 - passenger.

REPAIRS:
Str. 8/6—26/10/10.**G.**
Rebuilt to Class R24 Rbt.
Str. 16/11/17—25/4/18.**G.**
Str. 23/3—6/10/22.**G.**
At 1/1/23: J69/1. Westinghouse
brake. Condensing apparatus.
Str. 9/7—5/12/24.**G.**
Str. 21/1—18/3/27.**G.**
Additional rails on bunker.
Str. 30/11/29—18/1/30.**G.**
Westinghouse brake replaced
by steam plus vacuum ejector.
Condensing apparatus removed.
Str. 9—31/8/34.**G.**
Str. 5/9—6/10/37.**G.**
Str. 28/3—19/4/40.**G.**
Str. 26/7—24/8/42.**G.**
Str. 22/7—11/8/45.**G.**
Str. 22/3—7/5/49.**G.**
Str. 28/4—20/5/52.**G.**
Str. 3/9—12/10/56.**G.**

BOILERS:
305 (ex189).
305 (new) 26/10/10.
46 (exJ68 7046) 25/4/18.
2979 (ex7090) 5/12/24.
2977 (exJ68 7045) 18/1/30.
3037 (ex7393) 31/8/34.
3053 (exJ68 7046) 6/10/37.
3036 (ex7269) 24/8/42.
3098 (exJ68 7050) 11/8/45.
3069 (exJ68 8646) 7/5/49.
23743 (ex?) 20/5/52.
23745 (exJ68 68652) 12/10/56.

SHEDS:
Stratford.
Parkeston 14/6/45.
Stratford 20/10/45.
Parkeston 8/6/46.
Stratford 1/2/48.
Parkeston 28/8/49.
Stratford 28/1/51.

RENUMBERED:
7305 5/12/24.
8596 1/9/46.
68596 7/5/49.

CONDEMNED: 6/11/59.
Cut up at Stratford.

7190

Stratford.

To traffic 7/1900.
Class R24 - passenger.

REPAIRS:
Str. 10/3—3/9/13.**G.**
Rebuilt to Class R24 Rbt.
At 1/1/23: J69/1. Westinghouse
brake. Non-Condensing.
Str. 9/1—7/4/23.**G.**
Str. 5/3—25/4/25.**G.**
Str. 4/10—13/12/27.**G.**
Westinghouse brake replaced
by steam. Additional rails on
bunker.
Str. 18/10—12/12/30.**G.**
Str. 9/10—6/11/33.**G.**
Str. 21/11—24/12/35.**G.**
Vacuum ejector fitted.
Str. 7/12/38—3/3/39.**G.**
Rebuilt to J67/2.
Str. 10/8—6/10/43.**G.**
Str. 15/9—9/10/46.**G.**
Str. 7/7—13/8/49.**G.**
Str. 20/1—7/2/53.**G.**

BOILERS:
190.
190 (new) 3/9/13.
2969 (ex7342) 7/4/23.
2959 (ex7349) 13/12/27.
33 (exJ68 7038) 12/12/30.
40 (exJ68 7040) 6/11/33.
3036 (ex7087) 24/12/35.
2906 (exJ66 7325) 3/3/39.
2846 (exJ67 7336) 6/10/43.
2875 (ex8587) 9/10/46.
2897 (ex8523) 13/8/49.
23928 (ex?) 7/2/53.

SHEDS:
Norwich.
Stratford 16/12/27.
Walton-on-the-Hill 21/2/28.
Gorton 18/10/30.
New England 12/12/30.
Boston 9/1/31.
Cambridge 24/12/35.
South Lynn 22/12/47.
Norwich 26/7/53.

RENUMBERED:
7190 25/4/25.
8597 28/4/46.
68597 13/8/49.

CONDEMNED: 11/10/55.
Cut up at Stratford.

7191

Stratford.

To traffic 7/1900.
Class R24 - passenger.

REPAIRS:
Str. 1/2—22/5/13.**G.**
Rebuilt to Class R24 Rbt.
At 1/1/23: J69/1. Westinghouse
brake. Non-Condensing.
Str. 15/8/23—8/1/24.**G.**
Str. 26/5—24/9/27.**G.**
Westinghouse brake replaced by
steam. Add. rails on bunker.
Str. 5/10—16/11/29.**G.**
Str. 31/5—29/6/32.**G.**
Str. 13/4—21/5/35.**G.**
Gor. 1/7—5/8/39.**G.**
Gor. 31/10—4/11/39.**L.**
Height of chimney reduced.
Gor. 29/1—29/3/41.**G.**
Gor. 4/11—22/12/45.**G.**
Gor. 10/9—1/10/49.**G.**
Gor. 20/9—11/10/52.**G.**

BOILERS:
191.
191 (new) 22/5/13.
197 (ex7166) 8/1/24.
168 (ex7382) 16/11/29.
3057 (exJ68 7032) 29/6/32.
3035 (ex7086) 21/5/35.
2959 (ex7366) 5/8/39.
3095 (ex7198) 29/3/41.
3035 (ex8559 & sp) 1/10/49.
23842 (ex?) 11/10/52.

SHEDS:
Peterborough E.
Stratford 26/9/27.
Lincoln 12/12/27.
Stratford 21/5/35.
Trafford Park 6/9/35.
Walton-on-the-Hill 9/12/36.
Trafford Park 1/7/39.
Wrexham 6/12/40.
Trafford Park 29/3/41.
Brunswick 11/10/41.
Walton-on-the-Hill 26/3/44.
Gorton 20/1/46.
Trafford Park 2/1/49.
Brunswick 18/12/54.
Wresxham ?/1/57.

RENUMBERED:
191E 8/1/24.
7191 24/9/27.
8598 13/4/46.
68598 5/6/48.

CONDEMNED: 6/5/57.
Into Gorton for c/u: 11/5/57.
Cut up 1/6/57.

At Grouping, all except two just had Westinghouse brake for engine and for train working.

The exceptions were the two converted to steam brake in 1912, Nos.328 and 335 which became J69 due to their having the 180lb boiler.

Between 1923 and 1942, fifty-three Westinghouse fitted engines had a vacuum ejector added for train braking.

7192

Stratford.

To traffic 7/1900.
Class R24 - passenger.

REPAIRS:
Str. 8/9/11—4/1/12.**G**.
Rebuilt to Class R24 Rbt.
Str. 2/10—22/12/22.**G**.
At 1/1/23: J69/1. Westinghouse
brake. Condensing apparatus.
Str. 8/5—7/8/25.**G**.
Str. 1/9—14/12/27.**G**.
Additional rails on bunker.
Str. 9/10—26/11/29.**G**.
*Westinghouse brake replaced
by steam plus vacuum ejector.
Condensing apparatus removed.*
Str. 28/1—4/3/32.**G**.
Str. 6/9—11/10/35.**G**.
Str. 19/2—1/8/39.**G**.
Rebuilt to J67/2.
Str. 4/3—11/4/42.**G**.
Str. 25/9—21/10/44.**G**.
Rebuilt to J69/1.
Str. 15/11—14/12/46.**G**.
Str. 31/7—17/9/49.**G**.
Str. 21/6—18/8/51.**C/L**.
Str. 31/8—27/9/52.**G**.
Str. 10/2—17/3/56.**G**.

BOILERS:
192.
192 *(new)* 4/1/12.
305 *(exJ68 7042)* 22/12/22.
2967 *(exJ68 7050)* 4/3/32.
3042 *(ex7054)* 11/10/35.
2899 *(ex sp & J67 7201)*
1/8/39.
2893 *(exJ66 7309)* 11/4/42.
3040 *(ex7335)* 21/10/44.
3094 *(exJ68 7034)* 14/12/46.
3154 *(ex8576)* 17/9/49.
3154 reno.23716 18/8/51.
23751 *(ex?)* 27/9/52.
23794 *(ex?)* 17/3/56.

SHEDS:
Stratford.
Lincoln 14/12/29.

RENUMBERED:
7192 7/8/25.
8599 14/4/46.
68599 17/9/49.

CONDEMNED: 2/11/59.
Cut up at Stratford.

7193

Stratford.

To traffic 7/1900.
Class R24 - passenger.

REPAIRS:
Str. 11/3—7/7/14.**G**.
Rebuilt to Class R24 Rbt.
Str. 15/12/22—20/7/23.**G**.
At 1/1/23: J69/1. Westinghouse
brake. Condensing apparatus.
Str. 26/5—16/7/25.**G**.
Str. ?/?—6/1/27.**N/C**.
Steam heating fitted.
Str. 17/2—4/5/28.**G**.
Additional rails on bunker.
Str. 26/8—6/10/31.**G**.
Str. 19/3—28/4/34.**G**.
Str. 10/6—7/7/36.**G**.
Condensing apparatus removed.
Str. 27/8—3/10/38.**G**.
Rebuilt to J67/2.
Str. 10/1—10/2/42.**G**.
Vacuum ejector fitted.
Str. 17—26/3/42.**L**.
Str. 10/12/44—6/1/45.**G**.
Rebuilt to J69/1.
Str. 10/10—29/11/48.**G**.
Str. 31/5—27/6/53.**G**.
Str. 11/11—13/12/57.**G**.

BOILERS:
193.
2950 *(new)* 7/7/14.
2958 *(ex7392)* 20/7/23.
3041 *(ex7088)* 6/10/31.
2984 *(ex7388)* 28/4/34.
2989 *(exJ67 7331)* 7/7/36.
2871 *(exJ66 7288)* 3/10/38.
2810 *(ex7162)* 10/2/42.
3012 *(ex7055)* 6/1/45.
3036 *(ex8618)* 29/11/48.
23774 *(ex?)* 27/6/53.
23790 *(ex68512)* 13/12/57.

SHEDS:
Stratford.
Cambridge 21/8/28.
King's Lynn 15/9/46.
South Lynn 10/7/49.
King's Lynn 6/1/52.
Cambridge 19/7/53.
Stratford 1/2/59.

RENUMBERED:
7193 16/7/25.
8600 28/4/46.
68600 20/11/48.

CONDEMNED: 16/9/62.
Cut up at Stratford ??

7194

Stratford.

To traffic 7/1900.
Class R24 - passenger.

REPAIRS:
Str. 21/1—13/5/15.**G**.
Rebuilt to Class R24 Rbt.
At 1/1/23: J69/1. Westinghouse
brake. Condensing apparatus.
Str. 18/10/23—16/2/24.**G**.
Vacuum ejector fitted.
Str. 11/3—5/8/26.**G**.
*Westinghouse brake replaced
by steam (and vacuum ejector).
Additional rails on bunker.
Condensing apparatus removed.*
Str. 3/12/28—12/3/29.**G**.
Str. 26/6—29/7/31.**G**.
Str. 13/7—19/8/36.**G**.
Str. 14/11—19/12/40.**G**.
Str. 4/6—14/7/44.**G**.
Str. 27/6—18/8/47.**G**.
Str. 29/10—6/12/50.**G**.
Str. 14/2—11/3/55.**G**.

BOILERS:
194.
2956 *(new)* 13/5/15.
30 *(exJ68 7030)* 16/2/24.
2980 *(ex7340)* 12/3/29.
3055 *(new)* 29/7/31.
3014 *(ex7353)* 19/8/36.
3079 *(ex7166)* 19/12/40.
3090 *(ex7389)* 14/7/44.
3185 *(new)* 18/8/47.
23706 *(ex?)* 6/12/50.
23820 *(new)* 11/3/55.

SHEDS:
Stratford.
Neasden 27/9/26.
Annesley 2/6/27.
Neasden 16/6/27.
Immingham 28/1/32.
Ipswich 29/6/36.
Parkeston 26/2/37.
South Lynn 5/3/37.
March 26/3/37.
Stratford 9/6/37.
Parkeston 24/6/37.
Stratford 25/9/39.
Parkeston 8/9/40.
Stratford 13/4/41.
Parkeston 18/2/51.
Stratford 15/3/53.
Colchester 20/3/55.
Colwick 18/3/56.

RENUMBERED:
194E 16/2/24.
7194 5/8/26.

8601 8/9/46.
68601 6/12/50.

CONDEMNED: 1/10/59.
Cut up at Stratford.

7195

Stratford.

To traffic 7/1900.
Class R24 - passenger.

REPAIRS:
Str. 13/6—18/11/13.**G**.
Rebuilt to Class R24 Rbt.
Str. 2/10/22—15/2/23.**G**.
At 1/1/23: J69/1. Westinghouse
brake. Condensing apparatus.
Str. 8/9—23/10/24.**G**.
Str. 4/11/26—15/1/27.**G**.
Str. 24/1—18/3/30.**G**.
*Westinghouse brake replaced
by steam plus vacuum ejector.
Additional rails on bunker.
Condensing apparatus removed.*
Str. 20/8—14/9/34.**G**.
Str. 26/9—22/10/37.**G**.
Str. 10/8—6/9/41.**G**.
Str. 23/12/43—29/1/44.**G**.
Str. 28/6/45.**N/C**.
Str. 5/4—13/5/46.**G**.
Str. 27/2—2/6/48.**G**.
Str. 17/11—8/12/51.**G**.
Str. 19/8—2/10/54.**G**.

BOILERS:
195.
195 *(new)* 18/11/13.
2965 *(ex7383)* 18/3/30.
3041 *(ex7193)* 14/9/34.
3030 *(ex7390)* 22/10/37.
35 *(ex7369)* 6/9/41.
3037 *(exJ68 7027)* 29/1/44.
3097 *(ex7052)* 13/5/46.
3092 *(ex8537)* 2/6/48.
23726 *(ex?)* 8/12/51.
23708 *(ex68497)* 2/10/54.

SHEDS:
Stratford.
Hatfield 11/11/30.
Stratford 14/11/32.
Parkeston 15/2/42.
Stratford 25/11/44.
Norwich 20/6/46.
Lowestoft 11/9/46.
Norwich 23/11/49.
Boston 26/7/53.

RENUMBERED:
7195 23/10/24.
8602 10/5/46.
68602 29/5/48.

7195 cont./
CONDEMNED: 28/10/59.
Cut up at Stratford.

7196

Stratford.

To traffic 8/1900.
Class R24 - passenger.

REPAIRS:
Str. 8/6—5/12/16.**G.**
Rebuilt to Class R24 Rbt.
At 1/1/23: J69/1. Westinghouse
brake. Condensing apparatus.
Str. 22/10/23—23/2/24.**G.**
Vacuum ejector fitted.
Str. 26/9—18/11/25.**G.**
Str. 21/10/27—7/1/28.**G.**
Additional rails on bunker.
Str. 31/1—29/3/30.**G.**
Condensing apparatus removed.
Str. 4/7—12/8/32.**G.**
Str. 27/3—7/4/33.**H.**
Str. 3/4—14/5/35.**G.**
Str. 27/4—26/5/38.**G.**
Str. 4/3—13/5/39.**L.**
Str. 31/1—6/3/42.**G.**
*Trip cocks fitted. Condensing
apparatus re-fitted.*
Str. 17/6—21/7/45.**G.**
Str. 9/6—31/7/48.**G.**
Str. 29/7—30/8/51.**G.**
Str. 10/10—13/11/54.**G.**

BOILERS:
   196.
   2962 *(new)* 5/12/16.
   2956 *(ex7194)* 23/2/24.
   2998 *(ex7348)* 7/1/28.
   3028 *(ex7346)* 29/3/30.
   3050 *(ex7369)* 12/8/32.
   3023 *(ex7083)* 14/5/35.
   3092 *(ex7344)* 26/5/38.
   3041 *(ex7054)* 6/3/42.
   3046 *(ex7270)* 21/7/45.
   3065 *(exJ68 8648)* 31/7/48.
   23717 *(ex?)* 30/8/51.
   23726 *(ex68602)* 13/11/54.

SHEDS:
Stratford.
Parkeston 2/5/28.
Stratford 25/9/39.
Norwich 10/9/45.
March 26/7/53.

RENUMBERED:
   196ᴇ 23/2/24.
   7196 18/11/25.
   8603 8/9/46.
   68603 31/7/48.

CONDEMNED: 5/3/58.
Cut up at Stratford.

7197

Stratford.

To traffic 8/1900.
Class R24 - passenger.

REPAIRS:
Str. 29/12/11—12/4/12.**G.**
Rebuilt to Class R24 Rbt.
Str. 19/12/19—30/4/20.**G.**
At 1/1/23: J69/1. Westinghouse
brake. Condensing apparatus.
Str. 13/3—12/5/23.**G.**
Str. 21/3—16/7/24.**G.**
Vacuum ejector fitted.
Str. 1/10—31/12/26.**G.**
Additional rails on bunker.
Str. 23/11/28—28/2/29.**G.**
Str. ?/?—13/3/31.**G.**
Condensing apparatus removed.
Str. 13/6—7/7/33.**G.**
Str. 27/2—23/3/36.**G.**
Str. 2/9—26/10/39.**G.**
Str. 2—10/4/40.**L.**
Vacuum ejector removed.
Cow. ?/?—1/4/42.**L.***
Cow. ?/?—9/5/42.**G.***
Cow. ?/?—22/5/42.**G.***
Cow. ?/?—14/9/44.**G.***
* As WD 81 from Faslane.

BOILERS:
   197.
   197 *(new)* 12/4/12.
   2987 *(new)* 30/4/20.
   2954 *(ex7353)* 31/12/26.
   3049 *(new)* 28/2/29.
   3031 *(ex7272)* 13/3/31.
   2968 *(ex7265)* 7/7/33.
   3063 *(ex7268)* 23/3/36.
      36 *(ex7328)* 26/10/39.

SHEDS:
Stratford.
Neasden 6/7/25.
Doncaster 30/9/25.
Stratford 30/11/25.
Parkeston 6/5/27.
Stratford 25/9/39.
Sent to WD Melbourne 18/4/40.

RENUMBERED:
7197 16/7/24.

SOLD TO W.D.: 19/10/40.
*As WD 70081, to British
Industrial Solvents Ltd.,
Margam 12/1947. Scrapped
c.1953.*

7198

Stratford.

To traffic 8/1900.
Class R24 - passenger.

REPAIRS:
Str. 28/4—5/10/16.**G.**
Rebuilt to Class R24 Rbt.
At 1/1/23: J69/1. Westinghouse
brake. Condensing apparatus.
Str. 6/3—15/7/24.**G.**
Str. 1/4—10/6/27.**G.**
Additional rails on bunker.
Str. 25/8—17/10/28.**G.**
*Westinghouse brake replaced by
steam. Condensing apparatus
removed.*
Str. 2/7—18/8/31.**G.**
Gor. 11/10—18/12/33.**G.**
Str. 6/7—16/8/34.**G.**
Str. 4—21/9/34.**L.**
Str. 8/3—24/4/37.**G.**
Vacuum ejector fitted.
Gor. 5/5—1/6/40.**G.**
Str. 23/4—30/5/44.**G.**
Gor. 25/7—27/9/48.**G.**
Str. 28/1—16/2/52.**G.**
Str. 12/10—20/11/54.**G.**

BOILERS:
   198.
   2961 *(new)* 5/10/16.
      167 *(ex7167)* 15/7/24.
        50 *(ex7388)* 18/8/31.
   2975 *(ex7081)* 16/8/34.
   3095 *(new)* 24/4/37.
   2980 *(ex7273)* 1/6/40.
   3020 *(ex7355)* 30/5/44.
   3190 *(new)* 27/9/48.
   23736 *(ex?)* 16/2/52.
   23809 *(ex68537)* 20/11/54.

SHEDS:
Cambridge.
Trafford Park 2/11/28.
Wigan 21/11/28.
Brunswick 4/12/28.
Trafford Park 26/2/31.
Brunswick 26/5/31.
Trafford Park 26/6/31.
Hitchin 1/6/40.
Lincoln 26/7/53.

RENUMBERED:
   7198 15/7/24.
   8605 7/9/46.
   68605 27/9/48.

CONDEMNED: 4/7/58.
Cut up at Stratford.

7160

Stratford.

To traffic 6/1901.
Class R24 - passenger.

REPAIRS:
Str. 30/12/12—1/5/13.**G.**
Rebuilt to Class R24 Rbt.
At 1/1/23: J69/1. Westinghouse
brake. Non-Condensing.
Str. 19/3—6/10/23.**G.**
Str. 7/6—29/8/28.**G.**
*Additional rails on bunker.
Steam heating fitted.*
Str. 9/5—9/6/33.**G.**
Vacuum ejector fitted.
Str. 13—26/7/35.**H.**
Str. 11/9—7/10/36.**G.**
Str. 20/9—20/10/38.**G.**
Str. 8—29/7/40.**L.**
*Trip cocks and condensing
apparatus fitted.*
Str. 10/7—19/9/41.**G.**
Str. 19/11—9/12/44.**G.**
Str. 26—28/3/47.**N/C.**
Trip cocks re-fitted.
Str. 29/10—17/12/48.**G.**
Str. 26/5—28/6/52.**G.**
Str. 23/3—14/4/53.**C/L.**

BOILERS:
   160.
      160 *(new)* 1/5/13.
   2988 *(ex7055)* 9/6/33.
   3050 *(ex7196)* 26/7/35.
   3006 *(exJ68 7039)* 7/10/36.
   3058 *(ex7271)* 20/10/38.
   3100 *(exJ68 7032)* 19/9/41.
   3024 *(exJ68 7040)* 9/12/44.
   3012 *(ex8600)* 17/12/48.
   23748 *(ex?)* 28/6/52.

SHEDS:
Yarmouth.
Stratford 27/5/29.
Colchester 17/5/42.
Stratford 6/6/42.
Colchester 28/8/49.
Stratford 29/1/50.

RENUMBERED:
   160ᴇ 6/10/23.
   7160 *by* 2/6/28.
   8607 8/9/46.
   68607 11/12/48.

CONDEMNED: 5/5/58.
Cut up at Stratford.

For use as passenger pilots, in 1926 ten had the Westinghouse removed and became steam and vacuum braked. During 1929-30 a further twenty-one were altered from Westinghouse to steam and vacuum brake.

During 1927-29 another twenty-seven became shunting engines and were fitted only with steam brake. Between 1934 and 1940 nine of these had a vacuum ejector added, as did Nos.7328 and 7335 *see* page 141, middle.

Those shunting engines made steam brake only in 1927-29 also lost the 10-spoke balanced wheels in some cases, changing to 15-spoke as No.7370, or to 12-spoke as No.7057 *see* page 138, top.

No.7343 was made a shunter from 28th April 1928 and was one which kept the 10-spoke balanced wheels and still had them in April 1951. It was one of the twenty sent to Scottish area October 1927 to November 1928. Ten of these were steam brake only: Nos.7057, 7342, 7343, 7357, 7358, 7368, 7374, 7379, 7386 and 7392. The other ten had Westinghouse and vacuum ejectors *see* page 137, bottom No.7089, 7337, 7338, 7341, 7347, 7348, 7356, 7375, 7376 and 7391.

In their latter days, three of these Scottish based engines Nos.68503, 68524 and 68551 (*see* page 114, top) had their Westinghouse pump moved to the front of the left hand tank reason unknown.

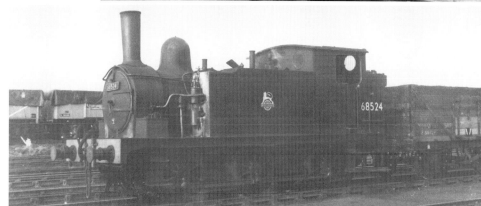

In October 1939, thirteen J69 were taken over by the War Department for use on military railway systems and in October 1940 were written off LNER stock. In May 1942 they were given WD numbers 78 to 84 and 86 to 91, subsequently increased by 70000.

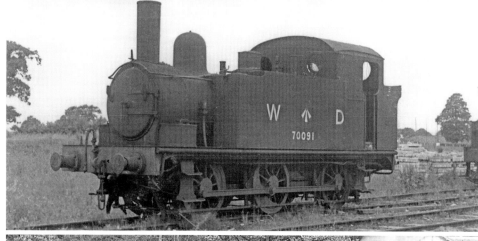

After the war they were disposed of to industry, six (plus one J68) continuing to work at Faslane on the Gareloch where the No.1 Military Port was taken over by Metal Industries Ltd., for their shipbreaking activities. M.I.LTD 2 was formerly WD 70087, LNER 7056 and was scrapped in June 1954.

7162

Stratford.

To traffic 6/1901.
Class R24 - passenger.

REPAIRS:
Str. 7/6—3/9/15.**G.**
Rebuilt to Class R24 Rbt.
At 1/1/23: *J69/1. Westinghouse
brake. Non-Condensing.*
Str. 25/8—8/12/23.**G.**
Str. 19/10—4/12/25.**G.**
Str. 9/9—10/12/27.**G.**
Additional rails on bunker.
Str. 10/4—6/6/30.**G.**
Steam heating fitted.
Str. 22/12/32—20/1/33.**G.**
Str. 16/3—2/5/35.**G.**
Vacuum ejector fitted.
Str. 11/8—2/9/38.**G.**
Rebuilt to J67/2.
Str. 14/11—13/12/41.**G.**
Str. 24/12/44—27/1/45.**G.**
Str. 12/10—26/11/48.**G.**
Str. 24/5—24/6/52.**G.**
Rebuilt to J69/1.
Str. 20/5—28/6/56.**G.**

BOILERS:
  162.
  2957 *(new)* 3/9/15.
   396 *(ex7271)* 8/12/23.
  3042 *(new)* 10/12/27.
  2954 *(ex7270)* 20/1/33.
  3024 *(exJ68 7031)* 2/5/35.
  2810 *(exJ67 7261)* 2/9/38.
  2896 *(ex7377)* 13/12/41.
  2918 *(exJ67 7164)* 27/1/45.
  23747 *(ex?)* 24/6/52.
  23714 *(ex68632)* 28/6/56.

SHEDS:
Cambridge.
Bury St Edmunds 5/10/52.
Cambridge 18/1/53.
Stratford 1/11/59.

RENUMBERED:
  162ᴇ 8/12/23.
  7162 4/12/25.
  8609 13/10/46.
  68609 20/11/48.

CONDEMNED: 16/9/62.
Cut up at Stratford ???

7163

Stratford.

To traffic 6/1901.
Class R24 - passenger.

REPAIRS:
Str. 29/9/21—6/1/22.**G.**
Rebuilt to Class R24 Rbt.
At 1/1/23: *J69/1. Westinghouse
brake. Condensing apparatus.*
Nor. 3/12/23—15/3/24.**H.**
Str. 25/9—11/11/26.**G.**
*Westinghouse replaced by steam
plus vacuum ejector. Condensing
apparatus removed.*
Str. 3/5—14/8/29.**G.**
Additional rails on bunker.
Str. 23/1—11/3/32.**G.**
Str. 17/4—19/5/36.**G.**
Str. 11/12/38—9/2/39.**L.**
Str. 19/2—13/4/40.**G.**
Rebuilt to J67/2.
Str. 31/10—24/12/42.**G.**
Str. 30/1—24/3/45.**G.**
Str. 29/9—20/11/47.**G.**
Str. 13/3—14/4/51.**G.**
Str. 3/11—3/12/53.**H/I.**

BOILERS:
  163.
  2960 *(ex7348)* 6/1/22.
   37 *(exJ68 7038)* 11/3/32.
  3032 *(ex7165)* 19/5/36.
  2881 *(exJ66 7283)* 13/4/40.
  2814 *(ex7339)* 24/12/42.
  2810 *(ex7193)* 24/3/45.
  2848 *(exJ67 8593)* 20/11/47.
  23904 *(ex?)* 14/4/51.

SHEDS:
Norwich.
Stratford 25/9/26.
Lincoln 23/12/26.
Frodingham 17/2/43.
Lincoln 30/11/45.
Hitchin 26/7/53.

RENUMBERED:
  7163 15/3/24.
  8610 1/9/46.
  68610 14/4/51.

CONDEMNED: 7/1/57.
Cut up at Stratford.

7165

Stratford.

To traffic 7/1901.
Class R24 - passenger.

REPAIRS:
Str. 13/3—25/6/12.**G.**
Rebuilt to Class R24 Rbt.
At 1/1/23: *J69/1. Westinghouse
brake. Condensing apparatus.*
Str. 2/2—7/4/23.**G.**
Str. 21/3—24/5/24.**G.**

Vacuum ejector fitted.
Str. 9—29/10/25.**L.**
Str. 22/1—7/5/27.**G.**
Additional rails on bunker.
Str. 4/4—5/7/29.**G.**
Str. 12/2—17/4/31.**G.**
Condensing apparatus removed.
Str. 27/6—25/7/33.**G.**
Str. 22/1—19/2/36.**G.**
Str. 29/6—28/7/38.**G.**
Str. 24/6—3/7/40.**L.**
*Trip cocks and condensing
apparatus fitted.*
Str. 12/12/41—13/1/42.**G.**
Str. 18/3—14/4/45.**G.**
Str. 24/3/47.**N/C.**
Trip cocks re-fitted.
Str. 23/5—1/7/49.**G.**
Str. 26/1—21/2/53.**G.**
Str. 15/4—14/6/57.**G.**

BOILERS:
  165.
  165 *(new)* 25/6/12.
  2993 *(ex7267)* 7/5/27.
  3056 *(new)* 5/7/29.
  3049 *(ex7197)* 17/4/31.
  3032 *(ex7351)* 25/7/33.
  3017 *(exJ68 7041)* 19/2/36.
  3027 *(ex7396)* 28/7/38.
  2986 *(ex7085)* 13/1/42.
  3165 *(new)* 14/4/45.
  3100 *(exJ68 8652)* 1/7/49.
  23762 *(ex?)* 21/2/53.
  23819 *(ex68556)* 14/6/57.

SHEDS:
Stratford.
Parkeston 20/9/27.
Stratford 21/8/38.
Colchester 26/3/39.
Stratford 10/3/40.

RENUMBERED:
  7165 24/5/24.
  8612 7/9/46.
  68612 1/7/49.

CONDEMNED: 26/6/61.
Cut up at Stratford.

7166

Stratford.

To traffic 7/1901.
Class R24 - passenger.

REPAIRS:
Str. 21/3—20/6/11.**G.**
Rebuilt to Class R24 Rbt.
Str. 14/2—7/5/20.**G.**
At 1/1/23: *J69/1. Westinghouse
brake. Condensing apparatus.*

Str. 30/8—23/11/23.**G.**
Str. 15/4—19/6/25.**G.**
Str. 18/8—5/11/27.**G.**
Additional rails on bunker.
Str. 8/2—29/3/30.**G.**
Str. ?/?—17/7/30.**N/C.**
Trip cocks fitted.
Str. ?/?—22/4/31.**N/C.**
Trip cocks removed.
Str. 5/10—9/11/34.**G.**
Str. 3—20/10/37.**G.**
Str. 17/6—27/7/39.**G.**
Str. ?/?—21/10/39.**N/C.**
Vacuum ejector fitted.
Str. 14—21/5/40.**L.**
Trip cocks re-fitted.
Str. 22/9—11/11/40.**G.**
Str. 21/2—12/3/42.**L.**
Str. 23/8—15/10/43.**G.**
Str. 24—25/3/47.**N/C.**
Trip cocks re-fitted.
Str. 4/3—31/5/48.**G.**
Str. 25/5—11/6/49.**C/L.**
Str. 1—26/1/52.**G.**
Str. 12/6—11/8/56.**G.**

BOILERS:
  166.
  166 *(new)* 20/6/11.
  197 *(ex7197)* 7/5/20.
  3023 *(new)* 23/11/23.
  3021 *(ex7269)* 29/3/30.
  2977 *(ex7305)* 9/11/34.
  3079 *(ex7360)* 20/10/37.
  2991 *(ex7385)* 11/11/40.
  2974 *(exJ68 7030)* 15/10/43.
  3188 *(new)* 31/5/48.
  23730 *(ex?)* 26/1/52.
  23882 *(ex68558)* 11/8/56.

SHEDS:
Stratford.
Colchester 11/7/42.
Stratford 2/1/43.

RENUMBERED:
  166ᴇ 23/11/23.
  7166 19/6/25.
  8613 7/9/46.
  68613 29/5/48.

CONDEMNED: 17/9/61.
Cut up at Stratford.

7167

Stratford.

To traffic 7/1901.
Class R24 - passenger.

REPAIRS:
Str. 16/4—31/8/10.**G.**
Rebuilt to Class R24 Rbt.

The passenger pilot at Liverpool Street station was ex Stratford 24th January 1948 as E8619 but in LNER green fully lined livery which it kept until it went to works 4th May 1953 for a General repair.

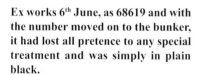

Ex works 6th June, as 68619 and with the number moved on to the bunker, it had lost all pretence to any special treatment and was simply in plain black.

Despite its somber paint job, the Liverpool Street crews kept it immaculately clean and polished where possible as this 20th November 1956 photograph proves.

In February 1957, Stratford repainted 68619, still black but now with full red, white, and grey lining. It was probably the first to use the BR crest instead of the emblem, and note that the lion is facing the wrong way.

No.68619's public image was further enhanced when, in September 1959, it was repainted in GER Royal blue with red lining and had the Great Eastern crest put on the bunker. The BR crest was also corrected. As No.7053 it was re-fitted with condensing apparatus and trip cock gear was put on 28th August 1940, the trip cock gear was re-fitted on 24th March 1947 and then carried to 30th October1961 withdrawal.

When No.68633 was withdrawn on 24th November 1960, Stratford carefully restored it to its original condition as G.E.R. No.87 and on 27th January 1962 it was installed in the Clapham Transport Museum where it remained to closure and removal to York National Railway Museum.

7167 cont./

At 1/1/23: J69/1. Westinghouse brake. Non-Condensing.
Str. 7/1—9/5/24.**G.**
Str. ?/?—?/3/27.**G.**
Additional rails on bunker.
Str. 26/4—13/5/32.**G.**
Str. 3—18/1/35.**G.**
Vacuum ejector fitted.
Str. ?/? 19/8/38.**G.**
Str. ?/?—?/10/39.**N/C.**
Vacuum ejector removed.
Str. ?/?—1/3/40.**G.**
After damage at Longmoor.
Str. ?/?—12/6/41.**G.**
Cow. ?/?—25/1/44.**L.***
* As WD 90 from Faslane.*

BOILERS:
  167.
  167 (new) 31/8/10.
2973 (exJ68 7045) 9/5/24.
3027 (ex7268) 13/5/32.
3082 (new) 18/1/35.
3015 (ex7387) 19/8/38.

SHEDS:
Norwich.
Stratford 18/1/35.
WD Longmoor (o/l) 14/10/39.

RENUMBERED:
7167 9/5/24.

SOLD TO W.D.: 19/10/40.
Sold 1946 to Metal Industries Ltd., Faslane. Became MIL5, later 3. Scrapped 1962.

7168

Stratford.

To traffic 7/1901.
Class R24 - passenger.

REPAIRS:
Str. 10/1—16/5/12.**G.**
Rebuilt to Class R24 Rbt.
At 1/1/23: J69/1. Westinghouse brake. Condensing apparatus.
Str. 23/1—8/3/24.**G.**
Vacuum ejector fitted.
Str. 22/1—15/4/26.**G.**
Str. 30/11/28—15/3/29.**G.**
Additional rails on bunker.
Str. 22/5—4/6/30.**L.**
Trip cocks fitted.
Str. 10/8—26/9/32.**G.**
Air-operated re-setting trip cock gear fitted.
Str. 14—25/11/32.**H.**
Str. 6—9/2/33.**L.**
Trip cock adjustment.

Str. 16/2—9/3/33.**L.**
Trip cock adjustment.
Str. 16/8—17/9/35.**G.**
Str. 19/11—28/12/39.**G.**
Str. 22—30/4/40.**L.**
Condensing apparatus, vacuum ejector and trip cocks removed.
Cow. ?/? 9/2/42.**G.***
Cow. ?/?—13/5/44.**L.***
* As WD 82 from Faslane.*

BOILERS:
  168.
  168 (new) 16/5/12.
  267 (ex7347) 15/4/26.
  269 (ex7268) 15/3/29.
  168 (ex7191) 26/9/32.
3054 (exJ67 7332) 17/9/35.
3033 (exJ68 7028) 28/12/39.

SHEDS:
Stratford.
Sent to WD Melbourne 2/5/40.

RENUMBERED:
7168 8/3/24.

SOLD TO W.D.: 19/10/40.
As WD 70082, sold to British Industrial Solvents., Margam. Became BIS 2. Scrapped 9/1955.

7051

Stratford.

To traffic 5/1904.
Class S56 - passenger.

REPAIRS:
At 1/1/23: J69/1. Westinghouse brake. Condensing apparatus.
Str. 5/3—9/10/23.**G.**
Str. 14/4—5/6/25.**G.**
Str. 17/9—13/12/27.**G.**
Westinghouse brake replaced by steam. Additional rails on bunker. Condensing apparatus removed.
Str. 21/6—24/9/30.**G.**
Str. 10/2—21/3/33.**G.**
Str. 23/12/36—20/2/37.**G.**
Str. 1/10—9/11/39.**G.**
Str. 27—30/5/40.**L.**
Vacuum ejector fitted.
Str. 26/9—24/11/43.**G.**
Str. 8/11—12/12/46.**G.**
Str. 20/11—23/12/49.**G.**
Str. 13/4—9/5/53.**G.**

BOILERS:
  51.
  29 (exJ68 7029) 9/10/23.
3069 (new) 21/3/33.

3094 (new) 20/2/37.
3088 (ex7361) 9/11/39.
3082 (ex7346) 24/11/43.
3089 (ex7083) 12/12/46.
23770 (ex?) 9/5/53.

SHEDS:
Stratford.
Walton-on-the-Hill 21/2/28.
Gorton 21/6/30.
Walton-on-the-Hill 18/10/30.
Trafford Park 21/3/33.
Walton-on-the-Hill 22/9/34.
Stratford 20/2/37.
Staveley 1/1/56.

RENUMBERED:
  51E 9/10/23.
  7051 5/6/25.
  8617 7/12/46.
68617 23/12/49.

CONDEMNED: 14/7/58.
Cut up at Stratford.

7052

Stratford.

To traffic 5/1904.
Class S56 - passenger.

REPAIRS:
Str. 22/3—11/10/18.**G.**
Str. 8/8—12/11/21.**G.**
At 1/1/23: J69/1. Westinghouse brake. Condensing apparatus.
Str. 9/5—7/7/23.**G.**
Str. 21/5—1/9/25.**G.**
Str. 21/10—23/12/27.**G.**
Westinghouse brake replaced by steam. Add. rails on bunker. Condensing apparatus removed.
Str. 6/12/30—30/1/31.**G.**
Str. 12/3—27/4/34.**G.**
Str. 31/8—27/9/37.**G.**
Str. 1/11—4/12/40.**G.**
Str. 28/10—27/11/43.**G.**
Str. 24/1—16/2/46.**G.**
Str. 19/9—30/10/48.**G.**
Str. 30/10—1/12/51.**G.**
Str. 7/9—6/10/55.**G.**

BOILERS:
  52.
  45 (exJ68 7045) 11/10/18.
3014 (new) 12/11/21.
2971 (ex7265) 1/9/25.
2959 (ex7190) 30/1/31.
3077 (new) 27/4/34.
3097 (new) 27/9/37.
  40 (exJ68 7029) 4/12/40.
3097 (exJ68 7040) 27/11/43.
3036 (ex7305) 16/2/46.

3195 (new) 30/10/48.
23725 (ex?) 1/12/51.
23720 (exJ68 68641) 6/10/55.

SHEDS:
Stratford.
Lincoln 23/2/31.
Frodingham 25/1/49.
Lincoln 4/8/49.
Staveley 24/2/52.
Lincoln 6/4/52.
Staveley 8/6/52.
Lincoln 13/7/52.
Darnall 28/8/52.
Lincoln 1/3/53.
Boston 9/3/58.
Colwick 15/6/58.

RENUMBERED:
  7052 1/9/25.
  8618 1/9/46.
68618 30/10/48.

CONDEMNED: 18/8/58.
Cut up at Stratford.

7053

Stratford.

To traffic 5/1904.
Class S56 - passenger.

REPAIRS:
Woolwich.12/12/19—17/6/20.**G.**
Str. 20/11/22—9/2/23.**G.**
At 1/1/23: J69/1. Westinghouse brake. Condensing apparatus.
Str. 5/12/24—14/2/25.**G.**
Str. 11/2—21/5/27.**G.**
Additional rails on bunker.
Str. 2/2—23/4/29.**G.**
Str. 29/9—7/11/31.**G.**
Str. 22/12/34—24/1/35.**G.**
Vacuum ejector fitted.
Condensing apparatus removed.
Str. 14/12/37—13/1/38.**G.**
Str. 7—28/8/40.**L.**
Trip cocks and condensing apparatus fitted.
Str. 22/2—29/3/41.**G.**
Str. 12—27/5/42.**L.**
Str. 17/12/43—5/2/44.**G.**
Str. 21—24/3/47.**N/C.**
Trip cocks re-fitted.
Str. 5/11/47—24/1/48.**G.**
Str. 6—9/10/52.**N/C.**
Str. 4/5—6/6/53.**G.**
Str. 3/4—22/6/56.**C/L.**
Str. 28/10—23/11/57.**C/L.**

BOILERS:
  53.
  55 (ex7055) 17/6/20.

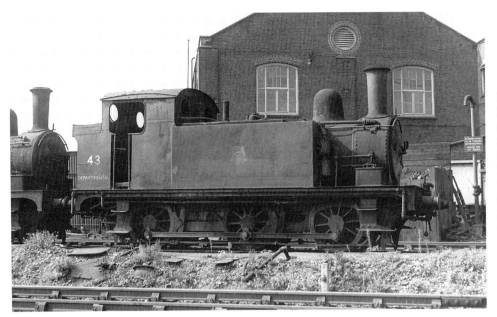

No.68532 (ex7355) withdrawn 16th December 1958, was transferred to service stock on 9th January 1959 and renumbered Departmental 43, also being fitted with a smokebox plate 43 but retaining the BR emblem on its tanks. Its service was brief as it was condemned on 21st August 1959. Note it was one with widened tanks and condensing chamber distinct from sides, and that it had extensions to the front footsteps.

The replacement was Part 2 No.68498 (ex7336) which was made Departmental 44 on 21st August 1959 and served as such to 16th September 1962 withdrawal. This was one not rebuilt with widened tanks so kept the 1000 gallons capacity.

No.68543 (ex7367) was taken from Running Stock on 2nd November 1959 to become Departmental 45 and it too was withdrawn on 16th September 1962 when the G.E. section closed to steam locomotives. As No.367, built April 1894, it was the first to have tank sides extended to cover the condensing chamber.

(above) Whilst a few continued in grey paint after Grouping, the J69's standing was such as to warrant LNER standard black with single red lining. No.193 was ex works 20th July 1923.

Unlike the other workshops, Stratford had not discarded the ampersand before they began adding the area suffix letter E. No.358E was ex works 18th September 1923. They did drop the ampersand as shown in the photograph of LNER 390E page 104, top - which was ex works 15th December 1923.

The ampersand was long lasting and was still on No.160 waiting to enter works on 9th May 1933, confirmed by tender lettering being in evidence. No.160 did have a general repair on 29th August 1928 at which it got the extra bunker rails but clearly missed both painting and re-numbering to 7160.

7053 cont./
3018 *(new)* 9/2/23.
3006 *(ex7368)* 23/4/29.
3059 *(new)* 7/11/31.
3081 *(new)* 24/1/35.
3103 *(new)* 13/1/38.
3078 *(ex7355)* 29/3/41.
3088 *(ex7051)* 5/2/44.
3060 *(exJ68 8650)* 24/1/48.
23772 *(ex?)* 6/6/53.

SHEDS:
Stratford.
Ipswich 23/4/29.
Colchester 8/5/29.
Stratford 24/1/35.

RENUMBERED:
7053 14/2/25.
8619 4/1/47.
E8619 24/1/48.
68619 6/6/53.

CONDEMNED: 30/10/61.
Cut up at Stratford.

7054

Stratford.

To traffic 5/1904.
Class S56 - passenger.

REPAIRS:
Str. 27/5—16/10/14.**G.**
Str. 12/7—6/10/22.**G.**
At 1/1/23: *J69/1. Westinghouse brake. Condensing apparatus.*
Str. 26/2—21/5/24.**G.**
Vacuum ejector fitted.
Str. 19/2—22/5/26.**G.**
Additional rails on bunker.
Str. 26/5—5/9/28.**G.**
Str. ?/?—?/3/30.**N/C.**
Condensing apparatus removed.
Str. 27/6—12/9/30.**G.**
Str. 21/1—1/3/33.**G.**
Str. 26/2—5/4/35.**G.**
Str. 23/12/37—14/1/38.**G.**
Str. 22/11—23/12/38.**L.**
Str. ?/?—?/10/39.**L.**
Vacuum ejector removed.
Str. ?/?—?/9/41.**H.**

BOILERS:
54.
2951 *(new)* 16/10/14.
2981 *(ex7364)* 21/5/24.
41 *(exJ68 7041)* 22/5/26.
3048 *(new)* 5/9/28.
3042 *(ex7162)* 1/3/33.
3091 *(new)* 5/4/35.
3041 *(ex7195)* 14/1/38.
3039 *(exJ68 7050)* ?/9/41.

SHEDS:
Stratford.
Ipswich 5/9/28.
Parkeston 26/9/28.
Stratford 26/3/39.
WD Longmoor *(o/l)* 14/10/39.

RENUMBERED:
7054 21/5/24.

SOLD TO W.D.: 19/10/40.
As WD 70086 sold to Metal Industries Ltd., Faslane in 1946 becoming MIL 1. Scrapped 6/54.

7055

Stratford.

To traffic 6/1904.
Class S56 - passenger.

REPAIRS:
Str. 16/1—17/10/19.**G.**
At 1/1/23: *J69/1. Westinghouse brake. Non-Condensing.*
Str. 30/8—27/10/23.**G.**
Str. 2/12/25—4/3/26.**G.**
Str. 15/3—27/7/28.**G.**
Westinghouse brake replaced by steam. Add. rails on bunker.
Str. 3—28/4/33.**G.**
Str. 11/7—13/8/37.**G.**
Vacuum ejector fitted.
Str. 4—18/11/38.**L.**
Str. 4—27/1/39.**L.**
Str. 15/6—30/7/41.**G.**
Str. 27/10—17/11/44.**G.**
Str. 20/9—25/10/48.**G.**
Str. 1—24/11/51.**G.**
Str. 1/1—2/2/57.**G.**

BOILERS:
55.
273 *(ex7273)* 17/10/19.
2988 *(ex7082)* 27/7/28.
3007 *(ex7385)* 28/4/33.
3073 *(ex7088)* 13/8/37.
3012 *(ex7345)* 30/7/41.
3026 *(exJ68 7037)* 17/11/44.
3062 *(exJ68 8641)* 25/10/48.
23724 *(ex?)* 24/11/51.
23738 *(ex68549)* 2/2/57.

SHEDS:
Ipswich.
Stratford 14/5/29.
New England 27/11/55.
Doncaster 4/12/55.
Retford 29/11/59.
Doncaster 13/3/60.
Langwith Jct. 27/3/60.
Canklow 7/8/60.
Retford 22/1/61.

Stratford 18/6/61.

RENUMBERED:
55E 27/10/23.
7055 4/3/26.
8621 2/1/47.
68621 23/10/48.

CONDEMNED: 16/9/62.
Cut up at Stratford ???

7056

Stratford.

To traffic 5/1904.
Class S56 - passenger.

REPAIRS:
Str. 25/4—9/10/19.**G.**
Str. 6/3—25/6/22.**G.**
At 1/1/23: *J69/1. Westinghouse brake. Non-Condensing.*
Str. 30/10/24—28/1/25.**G.**
Str. 26/11/26—18/3/27.**G.**
Str. 9/2—24/5/29.**G.**
Additional rails on bunker.
Str. 1/8—15/9/33.**G.**
Str. 10/2—14/3/38.**G.**
Cow. ?/?—26/2/45.**G.***
* As WD 87 from Faslane.

BOILERS:
56.
2983 *(new)* 9/10/19.
2994 *(ex7081)* 18/3/27.
3053 *(new)* 24/5/29.
2978 *(ex7395)* 15/9/33.
2955 *(exJ68 7038)* 14/3/38.

SHEDS:
Stratford.
WD Longmoor *(o/l)* 14/10/39.

RENUMBERED:
7056 28/1/25.

SOLD TO W.D.: 19/10/40.
As WD 70087 sold to Metal Industries Ltd., Faslane 1946. Became MIL 2. Scrapped 6/54.

7057

Stratford.

To traffic 6/1904.
Class S56 - passenger.

REPAIRS:
Str. 31/12/17—22/3/18.**G.**
At 1/1/23: *J69/1. Westinghouse brake. Condensing apparatus.*

Str. 9/5—1/9/23.**G.**
Str. 27/12/24—13/2/25.**G.**
Str. 10/2—12/5/27.**G.**
Additional rails on bunker.
Str. 9/8—5/10/28.**G.**
Westinghouse brake replaced by steam. Cond/g app.removed.
Cow. 23—26/10/28.**N/C.**
Footsteps and bunker handrails fitted.
Cow. 11/6—22/8/30.**G.**
Cow. 21/7—14/11/32.**G.**
Cow. 29/8—5/10/34.**G.**
Cow. 18/8—23/9/36.**G.**
Cow. ?/?—7/7/38.**L.**
Cow. 8/11—12/12/39.**G.**
Cow. 9—24/4/40.**L.**
Cow. 25/12/42—22/1/43.**H.**
Cow. 10/7—15/8/47.**G.**
Cow. 9—12/4/51.**C/L.**
Str. 8/11—11/12/52.**G.**
Str. 31/3—10/5/57.**G.**

BOILERS:
57.
2967 *(new)* 22/3/18.
2963 *(ex7345)* 1/9/23.
2963 reno. C1683 22/8/30.
C1687 *(ex7341)* 14/11/32.
3070 *(exStr & 7081)* 12/12/39.
3011 *(ex8525)* 15/8/47.
23756 *(ex?)* 11/12/52.
23841 *(ex68499)* 10/5/57.

SHEDS:
Stratford.
Scottish Area 16/10/28.
Eastfield 22/10/28.
St Margarets 1/3/29.
Doncaster 15/7/51.
Norwich 9/9/51.
Melton Constable 4/5/52.
South Lynn 26/7/53.
Barrow Hill 1/6/58.
Mexborough 29/6/58.
Langwith Jct. 24/1/60.

RENUMBERED:
7057 13/2/25.
8623 14/7/46.
68623 12/4/51.

CONDEMNED: 14/2/61.
Into Doncaster for c/u: 14/2/61.

7058

Stratford.

To traffic 6/1904.
Class S56 - passenger.

REPAIRS:
Str. 27/10—30/12/14.**G.**

(*above*) **Ex works 12th July 1924, No.7355 remained in grey and got its LNER number in the 19in. yellow painted figures. Note forward extension to front footsteps. No.7337, ex works in 1925 was still grey until it went for repair on 1st January 1931 from which it was out 21st February 1931 in unlined black. No.7371 - *see* page 96, top - was still grey to 18th August 1929.**

(*right*) **From June 1928 no more red lining was applied so No.7379, ex works 1st August 1928, went to Scottish Area in unlined black on 12th September 1928.**

After Cowlairs included painting in their maintenance of the twenty J69, they applied their custom of putting the engine number in 6in. shaded transfers on the back of the bunker, in the centre.

(above) **The unlined black on the passenger engines was at least given one coat of varnish until the 1939 war.**

This shows No.7345 in its war paint when ex works 30th September 1944. From July 1942 only NE was put on the tanks, Stratford still using 7½ in. letters. Buffers and front buffer beam were painted white to show up better in the blackout. Note tarpaulin screen in the cab to smother glare when the firebox door was open after dark.

Those reduced to NE at Gorton works got it in 12in. shaded transfers in this style. No.7273 was ex works 2nd June 1945 becoming 8581 on Sunday 17th March 1946 at Walton-on-the-Hill shed. By 2nd June 1945, blackout regulations had been lifted hence no white paint at the front end.

7058 cont./
Str. 11/3—30/6/21.**G.**
At 1/1/23: J69/1. Westinghouse
brake. Condensing apparatus.
Str. ?/?—?/5/23.**G.**
Str. 13/4—13/8/27.**G.**
Additional rails on bunker.
Str. 18/11—5/12/31.**G.**
Str. ?/?—?/11/36.**G.**
Vacuum ejector fitted.
Condensing apparatus removed.
Str. ?/?—6/1/40.**G.**
Str. ?/?—24/4/40.**L.**
Vacuum ejector removed.

BOILERS:
  58.
2952 (new) 30/12/14.
3010 (new) 30/6/21.
2999 (ex7367) 13/8/27.
3061 (new) 5/12/31.
3049 (exJ68 7047) ?/11/36.
3091 (exJ68 7030) 6/1/40.

SHEDS:
Stratford.
Colchester 3/12/39.
Stratford 10/3/40.
WD Melbourne (o/l) 25/4/40.

RENUMBERED:
  7058 by 2/5/25.

SOLD TO W.D.: 19/10/40.
As WD 70083 sold to Metal
Industries Ltd., Faslane 1946.
Became MIL 4. Scrapped 6/54.

_____

7059

Stratford.

To traffic 6/1904.
Class S56 - passenger.

REPAIRS:
Str. 13/8/20—24/3/21.**G.**
At 1/1/23: J69/1. Westinghouse
brake. Condensing apparatus.
Str. 8/2—7/9/23.**G.**
Str. 22/5—2/10/25.**G.**
Str. ?/?—30/12/26.**L.**
Steam heating fitted.
Str. 16/12/27—15/3/28.**G.**
Additional rails on bunker.
Str. 1—17/4/30.**L.**
Trip cocks fitted.
Str. ?/?—22/4/31.**L.**
Trip cocks removed.
Str. 19/7—25/8/32.**G.**
Vacuum ejector fitted.
Condensing apparatus removed.
Str. 15/4—23/5/35.**G.**
Str. 21/2—22/3/38.**G.**

Str. 27/6—25/7/41.**G.**
Str. 5/3—15/4/44.**G.**
Str. 11/8—14/9/46.**G.**
Str. 21/8—4/10/47.**L.**
Str. 1/1—11/2/50.**G.**
Str. 9/8—5/9/53.**G.**

BOILERS:
  59.
3005 (new) 24/3/21.
2995 (ex7386) 15/3/28.
3026 (exJ68 7033) 25/8/32.
2998 (ex7344) 23/5/35.
3037 (ex7305) 22/3/38.
3043 (exJ68 7044) 25/7/41.
3030 (exJ68 7033) 15/4/44.
3045 (exJ68 7046) 14/9/46.
3199 (new) 11/2/50.
23779 (ex?) 5/9/53.

SHEDS:
Stratford.
Norwich 18/8/33.
Yarmouth 10/10/46.
Cambridge 26/7/53.
Bury St Edmunds 3/10/54.
Cambridge 23/1/55.
Melton Constable 25/12/55.
Yarmouth 29/6/58.

RENUMBERED:
  7059 2/10/25.
  8625 6/9/46.
  68625 11/2/50.

CONDEMNED: 1/1/59.
Cut up at Stratford.

_____

7060

Stratford.

To traffic 6/1904.
Class S56 - passenger.

REPAIRS:
Str. 26/12/14—26/3/15.**G.**
Str. 13/11/22—18/1/23.**G.**
At 1/1/23: J69/1. Westinghouse
brake. Condensing apparatus.
Str. 22/1—30/4/25.**G.**
Str. 26/11—24/12/26.**G.**
Str. 21/10—31/12/27.**G.**
Westinghouse brake replaced
by steam. Add. rails on bunker.
Condensing apparatus removed.
Str. 16/8—17/10/30.**G.**
Str. 29/1—20/2/35.**G.**
Str. 23/4—21/7/39.**G.**
Str. 30/5—7/6/40.**L.**
Vacuum ejector fitted.
Str. 23/1—12/3/43.**G.**
Str. 28/3—6/5/43.**N/C.**
Str. 21/7—25/10/46.**G.**

Str. 28/10/49—14/1/50.**G.**
Str. 22/10—22/11/52.**G.**
Str. 24/4—27/7/56.**C/L.**
Str. 29/9—26/10/57.**G.**

BOILERS:
  60.
2955 (new) 26/3/15.
3029 (exJ67 7334) 17/10/30.
3010 (ex7366) 20/2/35.
2976 (ex7365) 21/7/39.
3034 (ex7328) 12/3/43.
3101 (exJ68 8653) 14/1/50.
23755 (ex?) 22/11/52.
23802 (ex68545) 26/10/57.

SHEDS:
Stratford.
New England 9/10/55.
Grantham 13/4/58.
Colwick 1/5/60.
Stratford 11/6/61.

RENUMBERED:
  7060 30/4/25.
  8626 19/10/46.
  68626 14/1/50.

CONDEMNED: 3/5/62.
Cut up at Stratford ?

_____

7081

Stratford.

To traffic 8/1904.
Class S56 - passenger.

REPAIRS:
Str. 7/5—23/7/20.**G.**
At 1/1/23: J69/1. Westinghouse
brake. Condensing apparatus.
Str. 4/11/26—18/2/27.**G.**
Str. ?/?—?/4/29.**G.**
Additional rails on bunker.
Str. ?/?—?/6/30.**G.**
Trip cocks fitted.
Str. ?/?—?/5/31.**L.**
Trip cocks removed.
Str. 17/11—8/12/33.**G.**
Vacuum ejector fitted.
Str. ?/?—?/12/35.**G.**
Str. ?/?—?/12/36.**L.**
Condensing apparatus removed.
Str. ?/?—?/8/39.**G.**
Str. ?/?—?/5/40.**N/C.**
Vacuum ejector removed.
Cow. ?/?—2/9/43.**L.***
Cow. ?/?—3/1/44.**G.***
* As WD 80 from Faslane.

BOILERS:
  81.
2994 (new) 23/7/20.

2975 (ex7396) 18/2/27.
3009 (exJ68 7048) 8/12/33.
3070 (ex7271) ?/12/35.
3016 (ex7363) ?/8/39.

SHEDS:
Stratford.
Colchester 10/3/40.
Stratford 8/9/40.

RENUMBERED:
  7081 by 31/10/24.

SOLD TO W.D.: 19/10/40.
Sold (still as WD 80) 2/1948 to
John Lysaght Ltd., Scunthorpe.
Reno.25. C/u 1958 or 1959.

_____

7082

Stratford.

To traffic 8/1904.
Class S56 - passenger.

REPAIRS:
Str. 7/6—28/12/17.**G.**
Wlwich. 24/12/19—17/7/20.**G.**
At 1/1/23: J69/1. Westinghouse
brake. Condensing apparatus.
Str. 11/6—18/8/23.**G.**
Str. 15/8—4/11/25.**G.**
Str. ?/?—3/1/27.**L.**
Steam heating fitted.
Str. 27/1—12/5/28.**G.**
Additional rails on bunker.
Str. 29/4—21/5/30.**N/C.**
Trip cocks fitted.
Str. 22/4/31.**N/C.**
Trip cocks removed.
Str. 8/8—7/9/32.**G.**
Vacuum ejector fitted.
Str. 17/7—2/9/35.**G.**
Condensing apparatus removed.
Str. 7/7—5/8/38.**G.**
Rebuilt to J67/2.
Str. 20/7—26/8/41.**G.**
Str. 22/3—22/4/44.**G.**
Str. 24/2—31/3/47.**G.**
Str. 27/8—23/9/50.**G.**
Str. 30/9—24/10/53.**G.**

BOILERS:
  82.
  358 (ex7358) 28/12/17.
2988 (new) 17/7/20.
3047 (new) 12/5/28.
3067 (new) 7/9/32.
2954 (ex7162) 2/9/35.
2866 (ex sp, J65 7157) 5/8/38.
2848 (exJ65 7157) 26/8/41.
2910 (ex7377) 22/4/44.
2878 (exJ66 8371) 31/3/47.
23900 (ex?) 23/9/50.

Cowlairs also used 12in. for NE only No.7343 being ex works 2nd December 1944 in this style and it was not re-numbered until 3rd November 1946 when it changed to 8505.

Not all Cowlairs engines were alike because No.7375 (8551 from 14th September 1946) only got 7½ in. NE when ex works 15th January 1944.

(below) From January 1946 LNER was restored at works paintings and the re-numbering began. No.8599 was put in this style when ex Stratford 14th December 1946.

No.8558 got LNER and its new number on 10th August 1946 when ex Stratford from a General repair.

(below) This was a Cowlairs painting ex works 15th August 1947 in normal LNER style. Note wide spacing made available because tank sides are flush with the cab.

No.8568 was ex Cowlairs 6th March 1948 and painted whilst they were still using LNER. It was well enough done to last until 27th February 1956 when this engine entered Stratford for its next - and last - repair. It was thus the last one in traffic with LNER and number. Note the closer spacing due to centering just on the widened tank side.

7082 cont./
23901 *(exJ67 68593)* 24/10/53.

SHEDS:
Stratford.
Norwich 7/9/32.
Lowestoft 18/9/32.
Norwich 8/12/40.
Yarmouth Beach 10/11/45.
Norwich 20/2/47.
Yarmouth 19/10/47.
Lowestoft 3/3/57.
Yarmouth 5/5/57.
Lowestoft 2/6/57.

RENUMBERED:
  7082 4/11/25.
  8628 1/9/46.
68628 23/9/50.

CONDEMNED: 24/2/58.
Cut up at Stratford.

7083

Stratford.

To traffic 8/1904.
Class S56 - passenger.

REPAIRS:
Str. 23/8/18—26/3/19.**G.**
Str. 7/10—16/12/22.**G.**
At 1/1/23: *J69/1. Westinghouse
brake. Condensing apparatus.*
Str. 2/8—22/11/24.**G.**
Str. 10/2—7/5/27.**G.**
Additional rails on bunker.
Str. 9/11—17/12/27.**L.**
Str. 8—20/3/29.**N/C.**
Vacuum ejector fitted.
Str. 24/5—11/7/30.**G.**
Str. 6/5/31.**N/C.**
Trip cocks fitted.
Str. 24/1—8/2/35.**G.**
Str. 25/6—30/8/39.**G.**
Trip cocks removed (to 7372).
Str. 10/10—1/12/42.**G.**
Str. 17/5—26/6/46.**G.**
Str. 26/9—29/10/49.**G.**
Str. 1/7—14/8/53.**G.**

BOILERS:
  83.
  2978 *(new)* 26/3/19.
  2991 *(ex7346)* 7/5/27.
  3023 *(ex7166)* 11/7/30.
  3085 *(new)* 8/2/35.
  3068 *(ex7352)* 30/8/39.
  3089 *(ex7372)* 1/12/42.
  3104 *(ex7372)* 26/6/46.
  3177 *(ex8556)* 29/10/49.
  23777 *(ex?)* 14/8/53.

SHEDS:
Stratford.
Colchester 10/3/40.
Stratford 8/9/40.
Colchester 20/7/41.
Stratford 2/11/41.
Colchester 6/6/42.
Stratford 11/7/42.
Colchester 2/1/43.
Stratford 25/11/44.
Colchester 7/12/46.
Stratford 15/2/47.
Colchester 12/4/47.
Stratford 16/5/48.
Colchester 16/6/48.
Stratford 8/10/50.
Colwick 11/12/55.

RENUMBERED:
  7083 22/11/24.
  8629 19/6/46.
68629 29/10/49.

CONDEMNED: 26/11/59.
Cut up at Doncaster ?

7084

Stratford.

To traffic 8/1904.
Class S56 - passenger.

REPAIRS:
Str. 7/2—26/5/20.**G.**
Str. 4/2—2/5/22.**G.**
At 1/1/23: *J69/1. Westinghouse
brake. Condensing apparatus.*
Str. 6/3—23/5/24.**G.**
Str. 23/9/26—29/1/27.**G.**
Additional rails on bunker.
Steam heating fitted.
Str. 25/8—15/11/28.**G.**
Vacuum ejector fitted.
Str. 19/5/31.**N/C.**
Trip cocks fitted.
Str. 5/12/32—10/1/33.**G.**
Str. 3/11—3/12/36.**G.**
Str. 6/4—21/5/41.**G.**
Str. 25/10—18/11/44.**G.**
Str. 19—20/3/47.**N/C.**
Trip cocks re-fitted.
Str. 23/5—1/7/49.**G.**
Str. 2—27/3/53.**G.**

BOILERS:
  84.
  166 *(ex7166)* 26/5/20.
  3011 *(exJ68 7049)* 15/11/28.
  3001 *(ex7355)* 10/1/33.
  3046 *(ex7385)* 3/12/36.
  2997 *(exJ68 7040)* 21/5/41.
  3159 *(new)* 18/11/44.
  3165 *(ex8612)* 1/7/49.

23766 *(ex?)* 27/3/53.

SHEDS:
Stratford.
Gorton 23/1/29.
Bidston 24/4/29.
Trafford Park 20/6/29.
Gorton 25/10/29.
Trafford Park 5/11/29.
Gorton 10/1/30.
Stratford 1/5/31.
Colchester 8/8/48.
Stratford 21/11/48.
Colchester 10/4/49.
Stratford 28/8/49.
Colchetsre 29/1/50.
Stratford 3/12/50.

RENUMBERED:
  7084 23/5/24.
  8630 3/1/47.
68630 1/7/49.

CONDEMNED: 1/1/59.
Cut up at Stratford.

7085

Stratford.

To traffic 8/1904.
Class S56 - passenger.

REPAIRS:
At 1/1/23: *J69/1. Westinghouse
brake. Non-Condensing.*
Str. 19/3—3/11/23.**G.**
Condensing apparatus fitted.
Str. 5/9—28/10/25.**G.**
Str. ?/?—3/1/27.**L.**
Steam heating fitted.
Str. 10/8—8/11/28.**G.**
*Vacuum ejector fitted. Additional
rails on bunker.*
Str. 19/5/31.**N/C.**
Trip cocks fitted.
Str. 16/8—12/9/32.**G.**
Str. 24/1—3/3/37.**G.**
Str. 19/4—20/5/39.**L.**
Str. 22/6—8/8/41.**G.**
Str. 14/1—8/2/45.**G.**
Str. 21—25/3/47.**N/C.**
Trip cocks re-fitted.
Str. 14/10—30/11/48.**G.**
Str. 20/3—11/4/53.**G.**

BOILERS:
  85.
  3032 *(new)* 3/11/23.
  2953 *(ex7369)* 8/11/28.
  3028 *(ex7196)* 12/9/32.
  2986 *(exJ68 7034)* 3/3/37.
  3103 *(ex7053)* 8/8/41.
  3052 *(ex7265)* 8/2/45.

3197 *(new)* 30/11/48.
23768 *(ex?)* 11/4/53.

SHEDS:
Stratford.
Gorton 23/1/29.
Stratford 1/5/31.
Parkeston 20/10/45.
Stratford 8/6/46.
Colchester 8/8/48.
Stratford 10/4/49.

RENUMBERED:
  85ᴇ 3/11/23.
  7085 28/10/25.
  8631 2/1/47.
68631 27/11/48.

CONDEMNED: 28/7/58.
Cut up at Stratford.

7086

Stratford.

To traffic 9/1904.
Class S56 - passenger.

REPAIRS:
Woolwich Arsenal. 31/12/19—
14/8/20.**G.**
Str. 8/8—13/10/22.**G.**
At 1/1/23: *J69/1. Westinghouse
brake. Condensing apparatus.*
Str. 19/3—10/6/25.**G.**
Str. 1/9—17/12/27.**G.**
*Westinghouse brake replaced
by steam. Add. rails on bunker.
Condensing apparatus removed.*
Str. 15/4—17/7/29.**G.**
Str. 20/6—22/8/31.**G.**
Str. 1/2—2/3/35.**G.**
Str. 11/11/39—13/1/40.**G.**
Rebuilt to J67/2.
Str. 8/2—4/3/44.**G.**
*Rebuilt to J69/1 but not officially
reclassified until 2/45.*
Str. 7/7—16/9/47.**G.**
Str. 11/6—28/7/51.**G.**
Str. 16/4—26/5/56.**G.**

BOILERS:
  86.
  2992 *(new)* 14/8/20.
  2990 *(ex7360)* 17/12/27.
  2986 *(ex7396)* 17/7/29.
  3035 *(exJ68 7044)* 22/8/31.
  2983 *(ex7387)* 2/3/35.
  2868 *(ex sp,J67 7020)* 13/1/40.
  2959 *(ex spare & 7191)* 4/3/44.
  3103 *(exJ68 8649)* 16/9/47.
  23714 *(ex?)* 28/7/51.
  23796 *(ex?)* 26/5/56.

Although Cowlairs could find pre-war style for 8623 *see* page 157, centre - two months earlier, on 21st June 1947, they had painted No.8504 in the post-war style of unlined Gill sans so as to obviate buying transfers which were expensive.

(right) No.8559 was ex Gorton in pre-war style on 3rd October 1947 and was shedded at Liverpool (Brunswick) which also had LMS engines which could have the same number. To obviate any confusion, in early March 1949 all ex LNER engines at Cheshire Lines sheds were altered to the BR number where this was not already borne, On Saturday 5th March 1949, the additional 6 was put on 8559 at the shed and explains the off-centre numbering and painted 6.

(below) Cowlairs continued its aversion to repainting until it became imperative into BR days. The NE dates from 2nd December 1944 and No.68505 was not put on until 26th February 1951. This engine had no further repairs and was withdrawn on 11th November 1953 so the NE survived its last nine years.

There were other Cowlairs examples. The near-invisible LNER dated from 6th June 1947 and 68503 was put on at a Heavy Intermediate repair on 10th December 1949 when Cowlairs were still painting LNER modification to Gill sans 6. It is probable this style remained to 3rd September 1952, when it went for a General repair.

Five got the regional prefix E in 1948, all at Stratford: E8495 (13th February), E8528 (5th March), E8548 (9th February), E8579 (2nd February), on black, and E8619 (24th January on green - *see* page 147, top.

7086 cont./
SHEDS:
Stratford.
Retford 14/3/28.
Gorton 13/1/30.
Trafford Park 18/3/35.
Brunswick 20/5/35.
Walton-on-the-Hill 23/8/40.
Trafford Park 24/7/41.
Gorton 22/12/41.
New England 4/3/44.
Stratford 11/3/51.
Staveley 2/11/52.
Stratford 30/11/52.

RENUMBERED:
 7086 10/6/25.
 8632 1/9/46.
 68632 28/7/51.

CONDEMNED: 8/5/58.
Cut up at Stratford.

7087

Stratford.

To traffic 9/1904.
Class S56 - passenger.

REPAIRS:
Woolwich Ar. 16/1—24/8/20.**G.**
Str. 14/12/22—3/3/23.**G.**
At 1/1/23: *J69/1. Westinghouse
brake. Condensing apparatus.*
Str. 25/10/24—30/1/25.**G.**
Str. 29/4—19/8/27.**G.**
Additional rails on bunker.
Str. 15—28/3/30.**L.**
Trip cocks fitted.
Str. 6/9—17/10/30.**G.**
Str. 22/4/31.**N/C.**
*Trip cocks removed. Condensing
app. removed ?*
Str. 8/8—13/9/35.**G.**
Str. 12—18/10/39.**G.**
Vacuum ejector fitted.
Str. 12/5—13/6/40.**G.**
*Trip cocks and condensing
apparatus re-fitted.*
Str. 30/7—2/9/44.**G.**
Str. 15—18/3/47.**N/C.**
Trip cocks re-fitted.
Str. 10/11/48—16/1/49.**G.**
Str. 13/8—11/9/52.**G.**
Str. 28/1—2/3/57.**G.**

BOILERS:
 87.
 266 *(ex7266)* 24/8/20.
 192 *(ex7352)* 19/8/27.
 3036 *(exJ68 7047)* 17/10/30.
 3026 *(ex7059)* 13/9/35.
 3047 *(exJ67 7331)* 13/6/40.

3058 *(exJ68 7043)* 2/9/44.
3102 *(ex8557)* 16/1/49.
23818 *(new)* 11/9/52.
23769 *(exJ68 68661)* 2/3/57.

SHEDS:
Stratford.
Colchester 25/11/44.
Stratford 8/6/46.
Parkeston 14/8/60.

RENUMBERED:
 7087 30/1/25.
 8633 25/4/46.
 68633 15/1/49.

CONDEMNED: 24/11/60.
Pres.in National Collection.

7088

Stratford.

To traffic 9/1904.
Class S56 - passenger.

REPAIRS:
Str. 22/11/18—18/3/19.**G.**
At 1/1/23: *J69/1. Westinghouse
brake. Condensing apparatus.*
Str. 10/12/24—7/4/25.**G.**
Str. ?/?—?/9/27.**G.**
Additional rails on bunker.
Str. ?/?—?/5/30.**N/C.**
Trip cocks fitted.
Str. ?/?—?/4/31.**N/C.**
Trip cocks removed.
Str. 6—28/7/31.**G.**
Str. ?/?—?/11/31.**L.**
Vacuum ejector fitted.
Str. 26/3—13/4/34.**G.**
Str. ?/?—29/4/37.**G.**
Str. ?/?—6/9/39.**G.**
Vacuum ejector removed.
Str. ?/?—4/12/41.**G.***
Str. ?/?—11/11/44.**G.***
* *for WD Longmoor.*

BOILERS:
 88.
 49 *(exJ68 7049)* 18/3/19.
3041 *(new)* ?/9/27.
2970 *(ex7372)* 28/7/31.
3073 *(new)* 13/4/34.
2975 *(ex7198)* 29/4/37.
3042 *(ex7192)* 6/9/39.

SHEDS:
Stratford.
Norwich *after* 5/32.
Stratford 13/4/34.
WD Longmoor *(o/l)* 4/10/39.

RENUMBERED:
7088 7/4/25.

SOLD TO W.D.: 19/10/40.
*As WD 70091 sold to John
Lysaght Ltd., Scunthorpe, 5/48.
Reno.26. Scrapped 10/1960.*

7089

Stratford.

To traffic 9/1904.
Class S56 - passenger.

REPAIRS:
Str. 8/7—29/10/21.**G.**
At 1/1/23: *J69/1. Westinghouse
brake. Condensing apparatus.*
Str. 21/11/23—31/1/24.**G.**
Str. 23/10/25—29/1/26.**G.**
Vacuum ejector fitted.
Str. 20/1—25/4/28.**G.**
*Additional rails on bunker.
Condensing apparatus removed.*
Cow. 24—31/5/28.**N/C.**
*Footsteps and bunker handrails
fitted.*
Cow. 23/1—1/2/29.**N/C.**
Steam heating fitted.
Cow. 19/7—22/8/33.**G.**
Cow. 29/9—29/10/37.**G.**
Cow. 2—25/10/40.**G.**
Cow. 2—25/5/45.**G.**
Cow. 28/1—8/2/47.**H.**
Cow. 29/6—16/7/48.**L.**
Cow. 11/5—3/6/50.**H/I.**
Str. 11—31/10/53.**G.**
Str. 10/12/57—9/1/58.**G.**

BOILERS:
 89.
 3013 *(new)* 29/10/21.
 3003 *(ex7354)* 25/4/28.
 3003 reno. C1684 1/2/29.
C1695 *(ex7368)* 22/8/33.
C1830 *(ex7356)* 25/10/40.
C1691 *(ex7356)* 25/5/45.
 3158 *(new)* 8/2/47.
23785 *(ex?)* 31/10/53.
23800 *(ex68567)* 9/1/58.

SHEDS:
Stratford.
King's Cross 10/9/24.
Stratford 10/11/24.
Ipswich 24/6/26.
Scottish Area 13/5/28.
Perth 30/5/28.
Dundee 30/10/39.
Perth 28/11/39.
Stirling 26/1/42.
Dunfermline ?/8/42.
Doncaster 24/6/51.

Norwich 9/9/51.
King's Lynn 26/7/53.
New England 11/3/56.
Grantham 25/1/59.
Colwick 1/5/60.
Stratford 11/6/61.

RENUMBERED:
 89E 31/1/24.
 7089 29/1/26.
 8635 1/9/46.
 68635 16/7/48.

CONDEMNED: 16/9/62.
Cut up at Stratford ?

7090

Stratford.

To traffic 9/1904.
Class S56 - passenger.

REPAIRS:
Str. 24/6/18—27/3/19.**G.**
Str. 16/8—4/11/22.**G.**
At 1/1/23: *J69/1. Westinghouse
brake. Condensing apparatus.*
Str. 6/6—16/9/24.**G.**
Vacuum ejector fitted.
Str. 20/5—14/7/25.**G.**
Str. 18/6—29/9/27.**G.**
Additional rails on bunker.
Str. 6/11/29—10/1/30.**G.**
Str. 8/10—25/11/31.**G.**
Str. 22/3—27/4/34.**G.**
Str. 1—31/8/36.**G.**
Condensing apparatus removed.
Str. 29/12/39—2/2/40.**G.**
Str. 23/1—26/2/44.**G.**
Str. 16—25/3/44.**L.**
Str. 28/7—10/9/47.**G.**
Str. 19/10—11/11/50.**G.**
Str. 3/6—5/8/55.**G.**

BOILERS:
 90.
 2979 *(new)* 27/3/19.
 2961 *(ex7198)* 16/9/24.
 2990 *(ex7086)* 10/1/30.
 3062 *(new)* 25/11/31.
 38 *(exJ68 7049)* 27/4/34.
 2984 *(ex7193)* 31/8/36.
 3067 *(ex7272)* 2/2/40.
 3050 *(exJ68 7044)* 26/2/44.
 3063 *(ex8561)* 10/9/47.
23705 *(ex?)* 11/11/50.
23728 *(ex68557)* 5/8/55.

SHEDS:
Stratford.
Colwick 18/7/25.
Leicester 30/10/25.
Stratford 4/12/25.

7090 cont./
Parkeston 24/6/26.
Stratford 24/12/39.
Parkeston 17/3/40.
Stratford 13/4/41.
Parkeston 20/7/41.
Stratford 2/1/43.
Colchester 8/1/44.
Stratford 17/10/48.
Colchester 10/4/49.
Stratford 28/8/49.
Colchester 8/10/50.
Stratford 3/12/54.

RENUMBERED:
  7090 16/9/24.
  8636 8/9/46.
68636 11/11/50.

CONDEMNED: 1/1/59.
Cut up at Stratford.

(top) **By 11ᵗʰ June 1948, when No.68552 was ex Cowlairs and repainted, the position of the number had been changed from tank to bunker, but it was still on the front buffer beam also.**

Stratford also moved the number to the bunker and fitted a cast plate on the smokebox door. This was the standard style until September 1949.

No.68560, ex works 13ᵗʰ August 1949, would be almost the last to be lettered with BRITISH RAILWAYS. Although prepared for a smokebox plate, one was not fitted.

The lettering was then superseded by the emblem, the 15½ in. size being used on Class J69. No.68573 was ex works 19th November 1949.

There was still variation in the brakes and wheel sets. No.68490 was steam brake only and had 15-spoke wheels without balance weights.

Whilst keeping 10-spoke balanced wheels, No.68508 was steam and vacuum braked.

Although No.68619 had the BR crest put on in February 1957, No.68499, ex Stratford 26th March 1957, still had the emblem applied. Note the inspection cover on the front sandbox. These were only put on by Cowlairs. This one had the 10-spoke balanced wheels and had Westinghouse and vacuum brakes.

No. 68575, ex works 9th March 1956, still had condensing gear, Westinghouse and vacuum brakes but 12-spoke wheels without balance weights. Its front sandboxes did not have inspection covers.

By mid-1957 there was a change from emblem to the BR crest, and with the lion facing the wrong way in heraldry. No.68513, ex works 14th September 1957, had crests followed by No.68500 (4th October 1957), 68626 (26th October 1957), 68578 (23rd November 1957), 68528 (7th December 1957), 68600 (13th December 1957), 68566 (21st December 1957), and 68635 (9th January 1958).

The BR crest was handed to face forward on both sides of the engine, and whilst correction of the heraldic mistake was made in 1959 and later, no J69 got this correction, No.68550 ex works 8th March 1958 being the last to have a heavy repair.

One small minor addition was made. This March 1961 photograph shows electrification warning flashes put on. The end of steam on the Great Eastern section on 16th September 1962 caused withdrawal that day of all nine survivors Nos.Dept.44 and 45, 68499, 68542. 68556, 68600, 68609, 68621 and 68635.

Stratford then built three more to the same design, Nos.137 to 139, during September and October 1908, plus No.130 in April 1910.

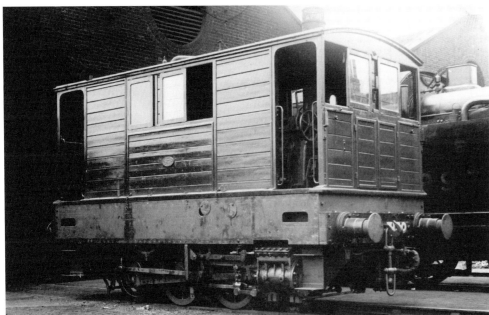

The single engine, No.7130 built in April 1910, had the different style buffers with stepped shank.

Another three, Nos.127, 128 and 131, were built in June 1914 at Stratford, and also had stepped instead of parallel shank buffers.

7135

Stratford.

To traffic 10/1903.

REPAIRS:
Str. 28/6—24/12/21.**G.**
Str. 13/8—4/12/26.**G.**
Str. 13—24/8/28.**G.**
Str. 28/5—5/9/30.**G.**
Str. 3/3—22/4/32.**G.**
Str. 28/6—11/8/33.**G.**
Str. 16/4—29/8/35.**G.**
Str. 8/1—3/3/37.**G.**
Str. 1/3—3/5/41.**G.**
Str. 29/6—10/8/42.**G.**
Str. 19/3—12/5/44.**G.**
Str. 31/3—10/5/46.**G.**
Str. 27/2—28/4/47.**L.**
Str. 19/11—24/12/47.**L.**
Str. 8/12/48—10/2/49.**G.**
Str. 4—22/2/51. **N/C.**
Str. 16/10—1/12/51. **G.**
Str. 8/11/53. *Not repaired.*

BOILERS:
135.
130 *(ex7130)* 4/12/26.
3705 *(new)* 24/8/28.
3704 *(exY6 07125)* 22/4/32.
126 *(ex7126)* 11/8/33.
128 *(ex7139)* 29/8/35.
3710 *(new)* 3/3/37.
3703 *(ex7138)* 3/5/41.
3709 *(ex7138)* 10/8/42.
3702 *(exY6 07125)* 12/5/44.
3706 *(ex7136)* 10/5/46.
3712 *(ex8221)* 10/2/49.
3712 reno.23983 1/12/51.

SHEDS:
Ipswich.
Colchester 21/3/37.
Ipswich 24/4/37.

RENUMBERED:
7135 4/12/26.
8216 10/5/46.
68216 5/2/49.

CONDEMNED: 30/11/53.
Cut up at Stratford.

7136

Stratford.

To traffic 11/1903.

REPAIRS:
Str. 10/4—20/5/22.**G.**
Str. 3/11/24—14/3/25.**G.**
Str. 24/3—9/7/27.**G.**
Str. 8/11/29—30/1/30.**G.**
Str. 31/5—16/6/34.**L.**
Str. 8/10—30/11/34.**G.**
Str. 17/9—28/10/39.**G.**
Str. 3/7—9/9/43.**G.**
Str. 10/2—18/3/46.**G.**
Str. 29/4—3/9/49.**G.**
Str. 28/2/53. *Not repaired.*

BOILERS:
136.
3700 *(new)* 20/5/22.
136 *(ex7125)* 30/1/30.
127 *(ex7130)* 30/11/34.
3711 *(new)* 29/10/39.
3706 *(ex7130)* 9/9/43.
3700 *(exY6 7134)* 18/3/46.
3716 *(new)* 3/9/49.

SHEDS:
Wisbech.
Colchester 17/11/28.
King's Lynn (Wisbech) 5/4/29.
March 27/7/52.

RENUMBERED:
7136 14/3/25.
8217 12/5/46.
68217 3/9/49.

CONDEMNED: 9/3/53.
Cut up at Stratford.

7137

Stratford.

To traffic 9/1908.

REPAIRS:
Nor. 12/4—9/6/23.**H.**
Str. 31/8/26—29/1/27.**G.**
Str. 19/4—20/6/31.**G.**
Str. 24/1—5/4/35.**G.**
Str. 1/6—26/7/41.**G.**
Str. 21—24/6/42.**L.**
Str. 18/8—8/10/42.**G.**
Str. 7/1—17/2/45.**G.**
Str. 17/6/49. *Not repaired.*

BOILERS:
137.
131 *(ex7131)* 20/6/31.
126 *(ex7135)* 5/4/35.
3713 *(new)* 26/7/41.
3701 *(ex7125)* 17/2/45.

SHEDS:
Yarmouth.
King's Lynn 20/6/31.
Yarmouth 3/10/31.
King's Lynn 30/5/33.
Cambridge 18/4/48.
King's Lynn 20/6/48.

RENUMBERED:
7137 29/1/27.
8218 12/5/46.

CONDEMNED: 19/9/49.
Cut up at Stratford.

7138

Stratford.

To traffic 9/1908.

REPAIRS:
Nor. 12/6—26/7/22.**H.**
Nor. 16/6—29/8/24.**H.**
Str. 10/3—10/8/28.**G.**
Str. 11/7—24/8/33.**G.**
Str. 15/11—21/12/40.**G.**
Str. 5/12/41. *Not repaired.*

BOILERS:
138.
3706 *(new)* 10/8/28.
3703 *(exY6 07126)* 24/8/33.
3709 *(ex7128)* 21/12/40.

SHEDS:
Yarmouth.
Norwich 19/5/40.
Yarmouth 9/1/41.
Ipswich 25/2/41.

RENUMBERED:
7138 29/8/24.

CONDEMNED: 12/1/42.
Cut up at Stratford.

7139

Stratford.

To traffic 10/1908.

REPAIRS:
Str. 8/1—6/5/22.**G.**
Str. 15/7—30/10/26.**G.**
Str. 9/9—7/12/28.**G.**
Str. 8/12/30—6/2/31.**G.**
Str. 20/12/32—27/1/33.**G.**

Str. 12/12/34—8/2/35.**G.**
Str. 22/5—28/6/38.**G.**
Str. 13/10—12/12/41.**G.**
Str. 21/12/43—19/2/44.**G.**
Str. 22/7—24/8/45.**G.**
Str. 9/4—2/5/46.**L.**
Str. 1/11—27/12/47.**G.**
Str. 3/9—4/11/50.**G.**

BOILERS:
139.
3701 *(new)* 30/10/26.
128 *(ex7128)* 6/2/31.
3708 *(new)* 8/2/35.
3705 *(ex7127)* 28/6/38.
3710 *(ex7135)* 12/12/41.
3711 *(ex7136)* 19/2/44.
3708 *(ex7131)* 24/8/45.
3705 *(ex8225)* 27/12/47.
23980 *(ex?)* 4/11/50.

SHEDS:
Ipswich.
Yarmouth 23/6/30.
Ipswich 13/10/30.
Colchester 25/11/35.
Ipswich 21/3/37.
Yarmouth 2/11/49.
Ipswich 15/2/53.

RENUMBERED:
7139 30/10/26.
8219 27/4/46.
68219 4/11/50.

CONDEMNED: 31/8/53.
Cut up at Stratford.

7130

Stratford.

To traffic 4/1910.

REPAIRS:
Ips. 17/6—7/10/22.**H.**
Str. 29/3—23/7/26.**G.**
Str. 26/1—25/3/27.**L.**
Str. 5/2—19/5/28.**G.**
Str. 8/11/29—11/1/30.**G.**
Str. 31/5—16/6/34.**L.**
Str. 28/9—9/11/34.**G.**
Str. 18/11—17/12/37.**G.**
Str. 17/1—25/3/43.**G.**
Str. 22/4—26/5/45.**G.**
Str. 4/9—7/10/47.**L.**
Str. 14/5—17/6/50.**G.**
Str. 8/2/53. *Not repaired.*

The class was completed in March 1921 when Stratford constructed three more, Nos.125, 126 and 129. Note that safety chains were provided and there was reversion to the parallel shank buffer type. Side skirtings and cowcatchers were normally left at the home shed when visits to Stratford works were made because those journeys were over lines which were fenced from public access.

The boiler had a raised dome on which the two Ramsbottom safety valves were mounted. The brake was Westinghouse on the engine and for train working, where such was needed. Unlike the side tank engines the toolbox was retained to withdrawal.

To comply with Board of Trade requirements when working where the public had access which was unrestricted, the motion had to be covered to almost rail level, and both ends had to be guarded by a cowcatcher. Until 31st December 1927, when passenger working on the Wisbech tramway ceased, this was strictly implemented as shown by No.7128 at the west end of Wisbech station.

The chimney was also to have a spark arrester fitted and all carried them to withdrawal.

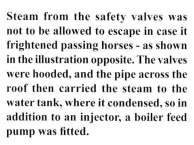

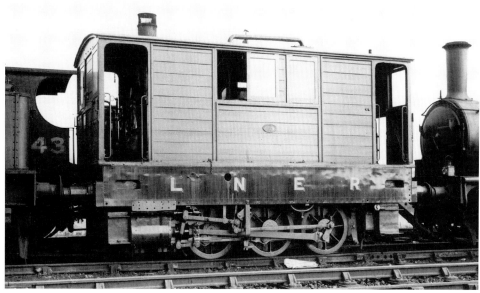

Steam from the safety valves was not to be allowed to escape in case it frightened passing horses - as shown in the illustration opposite. The valves were hooded, and the pipe across the roof then carried the steam to the water tank, where it condensed, so in addition to an injector, a boiler feed pump was fitted.

7130 cont./
BOILERS:
130.
125 (ex7125) 23/7/26.
129 (ex7129) 19/5/28.
127 (ex7125) 11/1/30.
3700 (ex7126) 9/11/34.
3706 (ex7129) 17/12/37.
3705 (ex7139) 25/3/43.
3714 (ex7128) 26/5/45.
3710 (ex8225) 17/6/50.

SHEDS:
Ipswich.
Cambridge 1/7/25.
Ipswich 27/7/25.
Cambridge 16/5/28.
King's Lynn 20/5/28.
Yarmouth 5/10/28.
King's Lynn 3/1/29.
Ipswich 31/1/50.
King's Lynn 28/5/50.
Yarmouth 25/2/51.
Ipswich 29/4/51.
King's Lynn 1/7/51.
Ipswich 23/9/51.

RENUMBERED:
7130 23/7/26.
8220 8/9/46.
68220 17/6/50.

CONDEMNED: 23/2/53.
Cut up at Stratford.

7127

Stratford.

To traffic 6/1914.

REPAIRS:
Ips. 14/4—11/7/21.H.
Str. 25/8—13/12/24.G.
Str. 27/8—3/12/27.G.
Str. 14/12/29—8/3/30.G.
Str. 3/5—25/6/32.G.
Str. 27/11/33—5/1/34.G.
Str. 12/9—25/10/35.G.
Str. 10/7—20/8/37.G.
Str. 23/2—24/4/42.G.
Str. 23/4—16/6/44.G.
Str. 27/5—4/8/46.G.
Str. 31/5—28/8/48.G.
Str. 28/3—28/4/50.C/L.
Str. 18/3/51. Not repaired.

BOILERS:
127.
126 (ex7126) 3/12/27.
129 (ex7130) 8/3/30.
3705 (ex7135) 25/6/32.
129 (ex7129) 5/1/34.
3705 (ex7126) 25/10/35.

3704 (ex7131) 20/8/37.
3707 (exY6 7134) 24/4/42.
129 (ex7126) 16/6/44.
3712 (ex7126) 4/8/46.
3709 (ex8226) 28/8/48.

SHEDS:
Ipswich.
Cambridge 30/7/24.
Ipswich 16/8/26.
King's Lynn (Wisbech) 24/3/27.
Ipswich 19/1/28.
Colchester 1/3/48.
Stratford 16/5/48.
Ipswich 3/10/48.

RENUMBERED:
7127 13/12/24.
8221 19/5/46.
68221 28/8/48.

CONDEMNED: 21/5/51.
Cut up at Stratford.

7128

Stratford.

To traffic 6/1914.

REPAIRS:
Nor. 17/7—13/10/23.H.
Nor. 13/4—13/6/24.H.
Str. 4/5—9/7/25.G.
Str. 19/6—22/8/30.G.
Str. 29/1—11/3/32.G.
Str. 14/1—22/2/35.G.
Str. 3/12/39—15/2/40.G.
Str. 14/11/43—14/1/44.G.
Str. 11/2—24/3/45.G.
Str. 12/2—29/3/49.C/H.
Str. 11/6—29/7/50.G.

BOILERS:
128.
3700 (ex7136) 22/8/30.
139 (ex7125) 11/3/32.
3709 (new) 22/2/35.
3712 (new) 15/2/40.
3714 (ex7125) 14/1/44.
3703 (ex7129) 24/3/45.
3713 (ex8223) 29/3/49.
3714 (ex8220) 29/7/50.

SHEDS:
Yarmouth.
Cambridge 10/7/25.
Yarmouth 1/8/25
King's Lynn (Wisbech) 15/6/31.
Ipswich 9/12/41.
King's Lynn 25/3/45.
Cambridge 11/4/48.
King's Lynn 6/6/48.
March 27/7/52.

Colchester 21/6/53.
Ipswich 15/11/53.

RENUMBERED:
7128 13/6/24.
8222 8/9/46.
68222 26/3/49.

CONDEMNED: 31/1/55.
Cut up at Stratford.

7131

Stratford.

To traffic 6/1914.

REPAIRS:
Str. 13/3—1/7/22.G.
Str. 23/2—13/6/25.G.
Str. 25/1—5/5/28.G.
Str. 27/11/30—23/1/31.G.
Str. 17/10—10/11/33.G.
Str. 5/12/34—17/1/35.H.
Str. 28/4—11/6/37.G.
Str. 28/2—19/5/43.G.
Str. 25/3—27/4/45.G.
Str. 18/1—6/8/49.G.

BOILERS:
131.
125 (ex7130) 23/1/31.
3704 (ex7135) 10/11/33.
128 (ex7135) 11/6/37.
3708 (ex7126) 19/5/43.
3713 (ex7137) 27/4/45.
3715 (new) 6/8/49.

SHEDS:
Cambridge.
Yarmouth 13/10/26.
King's Lynn (Wisbech) 16/2/27.
March 27/7/52.
Yarmouth 6/12/53.

RENUMBERED:
7131 13/6/25.
8223 8/9/46.
68223 6/8/49.

CONDEMNED: 19/7/55.
Cut up at Stratford.

7125

Stratford.

To traffic 3/1921.

REPAIRS:
Ips. 9/10—8/12/22.H.
Str. 14/12/25—27/3/26.G.
Str. 26/9/27—21/1/28.G.

Str. 28/7—26/10/29.G.
Str. 22/8—16/10/31.G.
Str. 8/2—24/3/33.G.
Str. 29/5—17/7/36.G.
Str. 9/6—19/9/41.G.
Str. 8/8—27/10/43.G.
Str. 1/12/44—12/1/45.G.
Str. 15/5—2/6/46.L.
Str. 9/6—7/7/46.L.
Str. 3/5—23/8/47.G.
Str. 7/11—12/12/47.L.
Str. 29/1—25/3/50.G.
Str. 2/3/52. Not repaired.

BOILERS:
125.
136 (ex7136) 27/3/26.
127 (ex7127) 21/1/28.
139 (ex7129) 26/10/29.
137 (ex7137) 16/10/31.
3701 (ex7129) 24/3/33.
125 (exY6 7133) 17/7/36.
3714 (new) 19/9/41.
3701 (ex7129) 27/10/43.
3710 (ex7139) 12/1/45.
3702 (ex7135) 23/8/47.
3717 (new) 25/3/50.

SHEDS:
Ipswich.
Colhester 15/10/34.
Ipswich 25/11/35.
Colchester 24/4/37.
Ipswich 15/12/37.

RENUMBERED:
7125 27/3/26.
8224 26/10/46.
68224 25/3/50.

CONDEMNED: 24/3/52.
Cut up at Stratford.

7126

Stratford.

To traffic 3/1921.

REPAIRS:
Str. 4/5—6/7/24.G.
Str. 22/11/26—26/2/27.G.
Str. 16/11/28—12/2/29.G.
Str. 28/1—17/4/31.G.
Str. 16/8—20/9/32.G.
Str. 5/1—21/2/34.G.
Str. 1/6—20/7/35.G.
Str. 27/11/36—21/1/37.G.
Str. 27/8—13/10/39.G.
Str. 18/4—23/5/42.G.
Str. 30/5—4/6/42.N/C.
Str. 20/2—1/4/44.G.
Str. 6/1—25/2/46.G.
Str. 21/9—8/11/47.G.

The class was extensively used on the dock lines at Ipswich, and from November 1928, also on the lines at Hythe quay, Colchester. Skirtings were not needed at these locations but cowcatchers were still carried.

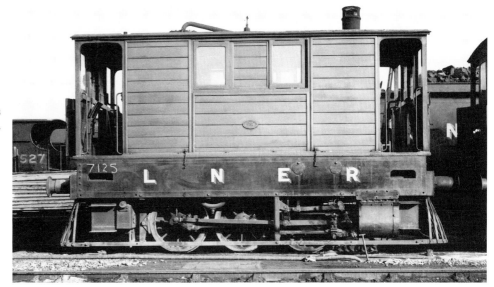

As the controls were in duplicate, this class could be driven from either end.

In some cases the safety chains were taken off, No.7127 being without them from its 3rd December 1927 repair.

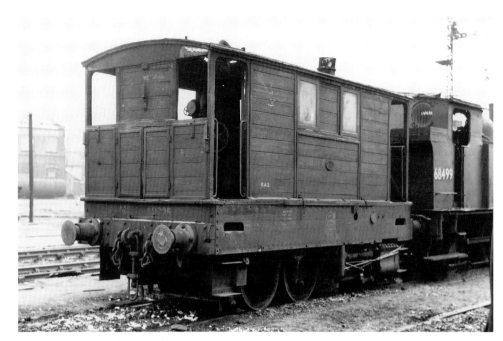

Others still had the safety chains through to withdrawal, in March 1955 in the case of No.68225.

No.68220 was the only one noted with a lid to its spark arrester. Note that it also kept the warning bell mounted on the roof. This 15th March 1953 photograph, taken after its 23rd February withdrawal, shows that it never lost the GER plate reading district No.4 which indicated it had at some time been allocated to Ipswich. At Grouping, GER engines carried one of the district allocation plates which were numbered 1 to 5, so did not identify the actual shed. The districts were No.1 Stratford, No.2 Peterborough, No.3 Norwich, No.4 Ipswich, and No.5 Cambridge.

Until during the 1914-18 war, the company's initials were displayed by shaded transfers on the deep side valance.

By Grouping the initials had been superseded by large painted numbers although the GE brass number plate was retained. District No.3 allocation plate indicates Norwich in which district it was shedded at Yarmouth.

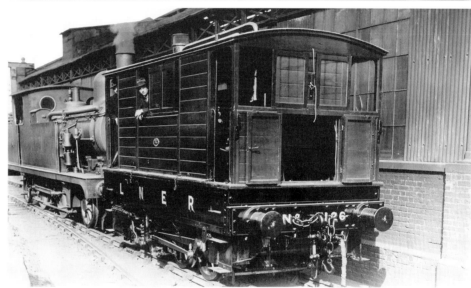

No.7126 was ex Stratford 6th July 1924 with its body work painted brown and the large number plate taken off. The replacement was the standard LNER 8⅝ in. wide plate which was useless except at very short range. Below footplate level was black with single red lining and even the ends of the buffer beam had a lined panel. By March 1927 all except No.7138 had a General repair at Stratford so presumably were lined.

From the June 1928 painting economies taking effect, lining was no longer applied. No.7137 was ex works 20th June 1931 and still had a district plate.

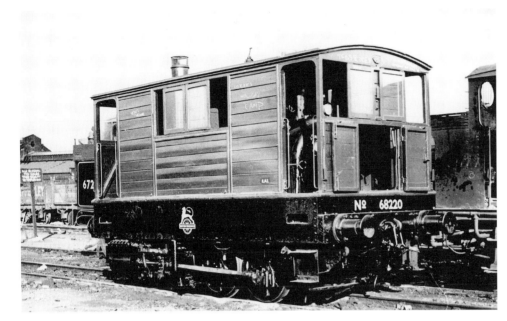

No.68220, here on 17th June 1950 from its final repair, still carries a No.4 plate.

From July 1942 only NE instead of LNER was put on the valance and by 16th June 1944 all had been so treated except No.7138 which was withdrawn on 12th January 1942.

In the 1946 renumbering J70 class were allocated 8216 to 8226 in order of building, No.7130 changed to 8220 on Sunday 8th September 1946 at King's Lynn shed.

No.7128 had NE from its 24th March 1945 General repair and changed to 8222 on 8th September 1946 at King's Lynn shed. It was ex works 29th March 1949 from a Casual Heavy repair and whilst given its BR number it had not been repainted.

7126 cont./
Str. 18/4—13/5/50.**G.**

BOILERS:
  126.
  135 *(ex7135)* 26/2/27.
  138 *(ex7138)* 12/2/29.
  126 *(ex7127)* 17/4/31.
  3700 *(ex7128)* 20/9/32.
  3705 *(ex7127)* 21/2/34.
  131 *(ex7137)* 20/7/35.
  3701 *(ex7125)* 21/1/37.
  3708 *(ex7139)* 13/10/39.
  129 *(exY6 07126)* 23/5/42.
  3712 *(ex7128)* 1/4/44.
  3705 *(ex7130)* 25/2/46.
  3710 *(ex8224)* 8/11/47.
  3711 *(exY6 8083)* 13/5/50.

SHEDS:
Ipswich.
Yarmouth 1/3/34.
Ipswich 4/5/34.
Yarmouth 26/9/37.
Ipswich 18/10/37.
King's Lynn 5/6/49.

Colchester 9/9/51.
King's Lynn 9/12/51.
March 27/7/52.
Ipswich 23/8/53.

RENUMBERED:
  7126 6/7/24.
  8225 11/5/46.
  68225 13/5/50.

CONDEMNED: 8/3/55.
Cut up at Stratford.

_____

7129

Stratford.

To traffic 3/1921.

REPAIRS:
Ips. 5/6—20/8/23.**H.**
Str. 20/12/26—5/3/27.**G.**
Str. 2/6—7/9/29.**G.**
Str. 13/4—6/6/31.**G.**
Str. 1/11—16/12/32.**G.**

Str. 25/8—28/9/33.**G.**
Str. 8/7—20/9/35.**G.**
Str. 9/4—4/6/37.**G.**
Str. 13/10—7/12/40.**G.**
Str. 24—28/12/40.**L.**
Str. 24/11/42—13/1/43.**G.**
Str. 3—30/1/45.**G.**
Str. 1/3—26/5/48.**G.**
Str. 25/9—10/11/51.**G.**

BOILERS:
  129.
  139 *(ex7139)* 5/3/27.
  130 *(ex7135)* 7/9/29.
  3701 *(ex7139)* 6/6/31.
  129 *(ex7127)* 16/12/32.
  3706 *(ex7138)* 28/9/33.
  131 *(ex7126)* 4/6/37.
  3701 *(ex7126)* 7/12/40.
  3703 *(ex7135)* 13/1/43.
  3709 *(ex7135)* 30/1/45.
  3708 *(ex8219)* 26/5/48.
  3708 reno.23982 10/11/51.

SHEDS:
Ipswich.

Cambridge 13/5/25.
Ipswich 20/11/25.
Colchester 15/12/37.
Stratford 25/11/44.
Colchester 18/12/44.
Stratford 8/6/46.
Colchester 23/6/46.

RENUMBERED:
  7129 5/3/27.
  8226 5/5/46.
  68226 22/5/48.

CONDEMNED: 2/8/55.
Cut up at Stratford.

_____

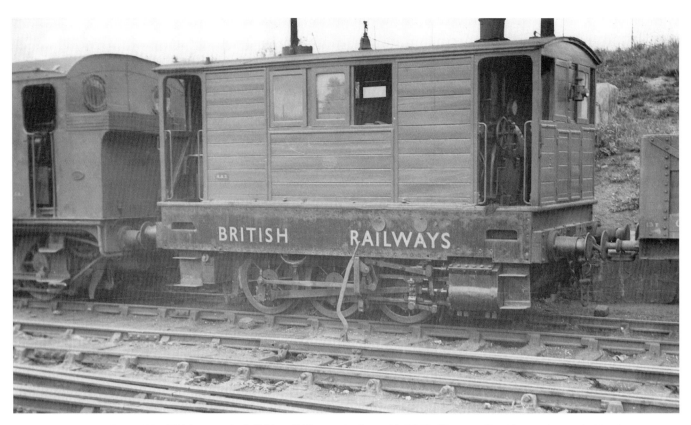

No J70 got an E prefix and No.68226, ex works 26th May 1948, was the first with BRITISH RAILWAYS lettering and still with a number on the buffer beam.

(below) No.7128 working at Elm Road, Wisbech, 9th August 1937.

Whilst BRITISH RAILWAYS was being used, the position for the number changed to above the buffer beam and applied to Nos.68216 (10th February 1949), 68217 (3rd September 1949) and 68223 (6th August 1949).

The emblem then took the place of the lettering and seven acquired it, these being Nos.68216 (1st December 1951), 68219 (4th November 1950), 68220 (17th June 1950), 68222 (29th July 1950), 68224 (25th March 1950), 68225 (13th May 1950), 68226 (10th November 1951). Note the BR shed allocation plate 32E, being Yarmouth (Vauxhall).

The fitting of a smokebox number plate did not apply to this class, but a semblance of it was put on the last two to have repairs. On Nos.68216 (1st December 1951) and 68226 (10th November 1951) the figures were centered and the number was put on. When No.68226 was withdrawn on 2nd August 1955, Class J70 was extinct.

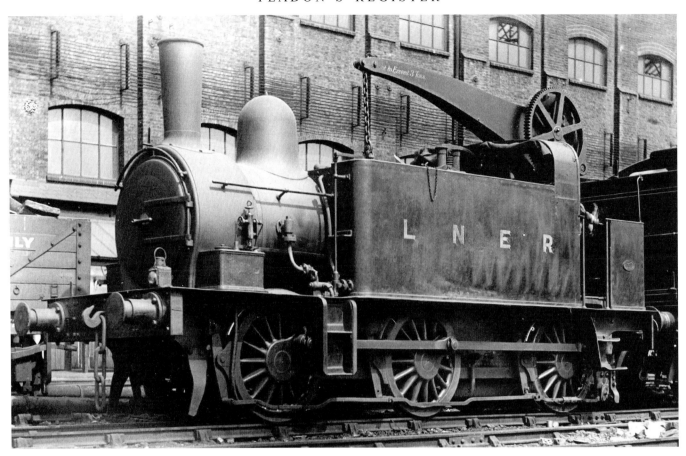

D was ex works 19th May 1923 still in grey but with plain tanks. C was out 17th November 1923 in unlined black with LNER on the tanks, followed by B (as shown here) on 19th July 1924. B differed from the other two in having its front guard irons fixed to the frame ends, C and D having them on the front of the buffer beam. Until into the 1930s stovepipe chimneys were carried by all three.

C changed to cast chimney with lipped rim when ex works on 11th September 1931, but still had a boiler with Ramsbottom safety valves, and a small toolbox atop of the right hand tank.

CLASS J 92

B (**204** to 1/10/1894)

Ruston & Proctor.

To traffic 5/1868.

REPAIRS:
Str. ?/3—?/12/1893.**G.**
Rebuilt to Crane tank.
Str. ?/?—?/3/09.**G.**
Str. 5/1—17/4/14.**G.**
Str. 19/10/21—18/2/21.**G.**
Str. 5/3—19/7/24.**G.**
Str. 2/1—18/5/28.**G.**
Str. 7/7—19/8/32.**G.**
Str. 15/7—15/8/35.**G.**
Str. ?/?—5/11/40.**G.**
Str. 22/2—12/4/47.**G.**
Str. 24/1—5/2/49.**L.**

BOILERS:
  B.
  B *(new)* ?/3/09.
1331 *(new)* 15/8/35.

SHED:
Stratford works.

RENUMBERED:
  8667 2/6/46.
68667 5/2/49.

CONDEMNED: 19/5/52.
Cut up at Stratford.

C (**205** to 1/7/1894)

Ruston & Proctor.

To traffic 7/1868.

REPAIRS:
Str. ?/6/1890—?/5/1891.**G.**
Rebuilt to Crane tank.
Str. ?/?—?/6/07.**G.**
Str. 10/6—22/9/13.**G.**
Str. 11/8—17/11/23.**G.**
Str. 13/6—11/10/27.**G.**
Str. 10/8—11/9/31.**G.**
Str. 12/9—10/10/35.**G.**
Str. ?/?—26/7/40.**G.**
Str. ?/?—8/3/44.**G.**
Str. 28/6—30/8/47.**G.**
Str. 24/1—11/2/50.**L.**

BOILERS:
  C.
  C *(new)* ?/6/07.
  213 *(new)* 27/11/12.
1332 *(new)* 10/10/35.

SHED:
Stratford works.

RENUMBERED:
  8668 2/6/46.
68668 11/2/50.
DEPT'L 35 27/9/52.

CONDEMNED: 10/11/52.
Cut up at Stratford.

D (**206** to 1/7/1894)

Ruston & Proctor.

To traffic 9/1868.

REPAIRS:
Str. ?/3—?/12/1893.**G.**
Rebuilt to Crane tank.
Str. ?/?—?/6/09.**G.**
Str. 28/12/12—5/5/13.**G.**
Str. 1/7—11/9/20.**G.**
Str. 29/1—19/5/23.**G.**
Str. 29/9/25—17/3/26.**G.**
Str. ?/?—5/3/28.**G.**
Str. 14/1—28/2/30.**G.**
Str. 15/1—8/2/34.**G.**
Str. ?/?—10/6/28.**G.**
Str. ?/?—30/9/41.**H.**
Str. ?/?—9/10/43.**G.**
Str. 26/4—14/6/47.**H.**
Str. 2—23/3/50.**H.**

BOILERS:
  D.
  D *(new)* ?/6/09.
1330 *(new)* 8/2/34.

SHED:
Stratford works.

RENUMBERED:
  8669 2/6/46.
68669 23/3/50.

CONDEMNED: 16/10/50.
Cut up at Stratford.

Ex works 8th February 1934, D had a new boiler with Ross 'pop' safety valves, and the tool box had been taken off, but it still had the old flush fitting smokebox door which it kept until ex works 30th September 1941. Note this 9th August 1934 photograph shows B (behind) still with a stovepipe chimney - albeit a shortened version - and this changed to a cast type when ex works 15th August 1935 with a new boiler and Ross 'pops'. When the boiler was changed, a Wakefield sight feed lubricator in the cab replaced the Roscoe type on the smokebox.

Shopped in 1943/4, all three got only NE on the tanks, the tarpaulins on each side of the crane were put on to stop glare from an open firebox door as an Air Raid Precaution measure.

At shoppings after March 1938 the LNER classification was painted in white two inch high numerals on the front buffer beam.

The tarpaulin covers for blackout purposes were not a new arrangement. This shows D with the same device having been put on for weather protection for the crew. The scant cab to allow for the crane to revolve was of little practical use. Although it is believed the cranes were never used in LNER years, the chain and hook remained on until early in 1946 as shown by the previous illustration on 13th October 1945.

(above) In the Thompson re-numbering scheme, B, C and D were allocated 8667, 8668 and 8669 and these numbers were all put on by Stratford shed on Sunday 2nd June 1946. Ex works 14th June 1947, No.8669 had LNER restored with that and the figures in shaded transfers, No.8667 in the same style was out 12th April 1947. Note the attempt to improvise more protection for the crew and that the chain and hook had now been taken off.

(centre) Ex works 30th August 1947, No.8668 did not get shaded transfers but had yellow painted and unshaded letters and figures in Gill sans style but with the LNER modified figure 6.

Ex works from a Light repair on 5th February 1949, No.8667's number had been changed to its BR equivalent, still in shaded transfers, and this is how it then remained until its 19th May 1952 withdrawal.

The other two got the BR emblem on the tank and the number transferred to the bunker side, with correct Gill sans figures, No.68668 ex works 11th February 1950 and 68669 out 23rd March 1950. None of them acquired smokebox number plates. No.68669 only lasted briefly being withdrawn on 16th October 1950.

No.68668 was transferred into the new Departmental series on 27th September 1952 and was then re-numbered to 35, but it was withdrawn on 10th November 1952 and J92 class became extinct. This illustration shows the engine on 10th January 1953, still very much intact.